ML
2075
E9

Evans,
Sound

S0-CAR-222

Soundtrack:
The Music of the Movies

SOLANO COMMUNITY COLLEGE

3 7045 00010 7674

Soundtrack: The Music of the Movies

MARK EVANS

Drawings of composers by Marc Nadel

CINEMA STUDIES SERIES • LEWIS JACOBS, CONSULTING EDITOR

Hopkinson and Blake, Publishers, New York

*All rights reserved
including the right of reproduction*

Copyright 1975 by Mark Evans

*Published by Hopkinson and Blake
329 Fifth Avenue, New York, N.Y. 10016*

*ISBN: 0-911974-19-9 (cloth), 0-911974-20-2 (paper)
Library of Congress Catalog Card Number: 75-5094*

Manufactured in the United States of America

LIBRARY OF CONGRESS CATALOGING IN PUBLICATION DATA

Evans, Mark.
  Soundtrack.

  (Cinema studies series)
    1. Moving-picture music—History and criticism.
I. Title.
ML2075.E9   782.8'1   75-5094
ISBN 0-911974-19-9
ISBN 0-911974-20-2 pbk.

Printed in the U.S.A. by
NOBLE OFFSET PRINTERS INC.
New York, N. Y. 10003

ML
2075
E9
46609

ACKNOWLEDGMENTS

My deepest thanks to Irvin and Ethel Talbot for their help, advice, and encouragement, to Harold Gelman and David Raksin for their invaluable assistance, and to Miklos Rozsa for writing the introductory remarks to this book.

For giving me access to countless private sources, I would like to express appreciation to: Daniele Amfitheatrof, William G. Blanchard, Scott Bradley, Alexander Courage, George Duning, Daniel Franklin, Joel Franklin, Gerald Fried, Hugo Friedhofer, John Green, John C. Hammell, Mrs. Carroll Knudson, George Korngold, William Lava, Frank Lewin, Leighton Lucas, Abraham Marcus, Diane Mathis, Patrick Moore, Paul and Dorothy Neal, Gunnard Nelson, Lionel Newman, Alex North, Dave Pepper, Edward B. Powell, David Raksin, Ruby Raksin, Miklos Rozsa, Edward J. Slattery, Frank Skinner, Paul Sprosty, Mrs. Max Steiner, Bill Stinson, Virgil Thomson, John Waxman, and Roy Webb.

My thanks also to Alexander Courage, for providing photographs, and to Paula Franklin, who edited this book with patience and grace.

Finally, a very special thank you to my understanding parents; a list of the things for which I thank them would be even longer than the history of film music.

M. E.

COPYRIGHT CREDITS

Ben Hur
Music by Miklos Rozsa
Copyright 1959
Metro-Goldwyn-Mayer Inc.
Rights throughout the world
  controlled by
  Robbins Music Corporation
Used by special permission

Captain From Castile
Music by Alfred Newman
Copyright 1948
Twentieth Century Music Corporation
Rights controlled by
  Robbins Music Corporation
Used by special permission

David Copperfield
Music by Malcolm Arnold
Copyright 1969
Reprinted by permission
of Omnibus Productions Ltd.
Twentieth Century Fox Productions Ltd.
for Twentieth Century Music Corp. Ltd.

Escape Me Never
Music by Erich Wolfgang Korngold
From film copyrighted by
  Warner Brothers Studios, 1947

The Ghost and Mrs. Muir
Music by Bernard Herrmann
Copyright 1947
Twentieth Century Music Corporation
Rights controlled by
  Robbins Music Corporation
Used by special permission

Laura
Music by David Raksin
Copyright 1945, Renewed 1973
Twentieth Century Music Corporation
Rights controlled by
  Robbins Music Corporation
Used by special permission

Lili
Music by Bronislau Kaper
Words by Helen Deutsch
Copyright 1952
Metro-Goldwyn-Mayer Inc.
Rights throughout the world
  controlled by
  Robbins Music Corporation
Used by special permission

Peyton Place
Music by Franz Waxman
Words by Paul Francis Webster
Copyright 1957
Twentieth Century Music Corporation
Rights controlled by
  Robbins Music Corporation
Used by special permission

Since You Went Away
Music by Max Steiner
Reprinted courtesy of
  American Broadcasting Companies

A Streetcar Named Desire
Music by Alex North
From film copyrighted by
  Warner Brothers Studios, 1951

*To Irvin Talbot, who in his distinguished
forty-five year career as Musical Director
of Paramount was regarded by all
who knew him as the Dean of Film Music*

Introduction

It is interesting to note that although the quality of film music today has declined, the public's nostalgia for the film music of the Golden Age of the movies is at a high peak. This new interest is not limited only to old film scores (which people are buying in the form of new recordings), but extends to composers as well—the previously unsung heroes of the film industry. For fifty years these composers, who supplied the soundtrack music that is now in such great demand, remained in the shadows while studio publicists flooded the newspapers with items about stars, producers, and directors. Even today the Hollywood trade papers and the Academy of Motion Picture Arts and Sciences often list film scores under "technical credits," as if the composers were mere technicians.

Mark Evans's book helps redress the balance by providing new insights into film music and analyzing the works of a great many composers, both known and unknown. I found in it the names of long-forgotten men who are at last being acknowledged for their contributions to the evolution of film music. With painstaking research, Evans also reveals what goes on behind the scenes in the studio music departments.

Overall, the book is a valuable reference work. Without taking sides or casting judgment, Evans presents the entire panorama of film music, both in Hollywod and abroad.

It makes most interesting reading.

MIKLOS ROZSA
Hollywood

Soundtrack: The Music of the Movies

Contents

ILLUSTRATIONS: *Drawings of composers,* pages 37, 65, 79, 163, 223; *excerpts from scores,* pages 25, 31, 53, 114, 123, 135, 147, 183, 205, 217; *movie stills,* pages 48, 94, 95, 139, 140, 188, 189, 209, 210, 236, 286, 287, 288, 289.

CHAPTER I

The Silent Film Era

The lights dim. A wistful, fragile young woman appears on the screen, while outside a storm rages. She answers a knock on the door, and a figure draped in a black cape enters. The man smiles—a sly, diabolical smile—twirls his handlebar moustache, and demands immediate payment of the mortgage. Menacing chords on the piano underline the drama of the encounter.

In a world that has survived televised moonwalks, Super Bowls, and films that could barely pass the Supreme Court's liberalized obscenity test, the fate of a distressed damsel in the clutches of a grasping landlord seems less than earth-shattering. A society that can witness on-the-spot coverage of earthquakes, floods, and riots can hardly be expected to react with nail-biting anticipation to the plight of one young woman, however noble and virtuous. But, during the first two decades of the twentieth century, silent films with similarly artless plots thrilled and delighted their audiences. Although the cynical and sophisticated may scoff at the melodrama of silent films, the medium is enjoying a vigor-

1

ous renaissance. College students as well as nostalgic older people are flocking to silent-film festivals. All of us—cynics and buffs alike—should remember that in the early days of the century, the most incredible aspect of moving pictures was that they *did move*.

It is doubtful that anyone could have foreseen the tremendous international industry that would arise as a direct result of the experiments in 1895 of the Lumière family. The first motion pictures produced by these Parisians were introduced to the public in a carnival atmosphere. Traveling showmen who wandered from town to village through the European countryside displayed the pictures on large wooden screens. The pitchman would recite a dramatic narration and usually sing to accompany the story told by the pictures. Such presentations clearly offered little competition to real theaters.

Actually, a type of sound film anticipated the silent motion picture as we know it. On October 6, 1889, Thomas Edison presented a sound film that could be viewed by one person at a time. Edison called his machine the "cintophonograph." The duration of the film was limited because of the phonograph, which could play only for a few minutes. But a subsequent invention, the Berliner gramophone, used longer records and thus enabled Charles Pathé in Paris and Oscar Messter in Berlin to attempt synchronization of the film strip and gramophone record.

At this early period of film history, developers of moving pictures were already beginning to think about the uses of music as accompaniment. Admittedly, it was often conceived more as a device to drown out the distracting sounds of noisy equipment than for any aesthetic purpose, but the relationship was established nonetheless. As early as 1895, in fact, the Lumière brothers themselves had invited an audience to meet in a basement café in Paris, where a pianist provided background music for their film program.

This occasion established a tradition that continued throughout the silent film era.

The musician's principal function was to emphasize highlights of the action on the screen, particularly to make the audience instantly aware that the fellow in the black cape, glowering at both heroine and viewers, was to be roundly hissed. Another highlight of the early melodrama was the chase sequence. Here it was the responsibility of the musician to see that the proper music accompanied the pursuit and identified hero and villain. (It should be noted, by the way, that the jerky pace of many silent films is misleading. Movies of the period were photographed at the rate of sixty feet of film per minute; reprints of today are often released at the current speed of ninety feet per minute.)

In 1896, a representative of the Lumière brothers arrived in England and arranged for a public presentation of the Lumière films. Their first public performance, on February 20, 1896, was so successful that by spring major music halls in England had started to present exhibitions of moving pictures. Music hall orchestras, which accompanied live performers, also played background for the new films.

During the early years of the century, experiments with sound continued as part of the over-all effort to popularize the new cinematic medium. Theater owners sometimes used gramophone records as accompaniments, drawing upon such varied musical sources as Gilbert and Sullivan operettas and Gounod's "Faust." A special record provided the accompaniment for the production *Little Tich and His Big Boots,* released in 1900 in England.

Motion pictures needed music. Not only did it drown out the noisy apparatus required to project the film. An instrumental background, whether provided by a record or by musicians—a soloist or an entire orchestra—also compensated for the lack of dialogue and conveyed mood. Theater

owners soon became aware of the potential of a score improvised by a pianist or organist, who would combine original themes or textures at the keyboard with excerpts from
familiar classics. Theater organists had tremendous repertoires, ranging from classics to popular tunes of the day,
often performed from memory. William G. Blanchard,
emeritus professor of music at Pomona College, began his
musical career in the Midwest, accompanying silent films
at the organ console. He recalls the era as "an attempt, and
often a fairly successful one, to put under the control of
one individual all the colors of an orchestra, plus percus-
sions of all kinds. Pipes included heavy reeds imitative of
the orchestral brasses; strings; all types of flutes; and a
species known as the tibia, which, with its throbbing tremolo,
was the hallmark of all theater organs. Percussion included
snare drums, xylophone, cymbals, bird whistles, fire sirens,
gun shots, and a piano, all of which could be played from
its two, three, four, and sometimes five, manuals."

Large theaters employed orchestras of varied size. The
conductor of such an ensemble was responsible for arranging the music, as well as for directing the players in actual
performance. The practice of using musical ensembles
began in a small way. A theater might start with a pianist
and then add some strings, and eventually expand as budget
permitted. Joseph Gershenson, later head of the music department at Universal Studios, began his career as violinist
in a violin and piano duo, to which a cello was later added.
The ensemble played agitatos, hurries, fight music, and
atmospheric pieces extracted from well-known operas or
overtures. Gershenson recalls: "One of the first pictures
I worked with was a film called *Wings,* which employed a
partial soundtrack on a disc, with sound effects, airplanes,
gun shots, etcetera. That was still in the experimental
period. The disc would seldom synchronize with the picture, and it was not unusual to hear gunshots during a

romantic scene instead of a battle. Music was almost always classical and symphonic in character."

Accompaniments were planned with varying degrees of care. David Raksin, who rose to prominence as a composer during the 1940s, first became interested in motion pictures when he watched his father direct a theater orchestra. He used a baton with a little electric bulb on the end, keeping a spare battery in his pocket. Musicians in the darkened pit followed the baton light. They had to be prepared to switch, in mid-phrase, from one piece to another depending on the exigencies of the filmed action. At their height, theater orchestras in major cities might employ as many as seventy-five musicians.

Although numerous composers and conductors transferred from silents to sound during the late 1920s, none of them had a more distinguished career than Irvin Talbot, who ultimately emerged as the dean of Hollywood's film conductors. His forty-five-year career with Paramount Pictures began in a Missouri pit orchestra. He recalls that in the early days of silent films, the conductor often had the responsibility of selecting music based on cue sheets furnished by a publishing service. Says Talbot: "The people responsible for making cue sheets had no ideas regarding the pictures in advance. They only knew if it was a comedy or drama. They used stopwatches, and had to select musical compositions which would conform to the timing of scenes in the film. These compositions were published by the synchronization service. The first one to do this was a man named Jimmy Bradford."

Cue sheets indicated to the conductor the length of the individual scenes, in proper sequence, and the basic mood required for each one. The conductor could then follow the musical guidelines or select his own music. A typical cue sheet might describe a scene thus: "Misterioso, heavy enters."

The conductor knew from the cue sheet that the villain

was about to make his appearance, and that he would be on screen for a given period. He would prepare just enough music to last the appropriate length of time, and then arrange for the orchestra to switch to another musical mood. "The most popular misterioso theme," recalls Talbot, "was 'The Slimy Viper,' and if the cue sheet called for that music, we would use the theme suggested or something similar."

The synchronization service was utilized by other noted film scoring pioneers, including Hugo Riesenfeld, David Mendoza, and Erno Rapee. They would select music from a library of orchestral scores, usually employing cue sheets as guides in determining whether a two-minute scene called for agitated chase music or a romantic melody. (Talbot eventually made his own cue sheets.)

A live orchestra presented unusual problems of synchronization. The conductor could be directing his ensemble in the performance of a gentle melody, when suddenly a chase began on the screen. The conductor had to signal the orchestra with a cut-off gesture so that musicians could flip over their printed parts to the next sequence. The conductor, of course, had already prepared for the sudden change, because the cue sheets had alerted him that an agitato would be needed to accompany a chase after a given number of minutes of the gentle melody.

Each theater maintained music in its own library. Such a library might contain many individual books, each one devoted to a specific mood such as chases, love themes, or comedy music. The responsibilities of synchronization depended to a great extent upon the capabilities of the theater's musical director. During his association with Hugo Riesenfeld, Irvin Talbot was asked to assemble compositions of appropriate length to match the timing of scenes in many films, including Cecil B. DeMille's epic, *The Ten Commandments*. These scores were then cleared for copyright, printed, bound, and made available to theater musical directors. If conductors lacked either the time or expertise to catalogue their own musical sequences, they could depend on scores that had been assembled by Talbot or one of his colleagues.

The expansion of the film industry led to the necessity of training specialists capable of dealing with the cinematic medium. Organization of the Paramount Theater circuit music department was a typical case in point. Nathaniel Finston became director of the department, with Irvin Talbot as musical director and conductor. His associate conductor was Josef Kowstner, his concertmaster, Frederick Fradkin, former concertmaster of the Boston Symphony. Jesse Crawford and his wife served as duo organists, and Max Terr was vocal coach.

Theatrical stage companies were formed almost every week by well-known Broadway producers such as John Murray Anderson, Frank Cambria, Vincente Minnelli, and Paul Oscard. The theaters were also testing condensed versions of Earl Carroll's "Vanities" and other stage shows. Talbot, who would train and assign the conductors after he had watched the performances, holds the record for breaking in theater conductors during the silent days. He also conducted more scores and vocal numbers for composers than any other conductor in the film industry.

Some of the great names of twentieth century music began their careers in the theater orchestras. The Capitol Theater, with Erno Rapee, David Mendoza, William Axt, and Roxy as artistic head, had a fine organization. Their concertmaster was a young man with conducting ambitions named Eugene Ormandy. The Capitol orchestra also maintained vocal soloists, among them Jan Peerce, Beatrice Belkin, and Major Bowes, and a solo dancer, Maria Gambarelli. Rapee even gave Sunday morning symphony concerts, performing such works as the Mahler symphonies; admission charge was $1.

In addition to conducting for silent films, musical directors at major theaters were also expected to provide accompaniments for live performers. Talbot, for example, worked with Bob Hope, Maurice Chevalier, Gertrude Lawrence, Fanny Brice, George Jessel, Eddie Cantor, James Melton, Walter Winchell, Bing Crosby, John Boles, Ethel Merman, Kate Smith, and Luisa Tetrazzini, all of whom performed at the Paramount Theater.

Inevitably, publishers and filmmakers realized that a much closer relationship between music and film could be achieved if music was composed or arranged specifically for a film. One of the more ambitious efforts was that of the French composer Camille Saint-Saëns, who wrote a score for strings, piano, and harmonium for the film *L'Assassinat du Duc de Guise* (1908).

Edison Films issued suggestions for music that could be used with certain scenes, even by a solo pianist. Two important collections were the Sam Fox Moving Picture Music Volumes by J. S. Zamecnik (1913) and the Kinobibliothek by Giuseppe Becci (1919). The former included "Indian Music," "Oriental Music," and "Spanish or Mexican Scenes"; there were also periodical publications of music for "Paris Fashions," "Aeroplane or Regatta Races," "European Army Maneuvers," and "Newsreels." The most popular material was extracted from sections of these volumes and labeled "Burglar or Sneaky Music," and the famous "Hurry Sequences." The Kinobibliothek consisted of arrangements and rearrangements of works of the masters that might be applicable to films. Although the pieces were not cued to specific scenes, they were related in a general way to the plot or story.

Some directors, it might be noted, employed small chamber ensembles in the studios themselves. The musicians did not record music to be heard by the theater audience, but rather played to inspire actors.

Gradually, directors became aware of the value of individual scores. In 1915, pioneer director D. W. Griffith produced his classic film *The Birth of a Nation*. An original score was prepared by Carl Elinor, but Griffith decided that he wanted to take a personal hand in writing and developing the music. He replaced the score with a series of pieces extracted from the symphonic repertoire, selected in collaboration with Joseph Carl Breil. This conflict between producer (or director) and composer continues in various degrees to the present day.

The final score of *The Birth of a Nation* consisted of a combination of excerpts from nineteenth-century symphonic pieces, patriotic tunes, and a romantic melody, "The Perfect Song," which later became the tune of the Amos and Andy radio program. For some of the sequences, Griffith used sections of works by Grieg and Wagner, including the "Ride of the Valkyries."

An unusual approach to the film medium was taken by Edmund Meisel, who replaced Yuri Faier as composer for Sergei Eisenstein's famed motion picture, *The Battleship Potemkin*. Meisel's music was to be performed live, played by a large symphonic orchestra during the screening of the film. The German government held that the silent film alone could be accepted as art, but that, with music, *Potemkin* became an "exercise in political inflammation."

By the end of the silent film era, a pianist in a small town could accompany *The Phantom of the Opera* by following instructions in a score printed by the Belwin Publishing Corporation. He might, for example, be advised to break a piece of pottery in order to frighten the audience when they saw the Phantom. If an orchestra were available, the timpanist could play crescendo rolls, with various members of the orchestra playing excerpts of a "Phantom" theme. But while Carl Laemmle's production was accompanied by excerpts of selections by Kilenyi, Vely, Berg,

Borchs, Baron, and Hinnicks, the trend was clear. More and more outstanding composers were being invited to compose individual scores for specific films. Among the most notable examples are *The Rubaiyat of Omar Khayyam* (Charles Wakefield Cadman, 1918), *Puritan Passions* (Frederick Shepherd Converse, 1923), *Entr'acte Cinématographique* (Erik Satie, 1924), *The Thief of Baghdad* (Mortimer Wilson, 1924), *L'Inhumaine* (Darius Milhaud, 1925), *Napoleon* (Arthur Honegger, 1926), *The Italian Straw Hat* (Jacques Ibert, 1927), *Krazy Kat at the Circus* (Paul Hindemith, 1927), and *The New Babylon* (Dimitri Shostakovich, 1928). A noteworthy collaboration was that between American composer George Antheil, known as the "Bad Boy of Music," and the French artist Fernand Léger, on *Ballet Mécanique* (1924).

The era of silent films came to an abrupt end with the arrival of sound, a new dimension that completely revolutionized the role of music and its relationship to the screen.

CHAPTER II

The Coming of Sound

The year was 1927. The President of the United States was Calvin Coolidge. Charles Lindbergh had just flown the Atlantic alone, and Americans who weren't talking about Lindbergh were probably discussing Babe Ruth, who had just hit his sixtieth home run. Despite Prohibition and a taciturn President, the nation was high on optimism and prosperity. On October 6, an audience attended the premiere of a new film, *The Jazz Singer*. The highlight of the evening was a moment when the star, Al Jolson, shouted, "You ain't heard nothin' yet, folks, listen to this!" and burst into singing one of his hit tunes, "Mammy." In this single moment, the silent film era came to its official end.

From the time of the first motion pictures, photographers had considered the use of sound as an integral element of film. The difficulty facing pioneers in the field was a lack of synchronization capability. Sound could be recorded on discs, but it was difficult to synchronize them with the screen action or amplify them in the theater so they could be heard. Even Edison had tried to coordinate moving pictures with gramophone records. The principle of photographing sound on film strips had been known before the turn of the century. (A Frenchman named Lauste applied it in 1911.)

It was technological advances in the 1920s that made the sound era possible. Two systems, sound-on-film and sound-on-disc, competed for adoption by film producers. One sound-on-film process developed out of the photoelectric cell, patented in 1920; it was the central element in the experiments of the inventor Lee De Forrest. De Forrest, who was interested in the simultaneous combination of recording and photography, developed a project he called Phonofilm. This sound-on-film technique allowed for the registering of sound impulses made up of fluctuating light patterns. The patterns were recorded as a continuous sound-track running alongside the visual track. In 1924 De Forrest collaborated with Irvin Talbot in a unique experiment. Leon Rothier, the Metropolitan Opera basso, sang "The Marseillaise" and "The Shadow Song," recorded under Talbot's baton and photographed under the inventor's supervision.

William Fox decided to use a different sound-on-film system, the German Tri-Ergon. Music for the motion picture *What Price Glory?* was recorded in 1927. In April of that same year, the company released Fox Movietone News, the first sound newsreel, employing the same technique.

The Warner brothers, meanwhile, became interested in a sound-on-disc method called Vitaphone, and decided to introduce it in their films. Both *The Jazz Singer* and *The Lights of New York* were prepared using this method. Yet the Warners' initial reaction to the whole idea of sound-on-disc was one of extreme skepticism.

At this time the idea of sound incorporated with motion pictures was still startling. Harry Warner visited Western Electric at the suggestion of his brother, Sam; he later admitted that he wouldn't have gone if he had known that he was being urged to consider the controversial films that could "talk." (When he first heard the twelve-piece ensemble at Bell Laboratories, Warner peeked behind the screen to see whether the staff had hidden an orchestra there.)

Warner's visit bore fruit. On August 6, 1926, Warner Brothers, in association with the Vitaphone Corporation, presented an important premiere. The program began with performances by Marion Talley, Efrem Zimbalist, Harold Bauer, Mischa Elman, Anna Case, and Giovanni Martinelli. They were followed by John Barrymore in the film *Don Juan;* it was accompanied by music synchronized by means of the Vitaphone. The score had been arranged by Major Bowes, David Mendoza, and William Axt, and was played by the New York Philharmonic, conducted by Henry Hadley. Critical reaction was enthusiastic. Olin Downes regarded the potentialities of the new process as endless. C. B. DuBois, president of the Western Electric Company, described the Vitaphone process as capable of creating a new art. Public acceptance came promptly, and executives of film production companies were quick to recognize that sound added a totally new dimension to the marketing of motion pictures. When Warner Brothers in Hollywood released news of their Vitaphone sound system, Nathaniel Finston was notified in New York that Paramount had suddenly decided that it too was going into sound.

Irvin Talbot assembled the score for Paramount's first sound film, *Warming Up* (1928), starring Richard Dix. He selected music and timed it in the projection room. He also hired an "orchestra" consisting of five musicians from New York and the Philadelphia Symphony. Recordings were made in a Baptist church in Camden, New Jersey, because of its excellent acoustics.

Early sound recording sessions were exercises in ingenuity. No one had ever developed procedures, so film music pioneers had to experiment as they went along. Talbot, who conducted nearly all of Paramount's Camden recording sessions, was aided by Nathaniel Finston, Max Terr, and two RCA engineers, all of whom sat in an enclosed recording room. Recordings were made on two 16-inch discs simultaneously. (One was a standby in case the first failed.) Source sound effects were added, too. For instance, *Warming Up,* a baseball picture, was enlivened with the sound of a bat hitting a ball. Pistol shots were simulated by a drummer. (An actual shot would have caused the stylus to jump the groove and spoil the recording.)

Responsibility for coordination between the motion picture and live performance rested totally with the conductor. As Talbot described it at the time: "From the moment the orchestra rises from the pit, propelled by electrically driven machinery, the music director is responsible for the success of the performance. Marked on the music on my conductor's stand is the cue for every change in lighting, for the raising and lowering of the curtains, for the lowering of the screen, for the commencement of the picture, for the use of the spot on the orchestra, or the white or colored spots on any special numbers which may be put on the stage. By means of a series of buttons on my desk, while directing the orchestra, I signal the stage or the projection room, as the case may be, a second in advance of the time for these changes. Thus a complete check is kept on every step of the performance. Should the electrician on the stage or the man in the projection room miss a cue on their plot, my signal checks them up on it. Furthermore, there can be no deviations or errors of judgment, for the electric buzzer gives its warning for each step of the performance."

Among his equipment, a master musical director might use as many as three speedometers coordinated with the projection room. They would enable him to see the speed at which the film was being run. If Talbot himself was not conducting, he could check on any show conducted by his assistants by means of a buzzer connecting the orchestra pit with his private room in the Paramount building.

In 1928 Paramount also began recording for First National Pictures. Nathaniel Finston then left for Hollywood to start one of the first studio music departments. He was joined by Andrea Setaro, recording supervisor; Sigmund Krumgold, organist; John Leipold and Herman Hand, composer-orchestrators; Ray Turner, pianist; and Henry Falk and Fred Doerr, librarians. With this talent signed on, the music department came into being.

Max Terr and Irvin Talbot remained in New York to finish First National commitments. Another task involved the Paramount picture *Shopworn Angel* (1928), starring Nancy Carroll and including a talking sequence. Neither West Coast executives nor New York exhibitors liked the picture, so it was turned over to Talbot. He gave it a dramatically varied score, and also inserted Fred Coots's popular song, "A Precious Little Thing Called Love." The film went on to achieve wide popular acclaim. The two musical directors received a telegram from Jesse Lasky who, along with Adolph Zukor, headed the studio. He declared that the music had been responsible for making the film a success, and promised two large bonus checks. (This would not be the first instance in which a producer would deem the composer or musical director responsible for saving a motion picture. Throughout the history of film music, composers have been called upon to add new dimensions to films; in fact, composer Bernard Herrmann has suggested that music supplements not what the technicians have done but, primarily, what they have been unable to do.) Soon afterward, in 1929, Paramount invited Talbot to Hollywood, where he pursued a long and distinguished career in film music as that studio's musical director. (Terr also joined the Paramount staff as an accompanist and arranger.)

Within three years after release of *The Jazz Singer,*

American and European audiences could point with pride to the latest technological phenomenon, "talking pictures." An American effort, *The Lights of New York* (1927), was the first all-talking sound film. In England, when film executives learned of the new technique, they decided to convert *Blackmail,* originally a silent production, into a "talkie." The latter, released in 1929, was not only the first British sound feature, but also called attention to a young director with a flair for suspense, Alfred Hitchcock. Hubert Bath, who had scored a part-silent, part-sound film entitled *Kitty,* also scored *Blackmail,* in association with Harry Stafford. In France, René Clair—a director who had originally opposed the use of sound—produced *Sous Les Toits de Paris* (1930), with music by Raoul Moretti and Armand Bernard. Producers in Germany, Italy, and Sweden also began incorporating sound in their features.

Some early sound films used music as a constant accompaniment to the action. Others abandoned music entirely, substituting dialogue instead. In still other cases, film dramas relied on a great deal of music and very little dialogue. Operettas furnished the basis for some of these. An English film, *Sunshine Susie* (1931), was based on a German operetta, "Die Privateskretorin." That same year saw the release of *Surf and Seaweed,* with a score by Marc Blitzstein, the American composer known for his operas. Most American filmmakers, however, turned to popular music as a point of departure, releasing such features as *Broadway Melody* (1930), *King of Jazz* (1930), and *Forty-Second Street* (1932).

Another rapidly developing branch of the sound film was the animated cartoon. In 1921, Max Fleischer's *Out of the Inkwell* had introduced a new animated star, Koko the Clown, who emerged from a bottle of ink to delight audiences. (In the 1930s Fleischer was to win fame as the creator of Betty Boop and Popeye the Sailor. His major animated features included *Popeye the Sailor Meets Sinbad the Sailor* and *Gulliver's Travels.*) Two years after Koko's debut, a young man from Kansas City arrived in Hollywood with a shirt, two pairs of socks, and a storehouse of imagination, ideas, and ambition. Walt Disney was destined to leave a unique mark on the art of the motion picture. Together with his brother, Roy, he founded a studio that specialized in a new type of cartoon featuring an original character. The star of the Disney films was Mortimer Mouse (soon renamed Mickey); by the time sound had arrived on the scene, Mickey Mouse was ready for his third film, to which a soundtrack was quickly added. The music included an arrangement of "Turkey in the Straw," improvised by Mickey and Minnie after a goat had swallowed the score. No one was sure how the goat reacted to his strange lunch, but there was no question about the reaction of the audiences to this 1928 film, *Steamboat Willie.*

The following year, the Disney studios released the first in a series of animated pictures called "Silly Symphonies." *Skeleton Dance,* not surprisingly, presented a group of skeletons—dancing to Grieg's "March of the Dwarfs." By 1933, Disney was ready to release one of his most popular cartoons, *The Three Little Pigs.* Its highlight was a taunting tune, "Who's Afraid of the Big, Bad Wolf?" which became a national favorite.

Studios soon realized that a popular song was an effective device in marketing a motion picture. Pat Sullivan's *Felix the Cat* had popularized another melody, "Felix Kept on Walking." Producers wanted a tune that could send the audience home whistling. The enthusiasm for hit tunes has prevailed to the present—a situation regarded by most composers as a mixed blessing.

The new emphasis on sound raised some problems. Recording sound was a new art, requiring people of considerable skill. No one had any experience in the field, yet specialists were needed. A scene containing a good deal of dialogue, for example, would be ruined by a large orchestra playing at full volume. In the theater, this problem did not exist. The conductor had only to raise his left hand, the first violins would execute a rapid decrescendo, and a soloist standing on stage could be heard by all. Unfortunately, the addition of sound made the use of live theater orchestras impractical and difficult to coordinate. Studios were forced to look for a method of regulating the volume and orchestral balance in scoring.

The demand for technical skills led to a new breed of specialist: the music mixer, more formally known as the musical engineer. Mixers were responsible for controlling the various microphones used in sound recording. Eventually, when music and sound were recorded separately, they also became responsible for combining the two. Initially, however, music and sound were recorded simultaneously.

Paul G. Neal, one of Hollywood's most experienced musical engineers, began his career during the early sound era. He recalled that the films of the late 1920s and early 1930s presented special problems to composer and engineer alike. "In the early days, one of the first big musicals was *The Rogue Song,* which featured Lawrence Tibbett. I had to go on the set with the two cameras working, an orchestra playing, and Lawrence Tibbett singing and moving around the set, all simultaneously. It made things more difficult and expensive. We refined the process gradually, but the equipment we used in those days was primitive compared to the techniques we are using today. In the early days, our recording was all through light valves and photographic film. Now all of our original recording is done on tape, which is much more sensitive. There is much less background noise, and we get rid of a lot of difficulties, because it is not necessary to put the musical score on photographic film until editing and cutting has been completed. Then, in dubbing, as many as twenty tracks may be combined to produce a final product."

It was inevitable that noted composers of serious concert music would become interested in sound films. Tastes in early film scores were as varied as the composers' styles themselves. In Germany and Austria, film composers included Karol Rathaus, Paul Dessau, and Hanns Eisler. Rathaus and Dessau preferred to use large orchestras in their screen scores. Eisler leaned toward an augmented chamber orchestra; sections of his music for *La Nouvelle Terre* dispensed with strings altogether. Eisler frequently composed large-scale sections of a film score that corresponded in style and scope to concert pieces. (The writing of extended musical sequences rather than short accompaniments to brief scenes has been characteristic among concert music composers writing for the screen.) Eisler's most important scores included *Song of Life* (1930), *La Nouvelle Terre* (1934), *The Four Hundred Million* (1939), and *Hangmen Also Die* (1942).

A film version of Kurt Weill's *Threepenny Opera* was produced in Germany in 1931. Frederick Hollander began his career in Germany, though he later moved to Hollywood. Hollander was most famous for the songs for *The Blue Angel* (1930). The film did not contain background music, but instead featured the haunting "Falling in Love Again"—sung by a new star named Marlene Dietrich—and a chorale theme based on music from Mozart's "The Magic Flute."

Even the Austrian composer Arnold Schoenberg wrote a piece called "Accompaniment to a Cinema Scene," an experiment in strict twelve-tone technique for an imaginary film. Schoenberg evidently had mixed feelings about writing for the screen. He never actually produced a film score, though he obviously toyed with the idea. In later years, when he settled in Los Angeles, his pupils urged him to write film scores in order to reap the tremendous financial rewards available in Hollywood. A famous tale among West Coast musicians was reported by Oscar Levant. Schoenberg reputedly offered Hollywood studios two conditions: first, he would accept a fee of $100,000; second, he demanded the right to keep his score unchanged. To forbid anyone to alter a single note of music was unheard-of. A Hollywood tradition has always allowed the producer, the director, their friends, and an assortment of relatives and business associates to interfere with the composer's intentions.

The leading composers of concert music in France also turned to the cinema. Erik Satie composed for the ballet "Relache" in *Entr'acte Cinématographique* (1924). A surrealist silent film fantasy, the sequence was directed by René Clair. Satie employed brief, clipped melodic phrases reminiscent of popular music. He also sought to relate the rhythm of his score to what he regarded as the natural rhythmic progression of the film. In one sequence, where a hearse breaks loose from a funeral procession and gallops away, Satie converts a melancholy horn tune into a furious burlesque.

All the members of the group that formed around Satie—known as "Les Six"—were attracted to motion pictures, especially Darius Milhaud, Arthur Honegger, and Georges Auric. Milhaud completed his first sound-film score in 1929 for a film entitled *La P'tite Lili*. His subsequent efforts included a French version of *Madame Bovary, L'Hippocampe,* and *Actualités*. Honegger contributed background scores for *Les Misérables, Crime et Châtiment,* and the controversial *L'Idée*. The last-named, banned for its left-wing political overtones, made use of the Ondes Martenot, an early electronic instrument. The score also demonstrated Honegger's ability to suggest the sounds of a speeding railroad train through orchestral instruments. (Honegger's concert work, *Pacific 231,* grew out of this music.) Honegger's

musical simulation of train sounds—like Stravinsky's carousel music in "Petrouchka" and Gershwin's traffic jam in
"An American in Paris"—became a model for composers
in and out of Hollywood. Auric's scores often resulted from
his collaboration with René Clair, who asked regularly to
provide background and incidental underscoring for his
pictures.

In Italy Giuseppe Becci, who had pioneered in Italian
silent films, continued working in the new sound medium.
Becci had grown up in a tradition of Italian opera, and his
film scores contained many lyrical melodies and "wordless
arias" for the orchestra. Dimitri Shostakovich began writing
movie scores in Russia in the late 1920s, although his better-
known works for the screen were to come.

By the mid-1930s, the first two important stages of film
music had come to an end. Silent films, with their experiments in sound synchronization, were a thing of the past.
The sound film, no longer a novelty, had developed improved techniques. A new and exciting period of film music
was about to begin.

CHAPTER III

The Rise of the Symphonic Film Score

During the 1930s, the scoring of motion pictures became established as a highly sophisticated art. Much of the credit belongs to the accomplished composers of symphonic and operatic music who agreed to try their hand at scoring films. Many of these pioneers moved to Hollywood from Europe, and their style was derived from the lush romanticism of Viennese opera. Prime examples were two of Hollywood's most active film composers, Erich Wolfgang Korngold and Max Steiner. Both men grew up listening to the operas of Wagner, Strauss, and Puccini, and the symphonies of Mahler. Both were particularly influenced by the harmonic idiom of Richard Strauss. Both preferred large symphony orchestras, with full, lush harmonies, extensive doubling of individual parts, and expressive melodic lines. Their scores often used the full string section for statements of lyrical themes and long, sweeping glissandos.

Both composers were child prodigies. Korngold was the son of Julius Korngold, a distinguished Austrian music critic. Steiner's grandfather, Maximilian Steiner, owned the famous Theater an der Wien, a Viennese music center; both his father and grandfather had been close friends of Johann Strauss and Offenbach.

Erich Wolfgang Korngold

Erich Wolfgang Korngold began composing at the age of six. By the time he was nine, he had written a cantata that earned the enthusiastic praise of Gustav Mahler, who declared the boy to be a genius. As a teen-ager, Korngold produced a variety of works worthy of a brilliant adult. The Emperor Franz Josef commanded a premiere performance by the Vienna State Opera of his musical pantomime, "The Snowman." Bruno Walter was one of the musicians to play his piano trio. At fourteen, Korngold completed his first symphony; by the age of nineteen, he could point with pride to three operas. Some of Europe's foremost musical masters, among them Strauss and Puccini, thought the works of the young Austrian displayed "astounding maturity."

Korngold moved to Hollywood in 1934, having been introduced to the medium of film by the Viennese director, Max Reinhardt, with whom he had collaborated in Europe. Much of his subsequent work was done at Warner Brothers, although the musical *Give Us This Night* was written for Paramount. His large output merits detailed consideration.

Korngold's first assignment was to adapt Mendelssohn's music for the Warner Brothers film, *A Midsummer Night's Dream*. This task called for considerable skill as an arranger, but Korngold's subsequent efforts were much more original. Among the Warner features of this period were many swashbuckling adventure stories, costume films awash with pirates and other sword-wielding heroes who specialized in rescuing Olivia De Havilland from impending disaster. Korngold's credits include music for *Captain Blood,*

Anthony Adverse, The Prince and the Pauper, The Adventures of Robin Hood, The Private Lives of Elizabeth and Essex, The Sea Hawk, and *The Sea Wolf.*

Korngold's scores invariably began with a full symphonic overture. He was fond of brilliant brass fanfares, followed by a long, sweeping melody played by the strings. Melodically, Korngold was an unabashed romanticist. We may speculate that if Richard Strauss had scored motion pictures, his film music might well have sounded like Korngold's. His melodies contained wide leaps, were harmonically tonal, and depended upon sequential resolution of appoggiaturas; he was also fond of enharmonic modulation. His music is breathless, expansive, and thoroughly expressive.

Korngold was a master at developing ideas that were valid both musically and descriptively. In *Elizabeth and Essex,* for example, he produced stirring martial accompaniments for the triumph of Essex and the Merry Men marching through Sherwood Forest. Descending melodic sweeps in the winds and strings depict the men descending from trees. Some composers can write excellent concert music, but lack a dramatic sense; others can write fine film music that does not stand on its own. Korngold, again like Richard Strauss, wrote music that did both.

Korngold could also be lyrically reflective. He experimented with the use of music below the pitch of actors' voices, as in his subtle accompaniment to the love scene in *Juarez.* He developed an ethereal background for strings and harp for *Between Two Worlds,* a remake of *Outward Bound.* For *Devotion,* a motion picture about the troubled lives of the Brontë family, Korngold composed brooding, delicate passages for the high strings, capturing the feeling of the English moors with his skilled transitions from bright to dark harmonic colors.

Korngold was also responsible for the music in *Of Human Bondage.* The love theme is expressive enough to

Escape Me Never, Erich Korngold

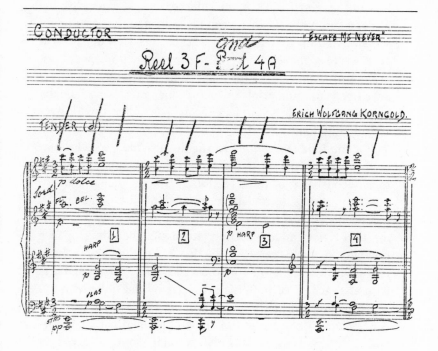

be the aria of an opera. Scored for violins, it is highlighted by wide leaps, reaching ever upward toward final resolution.

The Constant Nymph provided the source of inspiration for one of Korngold's major film scores. It concerns the life of a composer torn between his marriage to a prominent socialite and his love for a girl who has inspired him. Korngold wrote a major work, "Tomorrow," a tone poem for orchestra, women's chorus, and solo contralto voice. He developed the material in many thematic ways, finally allowing it to be heard in its entirety as a concert work over six minutes long.

For the film *Deception,* Korngold provided a cello concerto. It is played in a single movement, although structurally consisting of three sections. Its main theme is introduced by the cello, and then restated by the orchestra. A second theme is followed by a short pseudo-cadenza, leading to a lyrical middle section. Korngold then developed a polyphonic, fugal variation on his main theme, resolving into a virtuoso cadenza for solo cello. The work concludes with a statement of both main themes by the full orchestra.

Korngold's last major original score for Warner Brothers was *Escape Me Never* (1947). It contained a remarkable ballet, "Primavera," his only popular song, "Love for Love," and a glorious abundance of melodies—as many as ten individual themes, all developed in his customary symphonic style.

Perhaps the best way to understand Korngold's work is to consider his Academy Award-winning score for *Anthony Adverse.* Each major character, mood, or idea is represented by a specific theme. An ascending, scale-like melody that symbolizes Anthony is first introduced when the father of Anthony's mother is told that the boy died at birth; the theme reappears whenever references are made to Anthony's mysterious background. In Africa, Anthony becomes acquainted with Brother François, whose theme is a straightforward, chorale-like motif. The Casa da Bonny-feather is represented by a direct, sturdy melody, built over triadic accompaniment. The love song, originally scored for trumpet solo, is developed as a major romantic theme as well.

The world of film music was fortunate in having a pioneer as musically and artistically erudite as Korngold. For his very first assignment, *A Midsummer Night's Dream,* he made preliminary recordings of Mendelssohn's scherzo and nocturne, which were played over loudspeakers while the film was being photographed. He conducted pieces that were inserted after the film was cut, and also made simultaneous recordings. He invented a new technique for accompanying the spoken word, conducting the actor on the stage, making him speak his lines in the necessary rhythm; then he recorded the orchestral part, guided by earphones.

Korngold, one of the few composers for films who never used a stopwatch, avoided cue sheets and detailed timing. He preferred to improvise while watching footage in a studio projection room. His development of themes for a film's principal characters began while shooting was still in progress. Seated at the piano in the Warner Brothers music department, he would sketch out each musical sequence, then complete it at home.

To Korngold, a film script was like an opera libretto; conversely, he saw the film itself as a textless opera. There was a direct relationship between his melodic ideas and the emotions expressed on the screen, and his music at its best added a sharper and clearer definition to dramatic behavior. Korngold's view of the relationship between film and opera also affected the technical aspect of his scoring. Because of his extensive operatic background, he was accustomed to the spontaneity of live performances. He could follow flashes on the screen that indicated important high spots in a given cue, depending on his innate sense of timing to synchronize music and film in a virtually "live" performance.

"I have often been asked," Korngold said, "whether in composing film music, I have to consider the public's taste and present understanding of music. I can answer that question calmly in the negative. Never have I differentiated between my music for the films and that for the operas and concert pieces. Just as I do for the operatic stage, I try to invent for the motion pictures dramatically melodious music with symphonic development and variation of the themes."

Korngold's freedom in determining musical style and the placement of musical accompaniments was absolute. No other composer has ever enjoyed greater freedom in film composition. His work demonstrated the high level of achievement possible in motion picture music when an outstanding composer is given the facilities of a major film studio and the freedom to follow his best instincts.

Max Steiner

Like Korngold, Max Steiner started composing as a small boy. At fourteen, he attended the premiere of his first operetta, "Beautiful Greek Girl," at the Orpheum Theater in Vienna. The work was so successful that it ran for a full year. In 1914 Florenz Ziegfeld invited Steiner to come to the United States. His arrival in Hollywood in 1929 marked the beginning of a distinguished career; he was to produce over 300 film scores, probably more than any other composer. Steiner's first actual composing was on assignment at RKO, where he wrote music for a six-piece orchestra to fill the silences in English-language films that were being dubbed in Spanish.

Although films are now scored after shooting, this was not true in the early 1930s. Steiner often had to conduct his scores while the director supervised the shooting of the film. Music and dialogue were recorded while the picture was being photographed. If an actor forgot his lines or muffed the action, the music had to be re-recorded. If a musician hit a wrong note, the actors had to redo the scene. If the director was dissatisfied, a scene might require as many as fifty takes. Simultaneous music recording was abandoned, as directors and composers quickly found that they functioned best without having to depend on each other.

By 1934, Steiner had an impressive list of credits, not the least of which was the famed horror film, *King Kong* (1933). The score, recorded by an eighty-piece orchestra, contained a vast number of musical sound effects, all invented by Steiner; its throbbing, pulsating quality made it an immediate classic. Steiner's scoring also provided exotic atmosphere for *The Lost Patrol* (1934) the first dramatic musical background to be nominated for an Academy Award. At that time, however, no distinction was made between original dramatic music and arrangements of songs; the award went to Louis Silvers for his arrangement of Victor Schertzinger's songs in *One Night of Love*.

Steiner's success with *The Lost Patrol* led to another important assignment, music for *The Informer* (1935). Here he expanded an idea that had dominated his thinking about film music since the beginning of his career: coordination between the visual image and musical pulse. Such coordination had always been essential in animated cartoons, but Steiner wanted to achieve it in feature films as well.

The Informer, set in Ireland, was based on a novel by Liam O'Flaherty. It tells the story of Gypo Nolan, who decides to turn a friend over to the Black and Tans so that he can get the money he needs to emigrate to the United States. Gypo, portrayed by Victor McLaglen, is a lumbering, tragic sot who is ultimately gunned down in the street.

Steiner worked closely with the film's director, John Ford. He used Irish folk material and a hymn; the latter, with the addition of his own "Sancta Maria," serves as a basis for the ending, as Gypo goes to his death. Harp and celesta effects simulate the sound of dripping water, and the martial sounds of brass chords and drums are precisely timed to match McLaglen's steps. Steiner's score for *The Informer* won numerous awards and established a new relationship between music and action.

For scenes requiring absolute coordination, Steiner became one of the foremost exponents of the click-track technique. Carl Stalling and Scott Bradley had been the first to use this technique in cartoon scores. Steiner and Roy Webb pioneered its application to feature films.

The click-track is a device that enables synchronization of music and film with mathematical precision. Film exposure is measured in frames, traveling through the projector at a rate of 24 frames a second, 1,440 frames a minute. A click-track—holes punched in the sound-track on the edge of the film—can relate metronomic tempos to those of a film projector. The composer divides a given metronome speed into 1,440; the resulting figure is known as the frame-click beat. If a composer wants to write a chase sequence at a metronome speed of 144 beats per minute, he divides 144 into 1440, then requests the music cutter to provide a 10-frame click. The composer has the option of using a uniform click-track, with clicks regularly spaced, or a variable click-track, with clicks irregularly spaced.

When a film with click-track perforations passes through the projector, the conductor and musicians hear a clicking sound over their headphones, and they can record their music to a beat synchronized in advance with the exact timing of a film. It is even possible to photograph a scene

Since You Went Away, Max Steiner

in which musicians play or in which actors are engaged in physical action according to a temporary guide track recorded in advance to click-track specifications.

The click-track eliminated the element of chance from the film score. Music was no longer cut off in the middle or simply stopped, as it had been so often in the silent era. Coordination became an exact science. The composer who employs a click-track for a given sequence works from cue sheets often prepared by a music cutter. Frequently he uses a stopwatch in order to assure himself that a given piece of music will correspond exactly to important sequences. No precedent had existed in the establishment of such timing procedures. The men who pioneered in this field developed techniques which, despite some alterations, are still in use today. As one of the innovators, Steiner used the procedures with absolute precision, "catching" the minutest detail of screen action.

Steiner turned down offers to teach his techniques of film scoring in both Moscow and Peking. He stayed in Hollywood, where he remained one of the screen colony's most active musicians throughout the 1930s and 1940s. His music was inspired by his admiration for Wagnerian orchestration and melodic design. Steiner scores were nostalgic, emotional, and sentimental, often including lyrical themes or motifs built on an ascending scale. Among his numerous credits were two Oscar-winning scores of the 1940s—*Now, Voyager* and *Since You Went Away*. The *Now, Voyager* melody was set to lyrics by Kim Gannon, and, under the title "It Can't Be Wrong," was a top hit for six months. *Since You Went Away* was a sentimental film that brought tears to the audiences of the period. Thousands of young girls identified with Jennifer Jones as she raced along the railway platform beside the train carrying the boy she loved (Robert Walker) off to war. In this scene Steiner quotes such popular songs as "I'll Be Home for Christmas" and

Irving Berlin's "Together," interrupting them with military bugles. Motifs identified with various characters are combined with an orchestral imitation of a train, achieved through heavy chords in the brass. Steiner's emotional music and the poignancy of the scene itself had an unforgettable effect on those who saw the film.

Steiner also was responsible for the music in such classics as *The Charge of the Light Brigade, The Life of Émile Zola, Jezebel, Dark Victory, All This and Heaven Too, Casablanca, The Adventures of Mark Twain, Saratoga Trunk, Life With Father, The Treasure of the Sierra Madre, Johnny Belinda,* and *The Fountainhead.* All of these scores were hallmarked by Steiner's own special brand of sweeping melodic lyricism, an emotional outlook that matched the temper of the times and the general style of motion pictures being produced during the 1930s and 1940s.

The year 1939 was one of Steiner's busiest. With considerable assistance from his orchestrator, Hugo Friedhofer (now a prominent film composer in his own right), he fulfilled one of Hollywood's most demanding schedules. His agenda included a concert work, "Symphonie Moderne"; this lush, movie-concerto composition, based on a theme of Max Rabinowitsch, was featured in the film *Four Wives.* Steiner also composed his most important score of the period, that for the epic, *Gone With The Wind.* His music received considerable praise, and is highly representative of his method of scoring.

David O. Selznick, the producer of *Gone With The Wind,* had strong opinions about the use of music in his films, and his conflicts with composers were frequent. In the 1930s, he tried to find ways of including what he termed "the great music of the world" in screen scores. He preferred orchestral interpretations of classical music to original compositions. For *Gone With The Wind,* Selznick expressed a preference for a score based to a large extent on what he considered the strains and songs of the Old South, plus classical music. He suggested that Steiner consider using very little original music, relying mainly on two or three hours of sequences drawn from the symphonic repertoires.

Selznick's approach in dealing with composers gives some insight into the conditions under which even prominent musicians worked at this time (conditions of which the public was seldom aware). He suggested having a small instrumental ensemble play the themes for his approval, before execution of the final orchestration. His musical directions were highly specific: "Music and the effects of the fire are obvious and the word 'Sherman' [the second title] should be punctuated in music and effects terrifyingly." "Under no circumstances use any patriotic American music, with the possible exception of 'Marching Through Georgia,' the strain of which—you might consider having it off key— could recur through the other effects and music. This ought to blend off into the Tara theme as we dissolve to the cotton fields at Tara."

At one point, unsure whether Steiner would have the score completed by the deadline, Selznick invited Franz Waxman to write a score of his own as a sort of insurance. By the time Steiner's score was completed, however, Selznick was pleased with the music, which, contrary to his initial directive, was primarily original. He later suggested to William Paley, head of the Columbia Broadcasting System, that CBS consider releasing a commercial record based on the score, a highly unusual idea at the time; the record was not marketed until 1954.

Steiner's music for *Gone With The Wind* was lyrical and highly thematic. Every major character had a short theme, which Steiner scored for a variety of orchestral combinations and upon which he wrote variations as the occasion required. He used a variety of musical quotations—Southern tunes, patriotic songs, and even some Stephen Foster melodies. He later commented: "I think you will understand why I used a number of American songs belonging to the time and country with which Margaret Mitchell's novel deals. Of course, I have enormous quantities of my own music in this score, which is the length of a big opera. In the main, I have worked with seven principal character motifs of my own, and supplemented these with traditional folk songs which I use in part or entirely, or in some varied shape adapted by me to suit the situation." The seven principal themes represented Scarlett O'Hara; Rhett Butler; Melanie; and a love theme for Melanie and Ashley Wilkes; another love theme for Scarlett and Ashley; Scarlett's father, Gerald O'Hara; and finally, the nostalgic, memorable melody for Tara, the O'Haras' plantation. (Steiner felt that Tara was more than a home; he regarded it as an idea, a living entity that represented the proud tradition of the Old South.)

Curiously, Steiner's score was the only element of the film that failed to win an Oscar. The Academy Award that year went to Richard Hageman, John Leipold, W. Frank Harling, and Leo Shuken for the score for *Stagecoach*. Steiner's score, however, became a public favorite, and its continual re-releases on records have heightened its popularity.

Alfred Newman

A major Hollywood composer of the 1930s was Alfred Newman, who went to the West Coast at the invitation of Irving Berlin in 1930, after a successful career as a conductor on Broadway. Newman became music director at Goldwyn Studios. In this executive capacity, he was responsible for hiring some of the film colony's most outstanding younger composers. Thus he came to exert a profound stylistic influence on the nature of Hollywood film scores.

Newman's score for *Street Scene,* completed in 1931, was widely acclaimed. His use of Gershwin-style symphonic jazz, with a solo trumpet playing a lyrical blues theme, gave the film a special musical flavor. Eventually he adapted the principal melody into an orchestral composition, "Sentimental Rhapsody."

During the 1930s, Newman scored numerous motion pictures, including *Arrowsmith* (1932), *Les Misérables* (1935), *Dodsworth* (1936), *Stella Dallas* (1937), *The Prisoner of Zenda* (1937), and *Wuthering Heights* (1939). For the filmed adaptation of Brontë's novel, he composed darkly shaded orchestral music for the scenes taking place on the moors. One of his most memorable melodies, "Cathy," is from this score.

Newman would emerge in the 1940s, as both executive and composer, to become one of the most important figures in film music history.

Franz Waxman

Films of horror and suspense became exceedingly popular during the 1930s, for which no small credit was due to the work of Franz Waxman. Actually he was an extremely versatile and accomplished serious composer, equally at home in any genre.

Waxman, born in Poland, studied in Berlin and began his career as a pianist and songwriter. For a time, he was pianist with the Weintraub Syncopaters, a jazz orchestra. As a result, he became acquainted with Frederick Hollander, whose songs for *The Blue Angel* he conducted and orchestrated. In his first film score—for Fritz Lang's version of the Molnar classic, *Liliom* (1933)—Waxman revealed himself as an innovator by using the electronic Ondes Martenot.

Waxman went to Hollywood as musical director for the Jerome Kern musical, *Music in the Air*. He was then asked

A/ Franz Waxman

B/ Max Steiner

C/ Erich Wolfgang
   Korngold

A

B

C

to work on the horror picture, *Bride of Frankenstein* (1935), his score for which was praised by film music critics and laymen alike. It epitomized Waxman's mid-European romantic approach to film music. He developed individual leitmotifs for the main characters—Dr. Praetorius, the monster, and the monster's mate. The music includes a funeral march, an exciting chase sequence, and a chilling orchestral passage in which the timpani suggest the beating of a heart.

Waxman became musical director at Universal, conducted over fifty films there, and eventually branched out on his own as a film composer. His *Bride of Frankenstein* music was subsequently used by the studio, rearranged in different form, for other films.

Other American Composers

The American film industry tended to draw its native-born personnel from Broadway rather than the concert hall. Most serious composers, if they did film work at all, wrote mainly for documentaries. Roy Harris, for instance, scored *One Tenth of a Nation*. Another such composer was Virgil Thomson.

Thomson was invited by Pare Lorentz in 1936 to compose an original score for *The Plow that Broke the Plains,* a documentary dealing with the desolation of the eroded American terrain in the depression years of the 1930s. Thomson's music, characterized by sparse orchestration, hymns, folklike tunes, and simple, homespun harmonies, is infused with a feeling of pathos and loneliness. At the same time, it is more polyphonic than most film scores. He uses orchestral settings of such cowboy melodies as "I Ride an Old Paint" and "Git Along Little Dogies." A guitar gives a feeling of the West, as do blues sequences for saxophone and banjo. One of the more unusual musical touches in *The*

Plow that Broke the Plains occurs in a series of moving sequences depicting the devastation of the land. Here Thomson wrote a tango for orchestra, but at a slow, mournful tempo; using this dance rhythm, associated with the care-free 1920s, added a nice touch of irony.

Thomson's score for *The River,* another Lorentz documentary, is characteristic of his style. It includes quotations from "Dixie" and "A Hot Time in the Old Town Tonight," jazz-style trombone glissandos, and an imitation of the hammering sounds of a factory. There are also hymn tunes, often in various polyphonic settings.

Thomson returned to screen scoring in the late 1940s, when he worked on Robert Flaherty's documentary *Louisiana Story* (1948). This film depicts the experiences of a Cajun trapper faced with the oil derricks and machinery then appearing in the bayous of Louisiana. Thomson used authentic Cajun songs, arranged on occasion for the accordion, and a twelve-tone chorale that delights those who enjoy serial analysis. Thomson also wrote a fugue sequence for a fierce battle between a young boy and an alligator.

Thomson was not at home with the commercial films of Hollywood. As early as 1937, he questioned whether music could be thematically substantive and not intrude on the film itself. To him, Hollywood-style background scores were a form of musical journalese—expressive, but limited by the nature of the medium. Discussions about the virtues of self-effacing underscoring in motion pictures were just beginning. As a music critic, Thomson was among the first to raise the issue; he was certainly not the last.

A colleague of Thomson's, Aaron Copland, was also intrigued by motion picture music, and spent some time in Hollywood working on commercial films. While his experiences were not altogether happy, his stylistic influence on other composers was an important contribution.

Copland's first score was for a screen adaptation of John

Steinbeck's *Of Mice and Men* (1940). He then moved to another classic, Thornton Wilder's *Our Town*. It is to the credit of producer Sol Lesser that he decided to engage Copland, who was ideal for the job. Wilder had drawn his portrait of New England townspeople carefully. He sought to depict their joys and sorrows as part of the continuing tapestry of civilization, albeit a homespun segment embodying the essence of the American spirit. The playwright himself adapted his Pulitzer-Prize-winning work for the screen. It was peculiarly suited to the composer, whose natural idiom was direct and unsentimental.

Copland wrote music of austere dignity for *Our Town*. He broke with Hollywood tradition and composed a main title based on clear, folklike harmonies and polytriads. Because hymns were an integral part of the New England culture of the period, Copland drew upon what might be termed the atmosphere of hymnody. Unlike Thomson, however, he used no quotations, confining himself to writing tender, expressive, almost reverential sequences. For scenes depicting the open countryside, the composer's sounds are clean and crystal-clear: open brass, solo winds, and quiet strings. The music becomes more lively for the soda-fountain sequence, more contemplative for the visit to the cemetary. Like each person in Grovers Corners, the score of *Our Town* does its job, projecting a quiet serenity, stability, and the same enduring sense of rightness that pervades the play itself. Copland's music for this film is a splendid example of a composer adding quality to a motion picture without sacrificing musical value.

No discussion of the films of this era would be complete without mention of Charlie Chaplin, who of course left an imprint upon the art in many ways. For one thing, he had strong ideas about film music, especially the musical accompaniments to his own motion pictures. Chaplin was an eclectic artist in every sense, influenced musically by the popular songs of English music halls. David Raksin went to Hollywood to work with Chaplin on adapting the latter's music for *Modern Times* (1936).

The two men collaborated in what must be termed one of the most unusual joint efforts in film music. Chaplin whistled, sang, and played the piano, while Raksin notated Chaplin's themes and developed them. Raksin, who had a sophisticated taste in contemporary music, found himself in disagreement with Chaplin's English music-hall approach. The inevitable disagreement occurred, and Raksin left the film. But he returned, and the two men then worked closely together for months. Edward Powell joined Raksin in orchestrating the melodic and sentimental score. Raksin today is intensely loyal to Chaplin, and feels that his musical instincts were ideally suited to the type of films he produced.

German composer Hanns Eisler continued film scoring in the 1940s. Working with Bertolt Brecht, he produced incidental music for several plays. His scores for *Nature Scenes* and *The Children's Camp* were completed under the auspices of the New School for Social Research. For the former he wrote a chorale prelude, a scherzo with trio, an invention, an etude, and a sonata finale. Eisler's scores were the antithesis of the lush, Viennese style. One of his works, a twelve-tone serial score called "Fourteen Ways of Describing Rain," called for the same ensemble of instruments used by Schoenberg in *Pierrot Lunaire*—flute, clarinet, violin (alternating with viola), cello, and piano. For *Woman on the Beach* (1947), Eisler provided a fugue and a long sequence entitled "Scherzo and Recitativo."

In 1947, Eisler wrote "Composing for the Films," one of the important discussions of motion picture scoring in this period. The book details the composer's interest in screen accompaniments that use structured pieces of music, often built on a dissonant polyphonic style. Also in 1947, Eisler appeared as an unfriendly witness before the House Un-American Activities Committee; he was subsequently deported to East Germany, where he continued to write for films (and also composed the East German national anthem).

English Music

A major achievement in the synchronization of musical and visual ideas may be credited to Arthur Bliss, whose score for *Things to Come* (1936), based on the book by H. G. Wells, was singularly important in the development of British film music. He wrote in collaboration with the director, William Cameron Menzies. Because Bliss and Menzies worked so closely together, entire filmed sequences could be planned to make total use of the orchestra. This collaboration produced one of the first major British films in which a composer played an inherent role in the development of the film itself. Wells later praised both Bliss and his work, observing that the score was not intended to be merely attached to the film, but was rather an integral part of the creative design.

Bliss planned his orchestration carefully, employing a symphony orchestra, an extra percussion orchestra, and a large choir as well. Fourteen recording sessions were required to complete the score. It is interesting to note that consultations with the composer, and the respect shown for men like Bliss (and Korngold), were commonplace in the early years of motion pictures. Although the commercial significance of film scores has rapidly increased since those early days, the degree of a composer's influence on producers and directors has declined in proportion. The music for *Things to Come* underscores the drama in subtle ways. In a scene where children play with toys, happy melodies for harp, strings, and winds sound appropriately innocent; when a close-up reveals war toys, the music suddenly turns menacing. *Things to Come* includes a march theme that became popular on English radio, numerous humming effects in which the orchestra imitates machines, and a sequence for wordless choir, augmenting the strings, as a rocket leaves for the moon at the film's conclusion. Bliss arranged some of his music for concert performance, and the work justifiably received enthusiastic praise.

Two other English composers who were writing for films at this time were Benjamin Britten and Alan Rawsthorne. Britten provided important scores for the prewar English documentaries, *Coal Face* and *Night Mail*. His *Instruments of the Orchestra* emerged as a major concert work under the title "A Young Person's Guide to the Orchestra." In the film, the camera follows the various fugal entrances, with emphasis upon the visual aspects involving the conductor, soloists, and ensembles. Rawsthorne, known for his chamber music, wrote several outstanding scores for the screen, including *Uncle Silas, The Cruel Sea,* and the documentary *The Drawings of Leonardo.*

Prokofiev in Russia

Worthy of detailed consideration in a history of film music is the distinguished Russian composer Sergei Prokofiev. His scores were of special significance because he had already earned an international reputation for his concert music—the "Classical Symphony," piano concertos, and ballets—when he turned to the screen. Although he began his career as a nonconformist student, regarded as a shocking and rebellious young man, twentieth-century styles changed so quickly that his music was ultimately regarded as conservative, at least by some musicologists.

Prokofiev had an innate sense of theater, and brought to the screen considerable expertise as an orchestrator. But his scores provide a sharp contrast to works produced in Hollywood by composers steeped in Viennese romanticism. Prokofiev was neither Viennese nor romantic; he was Russian, and his film music retained the sharp, incisive dissonance and realistic, satirical, whimsical flavor identified with his concert works.

Two of the most important motion pictures of the 1930s from a musical standpoint were *Lieutenant Kije* (1934) and *Alexander Nevsky* (1938), both of which Prokofiev scored. The films differ totally in character, the former a stinging satire, the latter a paean to Russian nationalism. *Lieutenant Kije* concerns the misadventures of some courtiers of Czar Paul I. In order to avoid emphasizing an error of the czar, they invent a mythical figure named Lieutenant Kije, who can be conveniently blamed for the mistake. The plot was made to order for Prokofiev, who typically avoided an orchestra of Straussian proportions and instead strove for comedy, exploiting the extreme registers of the orchestra with solo passages for piccolo, tenor saxophone, and cornet. The fife and drum, combined with pompous and laughable effects, ridicule the mythical lieutenant and his distraught creators. Throughout, the composer slyly indicates the truth beneath the sham events taking place on the screen. The lieutenant's wedding music, for instance, suggests not solemnity but the mood of the local tavern. Romantic music includes solos for the double bass, hardly the most sentimental instrument in the orchestral palette. Ultimately, cornets signal the untimely interment of the poor lieutenant, a scene in which Prokofiev also includes the romance and wedding themes.

A far more serious mood dominates *Alexander Nevsky*. The film relates the efforts of a young thirteenth-century Russian prince of Novgorod, who led a struggle to drive an army of Teutonic Knights out of Russia. The latter, a group of Crusaders, were vanquished in a famous battle on ice, fought on the frozen Chudskoye Lake. The director, Sergei

Eisenstein, had quite specific ideas about the music. Prokofiev wrote: "His suggestions were often graphically expressed. He would say, 'Here it should sound as if a baby was being snatched from its mother's arms' or 'I want it to be like a cork dragged against a glass.'"

Prokofiev worked in a Russian tradition handed down from the time of Moussorgsky. His music is somber and grim, with hints of folk melodies. Orchestral voicings are often in open positions, creating the feeling of vast spaces, the terrain of the peasants and soldiers dominated by the Mongolians. The composer explained that he had considered using choral music of the period in order to achieve authenticity in scenes depicting the Crusaders, but finally decided that modern audiences would respond to the film more directly if he employed contemporary rhythms and harmonies; for this reason he composed a chorale of his own. To stress the fanaticism of the Crusaders, Prokofiev used brass fanfares, Gregorian harmonies, and sharp dissonance.

Alexander Nevsky contains several march sequences, culminating in the climactic battle on the ice. The episode features high tremolo figuration in the strings, suggesting the cold empty atmosphere of the frozen lake. Slowly the intensity grows as the cellos and basses, playing *sul ponticello,* introduce the music of the battle itself. Trumpet fanfares replace the chorale-motif as the battle becomes more violent. A string ensemble plays rhythmic figures that imitate the throbbing beat of horses' hooves as the cavalry gallops into combat. At the height of the conflict, the themes of the Russian soldiers and the Crusaders occur together, accentuating the violent antagonism between the opposing sides.

The association between Prokofiev and Eisenstein was an unusual one, for that or any other time. Since the director respected the composer, he gave Prokofiev the opportunity to write music that affected the entire development of the film. Some scenes of *Alexander Nevsky* were cut and edited to conform to a previously recorded music track; on the other hand, some musical sequences were written to accompany specific sections of the film. Prokofiev played an active role in the mixing and editing processes. He refused, however, to make decisions based on instrument readings of microphone recordings, preferring to depend solely on his ear. One of the few disagreements the two men had concerned the opening of the film. Eisenstein wanted a victorious, martial overture, leading into the opening sequence—the somber, tragic "Russia under the Mongolian Yoke." Prokofiev, on the contrary, thought the film should open on a happier, more dynamic note. Eisenstein refused; Prokofiev never wrote an overture.

Prokofiev and Eisenstein enjoyed a fruitful collaboration on the latter's *Ivan the Terrible* (1944) and *Ivan the Terrible, Part II* (1945). An example of their creative interplay involved a scene in *Ivan the Terrible* called "Oath Taken by the Boyars." Eisenstein rejected Prokofiev's initial music, which was to be prerecorded. The composer then asked the director for pictorial impressions of the scene. Eisenstein, a fine painter, provided a series of drawings, and Prokofiev completed the music to everyone's satisfaction. Prokofiev's music played a key role in the two films, especially in such important sequences as the procession of the people bringing a plea to Ivan and the delivering of three men from a burning, fiery furnace. Although his *Ivan the Terrible* is not so well known in the United States as *Alexander Nevsky,* some critics regard it as his finest score.

Other European Composers

In France and Italy, where composers of concert music had early become interested in motion pictures, they continued to maintain this interest—scoring both features and documentaries—to a greater extent than their counterparts in the United States. Some notable film scores come from the 1930s.

Maurice Jaubert was one who won wide acclaim in this period. After studying at the Nice Conservatory, he worked as director of music for Pathé and for the GPO Film Unit in London. Jaubert made little use of a symphonic orchestra in screen accompaniments, preferring a more intimate style to achieve a delicacy associated with contemporary French chamber music. He often wrote leitmotifs, and relied considerably on solo instruments. Among Jaubert's best known scores were those for *Le Petit Chaperon Rouge* (1929), *Le Quatorze Juillet* (1933), *Le Dernier Milliardaire* (1934), *L'Atalante* (1934), and *Carnet du Bal* (1937). His promising career was cut short when he was killed in action in 1940.

Arthur Honegger's scores of this era include those for the French films *Mayerling* (1935) and *Liberté* (1937), and the English classic of 1938, *Pygmalion*.

The Adventures of Robin Hood
Erich Korngold

The Informer
Max Steiner

CHAPTER IV

The Golden Age of Film Music

The 1940s were one of the most important decades in the evolution of motion picture music. Composers of great eminence had the opportunity to exercise their imagination in working with large orchestras. The outstanding scores of this period represent a high point of cinematic history. The entire industry was growing, the techniques of film-making constantly improving. Technical advances could only aid composers, whose resources expanded with every innovation in sound recording. Throughout this period, music was called upon to perform a variety of functions. A brief examination of some representative scores of the period will reveal the richness and variety of individual styles.

The major studios—Metro-Goldwyn-Mayer, Twentieth Century-Fox, Paramount, Universal, Columbia, Warner Brothers, and RKO—all had music departments, each of them with composers under contract. Tastes in film music, like tastes in motion pictures in general, varied at each studio. Each composer had his own individual approach to his craft. But certain trends became clear.

Many composers continued the romantic tradition of motion picture writing. Alfred Newman, Victor Young, and Frank Skinner were American-born exponents of this style. It was also favored by several leading Europeans, notably Miklos Rozsa, Franz Waxman, Dimitri Tiomkin, and Bronislau Kaper, who had made the trip to Hollywood. A different style grew out of a reaction against Viennese post-Straussian romanticism and in the direction of a more dissonant, rhythmic, and incisive form of harmonic expression. Aaron Copland exercised a prime influence on this style, although his own career in films was regrettably brief. Among the composers who exemplified the trend were David Raksin, Hugo Friedhofer, Jerome Moross, and, ultimately, Alex North.

Important works continued to be produced in England and continental Europe. Outside the United States, film scores were generally written by composers of concert music who never chose to specialize exclusively in scoring for the screen. Such men included Ralph Vaughan Williams, William Walton, Darius Milhaud, and Georges Auric.

On the whole, the principal composers of film scores during these years—in both America and Europe—found it necessary to deal with every type of aesthetic and technical challenge. The ways in which they met those challenges are a vital aspect of cinematic history.

Alfred Newman

Intensely dramatic music was required for the serious films of the 1940s. While some composers were concerned primarily with providing a musical background that could "catch" bits and pieces of action, another group of studio composers preferred to concentrate upon writing "mood" music that would comment in some way upon the feelings of the characters depicted on the screen. Foremost among the latter was Alfred Newman. Newman's career, with its promising start in the 1930s, reached new heights following his appointment in 1940 as general music director of Twentieth Century-Fox. As both a powerful studio executive and a composer-conductor, Newman set the tone and style for all the films produced by Fox during the years that followed.

Newman's favorite among his own scores—*The Song of Bernadette* (1943)—was also a landmark in motion picture music. A major contribution to the film's success was its music, which represents Newman at his best. *The Song of Bernadette,* based on the book by Franz Werfel, relates the story of the miracle at Lourdes. Newman and his long-time orchestrator, Edward B. Powell, made considerable use of the string orchestra, particularly with rollicking scherzos in scenes where Bernadette and her sisters race through the woods. Newman's approach to the famous vision scene won him wide critical acclaim. Here he demonstrated his ability to translate dramatic intensity directly into musical terms. Unlike many composers, even highly skilled ones, Newman had an innate sense of theater, and could infuse a screen sequence with tremendous power, pathos, or joy. Indeed, many feel that his greatest skill as a film musician was his capacity to evoke emotion. His scores were unapologetically romantic and lyrical. Although other critics have objected to Newman's unabashed emotionalism, his music transcends such criticism. He accomplished what he set out to do with superlative craft. Significantly, Newman's works are among those most admired by film musicians today. They have stood the test of time. Among his notable scores were those for *The Mark of Zorro* (1940), with assistance from Hugo Friedhofer; *How Green Was My Valley* (1941); *Blood and Sand* (1941); *Leave Her to*

Heaven (1945); *Dragonwyck* (1946); *The Razor's Edge* (1946); *Captain from Castile* (1947); and *Prince of Foxes* (1949).

Like Steiner and Korngold, Newman had been strongly influenced by Strauss. But unlike the lush, symphonic arrangements of the other two men, his works emphasized melodic strings. In fact, the hallmark of his style—strings in their highest register—became known as the "Fox string sound." The effect was exploited by many composers who worked regularly at Twentieth Century-Fox, but most fully by Newman and Powell.

Even a brief evaluation of selected Newman scores reveals a virtual encyclopedia of screen scoring techniques that have served as models for numerous other composers. His approach usually called for various leitmotifs, all of which could be subjected to considerable development, transposed to a variety of keys, augmented, diminished, played in all tempos, and inevitably arranged in several sequences for a yearning, lyrical, expressive string orchestra. Often countermelodies, in a lyrical mode appropriate for an operatic aria, would be offset against the main theme. Newman's melodies were characterized by wide leaps, often harmonized in thirds or sixths. Like Strauss, he knew how to manipulate the colors of the harmonic palette. His scores are always tonal; his uncanny ability to use deceptive cadences, to alternate between major and minor, and to infuse his music with a breathless, surging quality of emotionalism accounts for much of its unique quality.

Newman's melodic material for *How Green Was My Valley* was appropriately modal and folklike. In *Leave Her to Heaven,* he begins the film with a main title dominated by menacing horns and ominous timpani. He explores the use of brass in the scenes of suspense, and for the final sequence, in which a man released from prison joins his fiancée, he introduces a rich, lyrical theme to accompany

Captain from Castile, Alfred Newman

the little boat as it crosses the waters to reunite the lovers.

The music for *Dragonwyck* is highlighted by a dissonant opening based on a somber broken chord figure. A lilting waltz motif is identified with Miranda, the Connecticut farmer's young daughter who dreams of faraway places; it is eminently romantic, optimistic, and innocent. Like many Newman melodies, it propels itself upward through sequences, depending for harmonic expression on appoggiaturas resolving in a triadic context. Voices and high strings underline the eerie atmosphere of Dragonwyck, the manor house where much of the action takes place. Vincent Price's villainies are accompanied by an appropriately menacing leitmotif.

Newman's score for *The Razor's Edge* is also characteristic of his style. The famed Maugham novel upon which the motion picture was based relates the story of a young American, Larry Darrell, and his efforts to find himself and to discover the true meaning of faith. Newman's opening prelude exploits brass fanfares. A clarinet solo introduces the holy man visited by Darrell. Melodically expressive, it is scored for emphasis upon a triadic accompaniment. A climactic walk into the sunset is written dramatically for full orchestra, with the violins carrying the melody along a rising scale line. The love theme is also arranged for violins and also based on development of a scale line. Other favorite Newman devices are present, too: rich, full harmonizations, overlapping melodies and harmonies in the high strings, and brass chords.

One of Newman's finest scores accompanied *Captain from Castile*. The work he produced was decidedly Castilian, full of exciting Spanish rhythms and characteristic chord progressions. The opening, a stirring prelude, consists of a dialogue between strings and brass. Pedro de Vargas is represented by a lush melody, a true hero's theme. The love theme, "Catana," is harmonically darker and more chromatic. For Lady Luisa, the motif is gentle and stately, scored for solo woodwinds over strings. Newman accompanies a scene involving a magic ring with a more somber melody, harmonized in thirds and sixths. The love scenes between Catana and the captain in the New World received a completely lyrical treatment, harmonized and arranged for high strings. Vigorous string figures and a dynamic march for brass highlight the "conquest" scene.

Newman's score for *Prince of Foxes* is decidedly operatic. The themes are richly scored for a symphonic ensemble. Brass fanfares are identified with Cesare Borgia; Verano's melody is written in the style of an aria, again built on the development of scale-like motifs arranged in ascension. Andrea Orsini is portrayed through a strong, powerful march, with the melody assigned to the horns. Violins sing a lush melody identified with Camilla.

Bernard Herrmann

Discussions of film classics invariably begin with *Citizen Kane*. So much has already been written about this remarkable film and the contributions of the young and prodigious Orson Welles that further analysis seems unnecessary. But if the cinematic medium was never the same after the arrival of Welles in Hollywood, film scoring was never the same after the arrival of Welles's personal choice as composer, Bernard Herrmann.

Herrmann, like Welles, has become a Hollywood legend. He is a uniquely individualistic composer, an exception to all rules or generalizations. He began his career while still a teen-ager in New York, enjoying a meteoric rise as a composer and symphony conductor. He then joined the staff of the Columbia Broadcasting System. (He first became associated with Orson Welles as musical director of the famed Mercury Theater Radio Broadcasts, which was aired on CBS.) In 1940 he was appointed conductor-in-chief at the Columbia Broadcast Symphony, a position he was to hold for fifteen years. Herrmann regarded himself primarily as an artistic creator, and never allowed other professional obligations to interfere with composition. When he went to Hollywood, he had already completed a symphony, a violin concerto, and a dramatic cantata based on Herman Melville's "Moby Dick."

Armed with an encyclopedic knowledge of music and an uncanny ability to express emotions through sound, Bernard Herrmann was a natural for the film medium. He has consistently composed scores of impeccable taste, musicianship, and sensitivity, despite economic and social pressures to do otherwise. Many of the films on which he worked have become classics, a status for which his music was responsible to no small degree. His works will be discussed at length in this book because his contributions to the field of film scoring are unique.

The main title of *Citizen Kane* consists of a series of camera shots of Xanadu, Charles Foster Kane's exotic estate. The titles that come on the screen—"Mercury Production by Orson Welles" and "Citizen Kane"—appear without musical background. Herrmann begins the music a few seconds later, with a somber brass chord. The brass continue to play, joined gradually by contrabassoon, vibraphone, woodwinds, and strings. Horns eventually declare the motif that is closely identified with Kane. An ominous melody accompanying shots of Greek ruins and a cage of monkeys provides an impressive opening.

The sequence is typical of Herrmann's restraint. He had no desire to overload a scene with music; one of his greatest assets as a screen composer has always been his innate sense of timing, of always knowing precisely when (and when not) to use music for greatest effect. The music in *Citizen Kane* is always used as a linking device. In montage sequences, for example, it comments on characters as the camera cannot. A montage depicting Kane and his first wife at breakfast receives an unusual treatment: variations on a sentimental waltz become more dissonant and reach into the highest registers of the orchestra as the Kane marriage disintegrates from wedded bliss into frosty non-communication. Kane's newspaper empire expands; Herrmann accompanies shots of high-speed presses with a galloping can-can. At various times he also employs other dance rhythms, among them hornpipes, polkas, and square dances. He skillfully manipulates his main motifs, a four-note theme for Kane and a mysterious vibraphone theme identified with the word "Rosebud." (Although not usually a devotee of leitmotifs, Herrmann knows how to use them.)

The opera sequence provided an opportunity for dramatic use of music. For this tense scene, which he described as "a terrified girl lost in the quicksand of a powerful orchestra," Herrmann felt that no existing opera was appropriate, so he wrote an aria. A forty-second orchestral introduction precedes Susan Alexander's entrance and her disastrous operatic debut. Herrmann selected a light lyric soprano and asked her to perform in a key too high for her natural voice range. The heavy orchestral accompaniment, the high register, and the mismatching of voice and vocal material create exactly the right effect.

In the final sequence in *Citizen Kane*, Herrmann uses the strings to intensify the scene in which Kane's sled is tossed into the fire. He quotes the musical motifs identified with Kane's childhood, reminding the audience subconsciously of the true origin of "Rosebud." Kane's death is also accompanied by quotations of the motif. Ominous music brings the film to its conclusion.

Herrmann regards *Citizen Kane* as unique among his many films. In a recent interview, he said of Orson Welles: "He has no intellectual backbone as an artist; he's a great improviser in the sense that Beecham was a great improvisational conductor. The Mercury Players were a superb orchestra. When Orson had his own people around him, things happened." Clearly Herrmann admires Welles's enthusiasm and his extreme creativity. The composer's intensely romantic approach to film scoring was ideal for Welles's incredibly energetic and equally romantic direction.

Another Herrmann film released in 1941, the same year as *Citizen Kane,* was *All That Money Can Buy,* based on Stephen Vincent Benét's classic, "The Devil and Daniel Webster." The tale relates the sad plight of a New Hampshire farmer, Jabez Stone, who sells his soul to the devil in order to obtain good fortune. The pact lasts only for seven years, and when Mr. Scratch (the devil) comes to claim his soul, the farmer appeals to Daniel Webster, the famed statesman, to help him escape from the devil's contract. Scratch agrees to let the matter come to trial but brings in a jury composed of the spirits of some of America's most notorious murderers and traitors.

Herrmann's music for this film ranges from the delicate, folk-like, and tender to crashing sounds of raging fury, as the case demands. The theme for Scratch is wily, roguish, and nervously alive, darting mischievously in and out of the composer's musical tapestry. Whenever the devil appears he is accompanied by a special sound-effect derived from a singing telephone wire (recorded at 4 A.M.). To accompany the pastoral scenes of wheatfields and sturdy New Hampshire trees, Herrmann composed a lyric and expressive piece for oboe and strings. Again employing dance rhythms, he wrote an interesting piece of Americana, a diabolical scherzo incorporating sleighbells, for a sequence in which Scratch arranges a sleighride for his victims. An eerie, unearthly *danse macabre* in waltz tempo accompanies the death of Miser Stevens, another of the devil's clients. The music alternates between ethereal and thundering sections, the harmonies becoming increasingly discordant as Stevens grows more agitated. Ultimately, the miser is transformed into a butterfly and added to Mr. Scratch's collection. After the eloquent Webster convinces the jury to let Jabez Stone have another chance, a rollicking barn dance is interrupted by the devil, looking for new clients. (When the devil plays at the dance, four violin tracks are superimposed on each other.) In the final scene Scratch looks straight at the audience; it is obvious who is next on his agenda.

Herrmann's early scores won him grants and awards, an Oscar, and offers of new film assignments. Two of his most notable efforts during these years were his next collaboration with Welles, *The Magnificent Ambersons* (1942), and the Aldous Huxley-John Houseman adaptation of *Jane Eyre* (1944). In *The Magnificent Ambersons,* Herrmann's approach was similar to the one he used in *Citizen Kane.* Every note, every orchestral chord is an integral part of the film. It abounds with lyrical melodies, accelerating scherzos, and delicate, restrained underscoring. A waltz of Waldteufel served as a sentimental point of departure. For a Saturday night band concert, Herrmann wrote a symphonic piece using ragtime rhythms and spirited trumpet solos. A haunting meditation with a spiritual quality was scored for violins and harp, one of the composer's favorite combinations.

The music in *Jane Eyre* is gloomy and passionate, demonstrating his complete affinity with Brontë. Jane Eyre herself is represented by a poetic melody drawing upon modal harmonies, full of the spirit of the English countryside. A spirited orchestral accompaniment follows her across the foggy moors. For the mystery of the tower in Thornfield Hall, the fire, and the storm sequence, Herrmann turned to somber brass chords, thundering timpani, and an orchestra that virtually snarls and trembles with fear and fury. The love scenes between Jane and Rochester are played against rich, romantic melodies.

Also from this era is Herrmann's score for *The Ghost and Mrs. Muir* (1947), a departure from his other works of the time. He has described the music as his most romantic score. As always, Herrmann's harmonic vocabulary is his own, but here particularly it reflects the styles of the composers that have influenced him—the dark, cold brass of Vaughan Williams and Sibelius, the highly coloristic orchestration and identification with nature associated with Debussy and Delius. Herrmann wrote a light, sea-chantey motif for the ghost, an almost passionate melodic line as background for the relationship between Mrs. Muir and a suave, rather foppish writer. For Mrs. Muir's walks by the sea and, by extension, the passage of time symbolized by the ebb and flow of the water, Herrmann composed an impressionistic collage of cascading harp arpeggios, a glorious melody of horns, violas, and cellos, eventually taken over by the violins. For a sea storm, he turns to pyramid orchestration, starting in the lowest orchestral tessitura and gradually building to a culmination as waves crash against offshore rocks. Extraordinary effects are achieved through polymodal figures for the strings and winds, offset against open brass. A musical climax is reached through racing chromatic scales in the woodwinds and strings. Herrmann also wrote a melancholy composition for high strings and harp to accompany a scene in which Mrs. Muir remembers the ghost of long ago. It is a haunting melody, extended in arioso style, and achieves a touching poignancy with great dignity and restraint.

Early in his Hollywood career, Herrmann became known as an intense man with an explosive temperament. A number of serious and dedicated musicians, finding themselves in conflict with studio administrators who saw themselves primarily as businessmen, withdrew from the screen industry to work full time on concert music and teaching. Herrmann chose to remain. Like his friend Sir Thomas

Beecham, to whom he has often been compared, he never felt it necessary to be diplomatic in dealing with those he regards as musical charlatans. Colleagues have said that working with Bernard Herrmann is like sitting atop a volcano, but they acknowledge his genius. A veteran music editor claims that Herrmann is the strictest disciplinarian he has ever met, quickly adding, "Of course, I learned more from him than anyone else in my career."

Most stories about Herrmann that appear in print overlook some key elements in his character. He is not often described as a man who likes to provide a home for stray animals. Always a respecter of nonconformity, he has quietly and without fanfare championed the works of many young composers (as well as working to rescue Charles Ives from obscurity). Typically, he declines credit for such efforts, describing them merely as "what one artist should do for another." His interests have extended to forgotten nineteenth-century Europeans, Americans of all compositional styles, and a host of British composers little known in the United States.

Herrmann, with a romantic's view of art as the result of spontaneous creation, dislikes intellectualizing about it, especially when people try to explain what an artist means. He regards as misguided those critics who write long dissertations tracing the origins of musical themes or viewing musical structure as an end in itself. Similarly, he has little use for attempts to "academicize" film scores: "My colleagues who write double-fugues while two people are having tea on the screen are kidding themselves," he says.

Herrmann also has a hearty dislike for slipshod musicianship. He has constantly inveighed against re-orchestration or other distortion of classical works, a daily occurrence in the film industry. And, while Hollywood has its share of composers whose attitude toward producers may charitably be described as obsequious, Herrmann, predictably, is the exception. He is perfectly capable of administering a thunderous tongue-lashing to a producer who seems indifferent to quality.

Many successful screen composers lose interest in music unrelated to their source of income. Herrmann, on the contrary, has occupied himself with challenges of many kinds. He has introduced the public to forgotten works by romantic symphonists such as Raff and Gade. And he has produced a steady flow of serious music, culminating in his masterful opera based on "Wuthering Heights."

When "pop" scores became the fashion in the 1960s, Herrmann resigned his membership in the Academy of Motion Picture Arts and Sciences, declaring that he preferred to be judged by his peers, not his inferiors. He has not been recognized thus far by critics of the avant-garde, but his concert works, although outside the scope of this book, qualify him as a major American composer.

Herrmann is an intense and prolific worker who starts composing at dawn and completes his daily session by mid-morning. He prides himself on writing music that enters and exits from the soundtrack with extreme subtlety. A rugged individualist, he nevertheless regards the composer's role in developing a film as part of a team effort. In the 1960s, when engaged by Truffaut to score *Fahrenheit 451*, Herrmann asked the French director why he had not offered the film to one of his many avant-garde friends. Truffaut replied that the fashionable French modernists would give him music of the twentieth century—Herrmann's would belong to the twenty-first.

Victor Young

Another exponent of the romantic style was Victor Young, whose numerous screen scores earned him considerable popularity in the Hollywood of the 1940s and 1950s.

A violinist and conductor, born in Chicago but trained in Europe, Young was an extremely prolific songwriter with a remarkable gift for lyricism. His approach to a film was essentially uncomplicated: he sat down and poured out streams of long, romantic, emotional melodies. Studio music executives marveled at his ability to turn out one beautiful theme after another. They liked tunes they could whistle, and Young's work fit this category beautifully, especially after arrangement by his orchestrators, Leo Shuken and Sidney Cutner.

Critics who preferred a more dissonant or intellectual approach to cinema regarded Young's approach as overly sentimental. Ultimately his opulent scores became the prototype of "Hollywood music." But he understood that audiences and producers alike responded with tears and laughter to his expressive melodies. At his best, he added depth and vitality to films in the most direct way possible, by communicating with his audience. At the time of his death in 1956 he had contributed to some 300 motion pictures. He won the Academy Award posthumously, for his score for *Around the World in 80 Days*.

Young's associates agree that among his finest work was the music he wrote for the 1944 production of Ernest Hemingway's classic novel, *For Whom the Bell Tolls*. As always, the core of the orchestra is the string section, whose every resource is exploited. The themes are Spanish, with elements of Sevillian, Andalusian, Moorish, Catalan, and Aragonese styles. A solo guitar and cathedral bell increase the Spanish flavor of the work. As always, the score contains a love theme, an intense melody entitled "The Earth Moved," rendered by a solo violin against a background of strings playing tremolo figures in the uppermost registers. *For Whom the Bell Tolls* became a model for composers concerned with developing themes for other motion pictures dealing with a Spanish background.

Young's scores always contained numerous melodic variations on his themes, of every shade and hue. Although he was a highly skilled songwriter, he used his song melodies primarily as bases for development.

Miklos Rozsa

Foremost among foreign-born exemplars of the romantic tradition is Miklos Rozsa, generally respected as one of Hollywood's finest musicians. When he was only twenty-one in his native Hungary, he was signed by the German music publishers Breitkopf and Haertel (who still publish his concert music). Rozsa's friend Arthur Honegger was working in films, and Rozsa was so impressed with his score for *Les Misérables* that he wanted to try his own hand at the craft. He was told the inevitable: producers hire only composers with credits. Rozsa continued to write concert music. One of his ballets attracted the attention of French director Jacques Feyder, who invited him to dine. During dinner a beautiful German guest suddenly asked Rozsa whether her songs were ready. The lady's name, it turned out, was Marlene Dietrich; the songs were to be part of the score of Rozsa's first picture, *Knight Without Armor* (1937).

Rozsa was next involved with Alexander Korda's film *The Thief of Baghdad* (1940). The director, a German named Ludwig Berger, wanted a score by Oscar Straus, a composer of Viennese operettas. Korda wanted Rozsa, and Berger eventually accepted his material instead of the songs submitted by Straus. Rozsa's scores for *The Thief of Baghdad* and *Rudyard Kipling's Jungle Book* (1942) attracted considerable attention; they abounded with appropriate orientalisms, blended with Rozsa's own lyrical, chromatic texture.

It was in the area of psychological films, however, that Rozsa gained his greatest fame during the 1940s. Actually

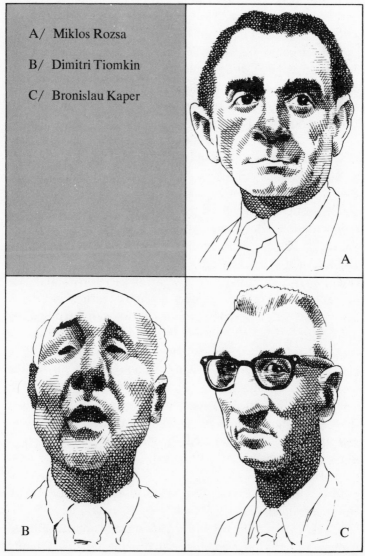

A/ Miklos Rozsa

B/ Dimitri Tiomkin

C/ Bronislau Kaper

(Nade)

he is adept at any type of scoring, but his career in Hollywood has been influenced by typecasting. His music is of such high caliber and demonstrates such consummate skill that producers tend to identify him closely with the type of film he has just scored. Thus he started with exoticism *(The Thief of Baghdad)* and then became identified with psychological suspense films *(Spellbound)*. Later, in the 1950s, he was to begin a long cycle of historical films. Rozsa is eminently Hungarian in musical outlook. The chromaticism of a Middle-European tradition inherited from his teacher, a follower of Max Reger, has remained with him throughout his career. But he has consistently adapted his musical style to various periods and idioms.

Rozsa won his first Oscar for *Spellbound* (1945), Hitchcock's thriller for which Salvador Dali had designed the dream sequences. Much of the attention focused on Rozsa's score resulted from his use of an electronic instrument, the theremin. His music is tense and impassioned, reaching a climax when Gregory Peck, obsessed with the color white, enters Ingrid Bergman's room carrying a razor, and discovers that she is sleeping under a white coverlet. The music here is scored for strings, with tremolos interrupted by muted brass. As the tension increases, Rozsa allows the brass to state his themes over terrifying, shrieking tremolo figures; he also begins a driving ostinato which carries the scene to its conclusion.

Rozsa, a nondrinker, used his imagination and fantasized about the agonies of alcoholism in *The Lost Weekend* (1945). Again he used the theremin, this time in a sequence in which Ray Milland discovers he cannot exist without a drink.

In this period, Rozsa also wrote scores for three Mark Hellinger films, *The Killers* (1946), *Brute Force* (1947), and *The Naked City* (1948). Hellinger produced motion pictures full of violence and crime, dramas about the nature of the underworld. Breaking with the traditional sentimentality and romanticism of Hollywood, they emphasized stark realism. By using brilliant orchestration and development of his themes, Rozsa created an atmosphere of forceful power and brutality. His motif for *The Killers* ultimately became the celebrated "Dragnet" theme, probably the single most famous musical motif ever to come out of television or motion pictures. The opening sequence of *Brute Force* is a hard, driving prelude, full of brass chords, a basso-ostinato upon which Rozsa builds his tension, and a nervous, pulsating rhythm. His music intensifies the characterization of the film. One sequence features the reminiscences of a well-meaning but blundering prison inmate who has been cheated by the woman he loved. Rozsa augments the scene with a Chaplinesque scherzo. When the prisoners gaze at the stars, dreaming of their past lives and their freedom, the background is a gentle, haunting nocturne, scored for strings. The use of the high register creates a feeling of physical height, of the sky and stars above the prison, seemingly close, yet light years away.

In *The Naked City*, Rozsa wrote some frenzied fugato passages, introducing one theme, developing it, and then combining it with a second theme. The fugato ends with the death of a gangster. The Hellinger film scores served as the basis for a concert suite, "Background to Violence," which Rozsa eventually scored for concert orchestra.

One of Rozsa's most distinguished efforts, *Madame Bovary* (1949), was inspired by the Hollywood version of Flaubert's novel. Rozsa had long admired the novel; he wrote an intense, whirling waltz for the famous ballroom scene, carefully following the descriptions of the sequence in Flaubert's work. Rozsa has always devoted intensive analysis to the psychological nature of the characters in the motion pictures he scores. The result has been unfailing sensitivity and scores of high musical quality.

Franz Waxman

Waxman's most renowned effort during the 1940s resulted from Selznick's invitation to write the score for
Rebecca, one of the major films of 1940. Waxman worked
primarily with leitmotifs. He did not, however, merely de-
vise themes for the orchestra to play in identification with
certain characters. Instead, he developed them in subtle
ways. For example, in one scene involving the path to
Rebecca's bedroom, he develops a theme first employed
when Rebecca's name is initially mentioned. When the
second wife, the principal character of the story, says,
"Last night I dreamed I went to Manderley again," Waxman
introduces a melody identified with the influence of the
mysterious Rebecca, who cast a spell over the house that
had once belonged to her.

Waxman's music was in some ways stylistically related
to the traditions established by Korngold. But Korngold
was Viennese, while Waxman was German, and the latter
turned more often to contrapuntal development and dissonances than the composers influenced by Strauss.

In *Dr. Jekyll and Mr. Hyde* (1941), Waxman employed
a chorus over the opening and closing credits. He explained
his unusual scoring by noting that the film emphasized the
triumph of man's best instincts over his worst. In *Suspicion,*
a Hitchcock film of 1941, Waxman used an electric violin
to create the element of fear. He placed great emphasis on
orchestral color, often choosing his instruments to create
sounds that would match the style of the scene as closely
as the melodic material. In fact, he indicated, he often
thought of the choice of color *before* writing the melodic
material. In *Pride of the Marines* (1945), he used a single
trumpet to create the feeling of loneliness that affects a
man who goes off to war. Waxman could be polyphonic
and complex (as in his fugue for *Objective Burma*) or

lyrical and expressive, writing melodies that called for grand leaps and exuberant strings.

Dimitri Tiomkin

One of Hollywood's classic ironies is that the composer of some of its most famous Western scores is a Russian. Dimitri Tiomkin, born in St. Petersburg, began his colorful career as a pianist, then turned to composition. He wrote for the ballet, toured Europe, and moved to Hollywood in 1929. Tiomkin is noted as a melodist who likes rich orchestration, and as a unique personality who enjoys a laugh on himself. His famous speech on accepting an Academy Award in 1955 (for *The High and the Mighty*) gave credit to the major classical composers, especially Tchaikovsky, from whom some Hollywood specialists had been borrowing for years.

One of Tiomkin's early scores was for Selznick's *Duel in the Sun* (1946). It abounds with lush instrumentation and melodious themes. Crucial scenes have basic musical motifs. A "casino dance" is scored for marimbas, xylophones, and Indian tom-toms, building to a frenzied and furious crescendo. For the love scenes between Jennifer Jones and Gregory Peck, Tiomkin wrote two more motifs, a "love theme" and a "conflict theme," ultimately combining them in contrapuntal style. In the musical accompaniment along the trail to the Spanish Bit, woodblocks and a solo accordion create the effect of walking horses. The trek to the sun is accompanied by a relentless, polyphonic ostinato for strings.

Copland, Friedhofer, and Raksin

Musical styles, like clothing, are dictated by fashion. At times producers insist on certain musical effects because they fear that a departure from the familiar will be unacceptable. For instance, Gershwin's music in "An American in Paris" was long the prototype for traffic jams. Honking autos had to be accompanied by a Gershwin-style gallop. Alfred Newman established another trend in *Street Scene,* with a lonely blues theme. The blues, suggesting the sophistication and worldliness of the big city, became the metropolitan prototype.

The whole approach to film scoring has relied heavily on established styles, and in the 1940s big symphonies and the romantic tradition were still the norm. This European mode was ideal for costume dramas or dramatic films, especially considering the heavy sentiment of features of the period. But it was less suitable for Westerns and other films of a peculiarly American genre. Another style developed, strongly influenced by Aaron Copland, particularly by his score for *The Red Pony* (1949).

The Red Pony, a screen adaptation of John Steinbeck's short story, is an atypical Western; there are no gunmen or Indians. There is a cowboy, but he doesn't do anything that motion picture cowboys usually do. The principal figure of the tale is young Tom Tiflin, who lives with his parents on their California ranch. Tom spends his time dreaming that he is a circus ringmaster or the general of a ghostly army, and looks forward to the day when Rosie, a mare belonging to ranch hand Billy Buck, will produce another colt. Tom's father gives him a red pony as a gift. Tom loves the pony, but it wanders out into the rain and becomes ill. When Billy Buck tries to operate on it, he is unsuccessful. Eventually the pony dies, and Tom is forced to fight off the buzzards who discover its body. At first Tom is bitter at Billy, but his resentment fades when Billy gives him Rosie's colt.

All the key sequences of the film are accompanied and underscored by Copland's tuneful and triadic music, which captures the spirit of cowboys and ranch life. Simple folk harmonies create a feeling of nature, directness, and simplicity. The film opens at daybreak on the ranch. Copland does not attempt to imitate the wind or singing birds in an impressionistic way, but instead begins his work with short musical phrases that are models of clarity. A busy background of woodwinds accompanies the breakfast sounds of frying eggs and crackling bacon. There is hardly a Western that does not include cowboys on horseback. For *The Red Pony*—no exception to the rule—Copland chose a steady rhythmic accompaniment to create a trotting effect. Over this he wrote two melodies, one in the style of a spirited cowboy song, the other more expansive; the first melody is played by the trumpet and the second by violins. The basic time stream of five alternates 3/4 and 2/4 measures. Copland wrote a gay melody for Tom's school friends, rearranging it for toy trumpet and tuba when Tom is depicted dreaming about his imaginary army. Copland turns from consonance to dissonance as Tom's encounters with nature become more realistic, bitter, and violent. Polytonal, polytriadic, and cluster effects are common. He develops one of his themes canonically, with clashing orchestrations, for a storm scene. When Tom fights off the buzzards, the music employs complex cross rhythms in the high registers of the orchestra.

Copland's approach to a film like *The Red Pony* is best understood by considering his overall perspective. Like Korngold, he was interested less in catching bits and pieces of action than in dividing a motion picture into sequences and developing accompaniments for each. Western feeling in *The Red Pony* derives from the irregularity and the ambling, awkward line of Copland's melodies, a free-wheeling angularity appropriate for the genre. Another point of interest is the composer's use of harmonic color to create the image of childhood. While Tom's world is logical, and he depends on his parents and other adults for security, this music is consonant. Dissonance is linked to the harsher experiences of life which Tom encounters in the process of growing up.

One of the most noted screen composers to write in the Copland tradition was Hugo Friedhofer. He began his musical career as a performing musician in his native San Francisco, moving to Hollywood when offered a job as an arranger at Fox. Later he went to Warner Brothers, where he orchestrated for Max Steiner and Erich Korngold. Eventually, producers recognized that Friedhofer was an accomplished composer in his own right and in 1937 he was invited by the Goldwyn Studio to write the background score for *The Adventures of Marco Polo*. He became respected by Hollywood musicians for his extensive knowledge of the screen idiom.

Friedhofer believes that music can provide a counterpoint to the visual action of a film. He disapproves of the idea that a person running on the screen must be accompanied by music that also runs. An acute critic, he once suggested that the difference between Tchaikovsky and Brahms was one of objectivity: Tchaikovsky says, "How unhappy I am"; Brahms says, "How tragic this is." Friedhofer's score for *The Best Years of Our Lives* (1946) was one of the more widely acclaimed works written for the screen. It became the model for numerous scores, serving as an example of what could be done in the realm of Americana. The film tells the story of three veterans returning from World War II. Although the script had elements of sentiment, emotion, and romance, it did not call for a lush musical accompaniment. Friedhofer chose to work with leitmotifs, but cast his themes in an American idiom and orchestrated them in the style of Copland. He did not adapt his melodies from folk songs, but rather composed original themes in a folk tradition.

The main theme of *Best Years* serves as the basis for the main title. Built on a series of triadic progressions, it is like the characters in the film: sturdy, direct, and straight-forward. Both the triadic melody and its hymnlike accompaniment are exploited in the score. A "Boone City" theme is constructed of two principal ideas, a five-note motif and a syncopated broken triad figure. A gentle melody harmonized in triads portrays the relationship between the family of Homer, a main character in the film, and his girl friend's family next door. Although the film does not include a love theme, it does contain a lyrical melody, "Peggy." Another melody, "Wilma," was recorded several times and became identified as the *"Best Years* theme." The scenes between Fred and Peggy are underscored by a blues-style melody not unlike Newman's famous *Street Scene* theme. For one sequence, where Homer smashes a toolshed window, Friedhofer, always a skilled and highly imaginative orchestrator, uses a variation of the familiar children's taunt that seems to have appealed to young people of every generation and every nation. Not all the scoring in *The Best Years of Our Lives* is thematic. Misterioso passages for strings, augmented by piccolos and trumpets (creating a martial feeling), are used for nightmare scenes to re-create the unhappy memories of wartime. Bombing sequences are scored so as to achieve the effect of battle without the sounds of war.

Friedhofer's music for *Best Years* won an Academy Award and was generally recognized as one of the first scores to achieve wide popularity despite its non-European style. Among his other scores of this period were such classics as *The Bishop's Wife* (1947), for which he wrote a lightly satirical score in the baroque idiom, and *Joan of Arc* (1948), the music for which was dramatic and sophisticated. Throughout Friedhofer's career, he has been identified as a man of extreme versatility, capable of dealing with many styles with equal finesse.

Another Hollywood composer who might be said to belong to the Copland school is David Raksin, who himself has provided a strong influence with his highly chromatic melodic writing. The final sequence from *Force of Evil* (1948) illustrates his style. It begins with a chromatic solo played by alto saxophone. Gradually the winds enter, introducing an important sixteenth-note motif. The accompaniment consists of a series of polytonal and polytriadic chord progressions. Dissonant sections are the result of linear melodic development, and there is considerable polyphonic imitation. In contrast, a lyrical "Nocturne" section is dominated by a long, flowing melody that outlines the harmonic accompaniment. Chords that support the melody are often triads with added 7ths, 9ths, and 13ths. The sophisticated tone of the score matches the contemporary mood of the picture. Raksin also wrote one of the screen's most distinguished melodies for *The Bad and The Beautiful* (1952), again characterized by wide melodic leaps and a choral foundation far more complex than the average film theme.

Other Concert Music Composers

Aaron Copland did very little work in Hollywood after *The Red Pony*. The relationship of other distinguished composers of concert music to the American commercial film world has ranged from brief to bizarre. In Europe producers were accustomed to assigning screen scoring to eminent composers of concert music. The film composer as such was relatively unknown. Vaughan Williams or Shostakovich might be writing either a film score or a symphony, and no one regarded the pursuit of both interests as incongruous. In Hollywood, however, the serious composer faced an adjustment. Depending upon his personality and temperament, he might adapt to the realities of the commercial music industry, or he might withdraw and devote himself to teaching and writing serious music. Korngold, for example, worked with great freedom at Warner Brothers, but subsequently retired to devote himself to his own music.

No genuine studio music departments exist today, but they were a powerful reality during the 1930s and 1940s. Survival in the film industry then required not only musical ability, but also the capacity to witness with some degree of stoicism the mutilation of one's work by studio administrators. A composer disinclined to follow a producer's instructions could be fired; his work could be emasculated by an executive with the musical acumen of a carnival barker. The composers who survived often had to shout down executives or do battle with the studio hierarchy. Actually, producers still assume that they understand the ways in which composers work. As late as the 1960s, David Amram encountered a bellicose production executive who refused to believe that he did not use helpers or ghost-writers.

Igor Stravinsky once offered to compose a film score for an enormous fee under his own name, or a fraction of the fee under a pseudonym. ("The music is cheap," he told producers. "It's the name that's expensive.") We can at least speculate about the type of film music Stravinsky might have written. His "Norwegian Sketches" were originally intended for use in a film. This suite shows the influence of Grieg, although the themes came from a collection of Norwegian folk music found by Stravinsky's wife in a second-hand bookstore. Another example is the slow movement of the composer's "Symphony in Three Movements," with passages for harp, solo winds, and string ensemble. In 1962, Stravinsky revealed that he had originally written this movement for the vision scene in *The Song of Bernadette* (although of course he did not score the film).

A number of other composers had brief or tangential relations with the film industry. One such was Karol Rathaus, widely known in Europe and the composer of an outstanding score for a German production of *The Brothers Karamazov*. He was not known as a film composer in the United States, and although he scored a number of documentaries in New York City, he remained undiscovered by the commercial film industry and devoted himself to teaching.

Mario Castelnuovo-Tedesco made a unique contribution to the motion picture industry. The renowned composer moved to the United States from his native Italy. A former pupil of Pizzetti, he had written numerous orchestral and chamber works, operas, solo concertos for leading virtuosi, and a number of compositions for voice and piano. Shortly after he arrived in California, he turned to motion picture scoring. His work included such challenging assignments as scoring a film version of "Carmen"—without using any of Bizet's music. He subsequently retired from film scoring to devote himself to teaching, and personally trained an entire generation of motion picture composers. Although he insisted that his pupils acquire a thorough foundation in composition and orchestration, he always encouraged them to develop their own styles. Among the most successful of the younger generation of screen composers who came to prominence in the 1950s, they included André Previn, Lionel Newman, Henry Mancini, John Williams, Jerry Goldsmith, Nelson Riddle, and George Duning.

Ernst Toch enjoyed an eminent reputation as the composer of symphonic and chamber works, operas, and incidental music both in his native Vienna and in Germany. He taught extensively in Europe and the United States, numbering several film composers among his pupils. Toch scored films in Hollywood in the 1930s, the most famous being *Peter Ibbetson* (1935). It contained some sensitively scored, highly ethereal dream sequences, and displayed the composer's highly personal style of polyphony and his use of voices for orchestral color. Like Korngold, Toch retired from film scoring, dividing his time between serious composition and teaching.

Alexander Tansman, a native of Poland, toured the world extensively as composer, pianist, and conductor. He completed many orchestral compositions prior to his first American film score, *Flesh and Fantasy* (1943). His "Scherzo" from this film was one of the first such orchestral pieces to be recorded. His other films included *Destiny* (1944), *Paris Underground* (1945), and *Sister Kenny* (1946).

The conductor who led Tansman's historic orchestral recording in 1943 was Werner Janssen, who himself had appeared with major American and European orchestras and had also written orchestral and chamber music. His score for *The General Died at Dawn* (1936) was one of the first serious accompaniments to a Hollywood film. He composed the music while the film was being photographed, in effect while reading the script. Scheduled to leave Hollywood for New York, where he was conducting the New York Philharmonic, he listened to his score at a proofreading rehearsal conducted by Irvin Talbot. Ernst Toch, Hugo Friedhofer, Heinz Roemheld, and Gerard Carbonara were given corrected cue sheets and assigned to edit and revise the sequences that Janssen had written to conform with the new cue sheets. The final recording session, also directed by Talbot, was devoted to the new edited sequences.

Other Hollywood Figures

The number of composers active on the West Coast during the 1940s was legion. A prolific writer was Frank Skinner, who had studied at the Chicago Musical College and then moved to New York, where he arranged stock orchestrations for music publishing houses. In 1935, he went to Hollywood, where he arranged *The Great Ziegfeld*.

Later he worked for Universal-International, composing all the music for the Deanna Durbin films. Skinner wrote the first major technical instruction book on motion picture scoring, "Underscore." Although other volumes had dealt with the aesthetics of film music, Skinner discussed in detail the precise mechanics of timing procedures and composing in accordance with them. He remained at Universal for many years, writing scores that ranged from horror films to Westerns to period pieces to features set in the present day. A modest craftsman, he devoted little time to promoting his reputation commercially, and even though his music often appeared on records, it was occasionally uncredited.

Cyril Mockridge studied at the Royal Academy of Music in London. In New York he served as musical director and orchestrator for the Broadway stage in the 1930s. In California he joined the Fox music department. Like Newman, he was especially identified with the "Fox string sound." His credits included *Cluny Brown* (1946) and *The Late George Apley* (1947).

Roy Webb began his career in New York, orchestrating such musical comedies as "A Connecticut Yankee." He subsequently joined the staff at RKO. After arriving in Hollywood in the early 1930s, he worked for many years at both RKO and Warner Brothers, composing numerous scores in the symphonic style. He was an exponent of precise timings and a pioneer in the use of the click-track. Associated with Max Steiner during the early years of his film scoring career, Webb had a somewhat similar musical style.

Leigh Harline attended the University of Utah and then joined the Utah Radio Orchestra. In Hollywood he was affiliated with the Disney Studios, where he wrote the background music for *Snow White and the Seven Dwarfs* (1939) and the entire score for *Pinocchio* (1940), including the hit song, "When You Wish Upon a Star." He re-

A/ John Green

B/ Irvin Talbot

C/ Alfred Newman

mained in Hollywood to score numerous other motion pictures on a free-lance basis.

Daniele Amfitheatrof, after studying composition with Respighi in Rome, conducted radio orchestras and major orchestras of Europe. In Hollywood, his credits included scores for *Letter From an Unknown Woman* (1948) and *Another Part of the Forest* (1948). He was identified with a lyrical, melodic style of writing, often exploiting the symphonic orchestra. Today he is writing concert music in Europe.

Herbert Stothart, born in Milwaukee, began his career on Broadway, contributing much of the musical score for "Rose-Marie." After providing the music for the Lawrence Tibbett feature, *The Rogue Song,* he became active in film scoring. Stothart scored numerous classic films at MGM, including the Jeanette MacDonald-Nelson Eddy features, and served as musical director for *The Wizard of Oz*. His style was melodic and highly lyrical. One of Stothart's most famous works, which he wrote with Rudolf Friml, was the "Donkey Serenade."

Adolph Deutsch was born in London, studied composition and piano, and moved to the United States as a boy. His compositions have been performed by major symphony orchestras, and he is interested in jazz and popular music as well. Active as a member of Warner Brothers, he has also composed and conducted for radio and the theater. Lyn Murray, also born in England, served as musical director for numerous radio programs in the United States. He provided incidental music for Columbia Workshop, wrote an opera with Norman Corwin, and conducted and composed for both vocal and instrumental ensembles. He subsequently scored and orchestrated many films.

Paul Sawtell studied in Berlin, Munich, and Chicago. He conducted and composed many motion picture scores, including those for the famous Tarzan films. In addition, he made frequent appearances as a guest conductor of symphony orchestras. Frederick Hollander had pioneered in film scoring in Germany. At Warner Brothers, he scored such noted American comedies as *The Man Who Came to Dinner* (1941).

Oscar Levant played a unique role in Hollywood film music. Though first known chiefly as a pianist, his subsequent reputation was that of a writer, composer, actor, and caustic observer of the Hollywood scene. He began his career as a pianist in silent film orchestras, but it was short-lived. When a conductor reprimanded him for a mistaken entrance, Levant retorted that he would play on cue if given proper notice. He was fired. Levant's compositions included an opera sequence for *Charlie Chan at the Opera* (1937), rendered on the screen by Boris Karloff (his voice dubbed by a studio singer).

The concert music of George Antheil was for a time regarded as outrageous by conservative critics. Antheil, who was also a piano virtuoso, embarked upon a successful career in motion picture music in the 1930s. He scored numerous films, among them *The Plainsman* (1936) and *Angels Over Broadway* (1940).

The Newman family contributed the talents of three of its members to Hollywood. Alfred Newman has already been discussed for his pioneering work in film music. His brother Emil was active as a composer and orchestrator. Lionel Newman, another brother, orchestrated films and has written numerous popular songs as well. Today he is general music director and head of the music department of Twentieth Century-Fox. In addition to his own composing activities for both films and television, he also conducts scores by other composers.

A complete listing of all the people active in film scoring in the 1940s would be impossible. No fine line existed between composers and orchestrators. A staff musician at a major studio might arrange or orchestrate scores, compose original accompaniments of his own, or conduct a recording session. Among the many who contributed to the development of motion picture music were Jeff Alexander, Leo Arnaud, Constantine Bakaleinikoff, Alexander Courage, Sidney Cutner, Murray Cutter, Sidney Fine, Robert Franklyn, Russell Garcia, Calvin Jackson, Howard Jackson, Jack Hayes, Lennie Hayton, Ray Heindorf, William Lava, Gus Levene, Arthur Morton, Maurice de Packh, Edward B. Powell, Leonid Raab, Ruby Raksin, Conrad Salinger, Hans J. Salter, Leo Shuken, Herbert Spencer, Morris Stoloff, David Tamkin, Nathan Van Cleave, and Eugene Zador.

Ralph Vaughan Williams

Hollywood, of course, had no monopoly on film music talent in the 1940s. In Britain, the pinnacle of film scoring was achieved when two of England's most distinguished creators, Ralph Vaughan Williams and William Walton, devoted major efforts to the screen.

Vaughan Williams's supreme achievement was to show how the colors of a full symphonic orchestra could be applied in an impressionistic style to convey the feeling of a landscape. In 1941 Muir Mathieson invited the composer to write music for English documentaries and features. He enjoyed great success with an early effort, *49th Parallel* (1941), and subsequently arranged its themes into a concert suite. After the war, Vaughan Williams turned to scoring major features, often blending choral voices with orchestral colors to produce unique effects. He approached the cinematic medium as a painter approaches his canvas, and chose to depend less on memorable melodies than on the use of the orchestra as a source of emotional color. As an exponent of atmospheric scoring, he wrote: "There are two ways of viewing film music: one, in which every action, word, gesture or incident is punctuated in sound. The other method of writing film music, which personally I favor, partly because I am quite incapable of doing the former, is to ignore the details and to intensify the spirit of the whole situation by a continuous stream of music. This stream can be modified (often at rehearsal!) by points of color superimposed on the flow."

For *Scott of the Antarctic* (1948) Vaughan Williams produced a symphonic masterpiece, a work that emerged after adaptation as his "Sinfonia Antarctica." Like Copland in his approach to *Our Town,* Vaughan Williams regarded his subject as one for which continuity was of singular importance. But of course it involved a very different form of unity than the progression of life in a simple New England town. For the film Vaughan Williams wrote music of austere majesty, long, lonely, sustained chordal passages suitable for an unconquerable landscape.

From the moment *Scott of the Antarctic* begins, the viewer cannot fail to be aware of the harsh world into which Scott and his men are about to immerse themselves. This is a confrontation between man and nature, between human beings and the primitive grandeur of the Antarctic wilderness. The loneliness of the region is underscored by a solo soprano vocalise, the frigid temperatures by disconnected xylophone notes. Against a background of vibraphone and wind machine, the harp, celesta, and percussion execute passages of icy delicacy, supported by a gentle halo of strings. Other melodies, scored for the brass, depict the bleakness of the polar region. Separate themes symbolize the two women whose lives were so important to the men on the expedition, Kathleen Scott and Oriana Wilson. Kathleen Scott, for example, is represented by an English horn theme played against harp accompaniment, suggesting the pastoral English countryside. Mournful deep bells produce a chimelike background for the death of Oates.

Why was Vaughan Williams's achievement so significant? The answer lies in the nature of the film itself. *Scott of the Antarctic* employed talented actors, but many of its key sequences were silent. Consider the scenes in which men oppose the ferocity of nature. Dialogue alone could not convey the gargantuan scope of their task, the feeling of impending danger, the loneliness of their existence. Each major cue, however, was underscored by Vaughan Williams's music. A moderately paced orchestral scherzo accompanies surfacing whales and comical penguins. Misty harmonies for strings and winds depict the surprise of the men in the Ross Island sequence; gradually, full brass and percussion expand the orchestral range and make the viewer subconsciously aware of the mystery, majesty, and potential danger of the landscape. For the concluding sequences, Vaughan Williams turned to a tragic, martial idiom. Every one of the orchestral effects—the string tremolos, the intense dynamics, the giant crescendos that resolve into ethereal silences—accent the bleak and beautiful images of this film.

The "Sinfonia Antarctica" was dedicated to Ernest Irving, who had originally engaged Vaughan Williams to write the score for *Scott of the Antarctic*. Actually, Irving had been critical of the music for *49th Parallel,* but after Vaughan Williams did the score for another Ealing film, *The Loves of Joanna Godden* (1947), the two men became close friends. (The composer had completed about fifty minutes of music for the dramatic scenes before the motion picture had even been shot. Although the two men had occasional disagreements, they got on remarkably well. Irving, for instance, suggested to the composer that his use of the singing voice in the orchestra would distract from dialogue on the screen.) In his dedication of the concert piece, Vaughan Williams said that he hoped the score would not prove to be a white elephant. Irving responded that his objections to the original white elephant arose not from its color, but from its appetite.

Vaughan Williams was involved in several other films during the 1940s and 1950s. He adapted his music for *Coastal Command* into a twelve-minute concert suite. For *Stricken Peninsula,* the composer employed Italian folk music scored for brass band. He collaborated with Ernest Irving in providing the music for *Bitter Springs,* set in the Australian Outback. Irving wrote several sections on his own, often developing variations on a melody by Vaughan Williams. In his score for *The England of Elizabeth,* Vaughan Williams incorporated orchestral treatments of the sixteenth-century songs "It Was a Lover and His Lass" and "The Wind and the Rain." This was not the first time he had used folk songs; *The People's Land* included such familiar tunes as "John Barleycorn" and "The Springtime of the Year." Two themes deleted from his film score for *Flemish Farm* were eventually used in his Sixth Symphony, which he began sketching shortly after the film was completed. As a commentator, Vaughan Williams described English musical life in the documentary, *Dim Little Island.* (In later years, he denied ever having heard of the film, but Gerald Cockshott remarked that "The voice is Vaughan Williams's and his part of the narration is so characteristic of his beliefs and of his style that he must have either written it or revised it to his own requirements.") Vaughan Williams's last film contribution was his set of ten Blake songs, for tenor and piano, for *The Vision of William Blake.*

William Walton

Shakespeare's plays have inspired composers ever since musicians first became familiar with them. The 1930s and 1940s saw several screen adaptations of Shakespearean plays, in which music played an extremely important role.

Foremost among the composers to work on these films was William Walton. In 1944 he collaborated with Laurence Olivier on the latter's production of *Henry V*.

Walton, whose style was more restrained and less rhapsodic than that of Vaughan Williams, had been writing motion picture music since the 1930s. He once observed: "The thing I quickly realized about film music was that it need not necessarily be good or bad, but it had to be appropriate." But composing for a Shakespeare play was uniquely challenging. Here above all the music cannot overshadow the dialogue. Because the audience must concentrate on the words, the score has to do its job without submerging the actors.

The composer approached this challenge with aplomb. At the beginning of the film, a handbill blown into the foreground by a breeze unfolds to reveal an announcement of a performance of *Henry V* at the Globe Theater. A racing flute solo is heard in the background, then the sound of plain chant as the camera reflects a view of Elizabethan London. An orchestra joins the voices, and on the screen musicians tune up instruments of the period: a chest of viols, a recorder, and a straight trumpet. (The subsequent overture, however, is scored for a modern symphony, although it employs old English modal harmonies and dance rhythms.)

In *Henry V*, Walton wisely used his music primarily as a linking device. The first chorus speech is followed by some spirited orchestral passages, but they enter gently. Chordal progressions often underscore the long speeches delivered by Olivier as the young king. Walton wrote two expressive pieces for strings, a passacaglia for the death of Falstaff, and a simple, haunting folk melody entitled "Touch Her Soft Lips and Part." The battle scenes are punctuated by music that increases their excitement; at one point, however, Walton surprises us by stopping the music completely, so that the only sound is that of arrows whistling toward their targets. At the end of the film, the "Agincourt Song," a traditional melody associated with the famous battle, is used in a special arrangement to underscore the credits.

Walton and Olivier worked together again on *Hamlet* (1948) and *Richard III* (1954). In both films Walton's music was consistently up to his high standard. A highlight of *Hamlet* was the tragic funeral march that opened and closed the screen play. To underscore Hamlet's soliloquy, Walton alternated the music of low strings with sound effects of crashing waves near Elsinore Castle. Ethereal sequences for woodwind solos, harp, celesta, and strings were later incorporated in a tone poem, "Hamlet and Ophelia." For *Richard III,* Walton created a stirring prelude in the spirit of royal pomp, several tender melodies for strings (among them "I Would I Knew Thy Heart"), and a wonderful period piece entitled "Music Plays." The latter is classic Walton in that it is music of high quality, conveys a sense of the period, and is full of the excitement of Elizabethan theater. Walton eventually arranged many of his favorite sequences from Shakespearean films for concert performance.

Walton regarded his collaboration with Olivier as the most rewarding of his experiences in films. He characterized Olivier as a man who invariably knew what he wanted as a director—and who was nearly always right. Muir Mathieson recalls an instance when Walton added some Italian instructions to a sequence for *Richard III.* When Olivier asked Walton to explain the directions, "Con prosciutto, agnello e confitura di fragiole," the composer, looking exceedingly distressed, replied, "Ham, lamb and strawberry jam!"

Although Walton's epic scores are more widely known, he also provided the music for such classics as *Major Barbara* (1941) and the 1935 version of *Escape Me Never.*

Other English Film Composers of the "Golden Age"

One of the most famous English film adaptations of a celebrated classic was *Oliver Twist* (1948). Its characteristically British humor came from the pen of Arnold Bax, a noted composer of concert music. Using the piano as a solo instrument, Bax wrote a theme for young Oliver and adapted it in variations for numerous scenes in which the boy appeared. The composer also wrote a spirited string sequence to underscore a scene in which juvenile pickpockets attempt a robbery.

Richard Addinsell scored numerous films in England during this period. He is most persistently identified with a work that is least representative of his personal style, the "Warsaw Concerto" (discussed in Chapter V). His score for *Blithe Spirit* combined mystery and humor, with ghostly passages for woodwinds and vibraphone, and a comic theme for Madame Arcati's bicycle ride.

Comedies were the forte of William Alwyn, whose score for *The History of Mr. Polly* contains a notable fugue for woodwinds, an accompaniment to Mr. Polly's early attempts at punting. Alwyn's other important films included *Captain Boycott* (which included material based on traditional Irish melodies), *The October Man, Madeleine, The Rocking Horse Winner,* and *Night Without Stars.*

John Ireland, one of England's best known serious composers, provided much of the excitement in *The Overlanders,* with distinctive music for a cattle stampede. Benjamin Frankel displayed extreme versatility in both serious and comic films, ranging from *London Belongs to Me* to *The Clouded Yellow* (with a piano melody in the style of Poulenc) to *Appointment With Venus* (for which he provided a pastoral theme for the central figure of the film, a cow.) Frankel's score for *The Man in the White Suit* contained a new sound effect, the "guggle," developed by

Mary Habberfield, sound editor at Ealing Studios, and augmented by a tuba and bassoon.

Anthony Hopkins demonstrated a unique flair for comedy scores, achieving humor through the use of serious music out of context. Other English composers active in this period included Leighton Lucas, Clifton Parker, and Lambert Williamson.

French Film Composers

The collaboration between Olivier and Walton brings to mind another remarkable association between director and composer, that of Orson Welles and Jacques Ibert. When Welles invited Ibert to join him on a film version of *Macbeth* (1948), Ibert viewed the prospect as a challenge. He observed: "There could be no question of writing a score having the grandiloquent quality of a symphony or lyric melodrama. Above all, I had to respect the general atmosphere that would be expressive without being too emphatic—purely cinematographic, blending with the tragedy without overwhelming it. Therefore, in composing this score I have tried to carry out this essential requirement and to translate in appropriate musical terms the impressions felt at viewing the film itself."

Ibert, famous for his colorful orchestrations, naturally used many unusual scoring effects. His choice of instruments always added color to the play's characterizations. For example, his theme for the witches was written for celesta (which played the melody), broken chord figurations in piano and harp, and a background that emphasized eerie viola harmonics. In the scene where Macbeth drinks to excess, Ibert used a tuba solo played against dissonant string chords. The blaring tuba creates a vivid impression of pompous grotesquerie.

Other major French contributions to motion picture scoring were made by members of "Les Six," who continued their interest in the cinematic medium. Darius Milhaud's film scores include those for *The Beloved Vagabond* (1936), *Rasputin* (1938), and his most famous, *The Private Affairs of Bel-Ami* (1946). Milhaud, whose technique and use of polyphony were similar to Satie's, preferred to develop short motifs rather than long melodic lines. His motion picture music was unobtrusive, often relying upon series of gently moving chord progressions to provide a quiet harmonic undercurrent. Occasionally, however, he varied the mood with jaunty, dancelike tunes and dissonant variations on his thematic material.

As noted earlier, Arthur Honegger made important contributions to the film medium. So did Francis Poulenc, who worked with Jean Anouilh on *Le Voyageur sans Bagages* (1943). But it was Georges Auric for whom motion picture music constituted a major career. Auric's music for Cocteau's *Le Sang d'un Poete* (1930) had made him a leading film composer in Paris. His scores for the same writer's *La Belle et La Bête* (1946) and *Orphée* (1950) were major works in the history of the French screen.

Auric's approach to film music was the reverse of that expected in Hollywood: he introduced musical themes only when absolutely necessary. (Technically, he went so far as to write melodies without chordal accompaniment.) In *La Belle et La Bête,* Auric achieved his orchestral effects through sensitive harmonic color and detailed scoring for strings. The beast was represented by a menacing melodic motif in the basses. His score was both tonal and melodic, but restrained string tremolos, harp figuration, and unresolved harmonic progressions created a quality of mystery and suspense. In *Orphée,* Auric employed quotations, including the D minor trio from the "Dance of the Blessed Spirits" in Gluck's "Orphée." Jazz was introduced in a café sequence, and drums from Katherine Dunham's band accompanied the death of Orpheus in a most dramatic style.

One French production of the 1930s involved, if briefly, Maurice Ravel. A film company invited him to submit samples for a projected motion picture starring the famous singer Chaliapin as Don Quixote. (The composer was unaware that the company had also asked Manuel De Falla, Jacques Ibert, Marcel Delannoy, and Darius Milhaud to prepare sketches.) Ravel began working on a cycle of songs, "Don Quichotte à Dulcinée," in 1932. This three-part group—one romantic, one epic, and one centered on drinking—was written as an example of the type of work he intended to do for the film score. Ultimately, the producers decided to employ Ibert. They explained that Chaliapin regarded Ravel's music as "undramatic," and that the composer had taken too long to complete the sample manuscript. Ravel died in 1937, so we can only speculate on how he would have handled a complete score.

Dimitri Shostakovich

In a class by himself as a film composer is Dimitri Shostakovich. Because he works exclusively for Soviet film producers, his scores have received comparatively little attention outside Russia until recently.

Shostakovich began his musical career as a pianist for silent films in his native Leningrad. His scores include those for such important Soviet films as *Alone* (1930), *Counterplan* (1932), *Volochayev Days* (1938), *Zoya* (1944), *The Young Guard* (1947-48), *Ivan Michurin* (1948), *Pigorov* (1948), *The Fall of Berlin* (1949), *Bilinski* (1953), *The First Echelon* (1950), *The Gadfly* (1955), and *Hamlet* (1964). His works for the screen are similar in tone and style to his concert music: brilliantly scored sequences for symphonic orchestra bouncing with tuneful scherzos, polkas, and waltzes. His own personal harmonic style, with surprising accents and dissonances, is cast in a completely tonal framework. A characteristic of his approach is the insertion of musical ideas while thematic material is developed in the background. In scenes of great emotion, the composer prefers long, melancholy lines for strings rather than heavy orchestral effects. Shostakovich's inclination to write closed forms and whole compositions in film scores is characteristic of serious composers, who tend to think of film scores beyond the life of the film.

In *Zoya* Shostakovich used a chorus, incorporating the Internationale and a choral excerpt from Glinka's opera, "A Life for the Tsar." This film also boasts a pulsating symphonic march. For scenes depicting the loss of soldiers in battle and the impact of their deaths, he wrote sentimental melodies for strings. The work exemplifies his use of brilliant passages for strings, brass fanfares, underscoring that includes hymnlike themes identified with the Russian army, and unison writing, often for antiphonal effects.

Pigorov is notable for straightforward melodies, including a lilting waltz and a furious scherzo scored for full symphonic orchestra. For *The Gadfly,* Shostakovich wrote a barrel-organ waltz. Related in spirit to Stravinsky's "Carousel" in "Petrouchka," it is a rather sentimental melodious theme for strings and winds augmented by celesta and bells.

Shostakovich's score for *Hamlet* is illustrative of his approach to films in general. Somber unison scoring for strings and brass opens the grim prelude. The palace ball is enlivened by a fast-paced, tuneful melody in 6/8 for strings. When the ghost appears, the accompaniment consists of alternating tremolos scored for full orchestra and menacing muted chords for brass and piano. A dancelike theme arranged for flute and strings provides background for the garden sequence. In contrast, music for the poisoning sequence stresses relentless ostinatos, both rhythmic and harmonic, motor rhythms, and antiphonal dialogues between the winds and strings. Shostakovich wrote brass fanfares and tuneful dance music for the arrival of the players, lyrical passages for strings and cembalo as background for Ophelia, and stormy tremolos and figurations for full orchestra to accompany Hamlet's duel and death.

Like many Soviet composers, Shostakovich has adapted his film music into suites or concert pieces. *Memorable Year 1919* was a film score subsequently arranged in a five-movement suite, including a tender "Romance" and a lively tarantella. *The Fall of Berlin* contained extensive choral passages, similar in tone to *Alexander Nevsky;* Shostakovich used them in an oratorio he later wrote.

The Song of Bernadette
Alfred Newman

Hamlet   *Joan of Arc*
Dimitri Shostakovich   Hugo Friedhofer

For Whom the Bell Tolls
Victor Young

Jane Eyre
Bernard Herrmann

Captain from Castile
Alfred Newman

CHAPTER V

Some Special Perspectives on Film Music

In contrast to concert music, the motion picture score has to fulfill a variety of needs. It is thus important to consider film music from various perspectives independent of the historical development of the form. So we pause briefly in our chronological journey to examine some representative examples of film scoring that are of both historical and stylistic significance.

The performance of concert music and opera in a film presents special musical problems. So does the animated cartoon, with its constant starts and stops and abrupt action. Ballets or other dance sequences provide unusual challenges to the composer as well as the cinematographer. Introducing jazz, essentially an improvisatory art, to the film medium leads to a host of aesthetic questions. And scoring for the historical film is yet another specialized art.

Concert Music in Motion Pictures

From the beginning, motion picture music has had a special relationship to music of the concert hall. The lives of famous composers, or of fictional musicians, have long appealed as the source of plots. For the latter, several composers have written original music to appear in filmed concert sequences. In either instance, the training of Hollywood actors to "perform" the compositions offers an interesting sidelight on the workings of film land.

Hollywood has not been noted for its accuracy when dealing with the lives of master composers. Indeed, alterations and distortions of factual material in such films have been discouragingly common. At best, composers' lives have been romanticized, cast very much in the nineteenth-century mold. A notable exception was *Magic Fire* (1955), based on the life of Richard Wagner. Producer-director William Dieterle invited Erich Korngold to supervise the music. By this time Korngold had retired from film scoring and was devoting full time to his symphonic writing. He agreed to come out of retirement on condition that he would have authority to see that Wagner's music was not altered or rearranged. He insisted that it be used in its original form, without any additions or changes.

Korngold used, as background music for each scene in Wagner's life, excerpts from works the composer was writing at the time. Appropriately, he introduced leitmotif techniques into the score. When Wagner is considering the possibility of a theater devoted to his work, it is to the accompaniment of the "Valhalla" motif of Wotan. At Wagner's wedding, musicians play his own wedding march. Korngold himself recorded all the piano solos played by Liszt, Wagner, and von Bülow, and even made an appearance in the film as Hans Richter, conducting the first performance of "The Ring of the Nibelungs" in Bayreuth.

Although many motion pictures featured performances of concertos by composers such as Tchaikovsky, Rachmaninoff, and Grieg, a number of works were written specifically to be performed as concert music on the screen. In 1940 the English composer Richard Addinsell composed a concerto movement for the film *Dangerous Moonlight*. Subsequently retitled the "Warsaw Concerto," it enjoyed spectacular success in pops concerts. The piece found numerous detractors; critics insisted that the capsule concerto was not really a concerto but a rhapsody—whose musical quality they questioned. The public was pleased, however, and the success of the work encouraged the commissioning of similar compositions by various studios.

Sir Arthur Bliss composed a concert piece for *Men of Two Worlds* scored for piano, orchestra, and male chorus. Other such works included the Cornish Rhapsody (Hubert Bath, in *Love Story*) and the piano concerto from *Hangover Square* (Bernard Herrmann). Franz Waxman based a concert rhapsody on themes he had used in the Hitchcock film, *The Paradine Case*. An unusual film about musicians was the Warner Brothers feature, *Deception*. Korngold, again the composer, wrote an entire cello concerto for this motion picture.

Most concert music written for performance in motion picture scenes was influenced either by European styles or by Gershwin. A new trend began when John Green transcribed Aaron Copland's "El Salon Mexico" for piano solo with orchestra, so that it could be performed in a concert sequence for the film *Fiesta*.

A number of directors outside the Hollywood mainstream explored the relationships between visual images and serious concert music. Several experiments combined impressionistic images with large-scale musical works. In 1949, for example, Jean Mitry produced *Pacific 231*, a filmed study of trains inspired by Arthur Honegger's orchestral composition. Three years later he tried a similar experiment with the piano music of Debussy; using two Arabesques and "Reflets dans l'Eau," he produced a three-movement screen interpretation utilizing photographic views of moving water. The following year, Renzo Avanzo created a visual interpretation of Respighi's "Fountains of Rome" with photographs of fountains provided by Claude Renoir.

For a long time, audiences seemed unaware that actors or actresses who "played" an instrument or "sang" in their screen performances were not really performing. But of course intense behind-the-scenes activity was necessary to prepare someone for this type of undertaking, especially when a star with no musical training was expected to convey the impression of being a talented performer.

In order to prepare someone for such a performance, a studio turned to uniquely gifted specialists for coaching. One was MGM's music supervisor, Harold Gelman. Gelman's activities ranged from intensive research on copyright data to helping composers determine the authenticity of music used in historical films. He was also called in to make virtuosi out of people who might not read a note of music. Once Gelman was asked to give calliope lessons to Walter Pidgeon. Although Gelman had begun his career as a Juilliard-trained concert pianist, the calliope had never been a required instrument. Nothing daunted, he did some quick research and acquired enough expertise to help Pidgeon "play" like an expert.

Says Gelman: "I don't think anyone knows that these performances are the result of careful planning. Music sequences are prerecorded. Then the singer must mouth back the words in synchronization with the recording, so that the photographer can capture his image and make it appear that he is really singing. I had to spend many hours watching singers open their mouths, to make sure they did it at exactly the right time. What could be worse than a singer appearing to say 'ooh' when the sound was 'ah'?"

During his first years at MGM, Gelman trained both instrumentalists and singers. He gave piano lessons to Elizabeth Taylor, Michael Wilding (who portrayed a blind pianist), and June Allyson (who had to appear to be playing the Grieg Piano Concerto). Actors usually mouthed lyrics to recordings by other singers. Eleanor Parker, for example, could "sing" in several different languages. (She didn't speak them, but she learned them phonetically.) Even if an actress were an accomplished vocalist, she would prerecord her songs and then be photographed mouthing the words to her own recording. Gelman was on hand to supervise such recordings by Katherine Grayson and Jane Powell. Even gifted instrumental performers like José Iturbi would first record the music and then go through the physical motions of playing to the prerecorded track.

In general, Gelman found his famous pupils to be cooperative. "When an actor came to me for assistance," he recalls, "he was usually a willing pupil. It was hard to do this in a way that was believable. I have never met one actor who wasn't a little bit scared about this whole proposition. If he wasn't a musician, looking like a virtuoso while going through the physical motion of playing seemed quite formidable. They were all good students."

Well, almost all. Lauritz Melchior, the celebrated tenor, had enormous difficulties mouthing lyrics, even though he had easily made the original recording. In another case, a character actor who was supposed to portray Franz Liszt could not bring himself to practice sitting at the piano or manipulating his fingers. On the day of the filming, he was completely incapable of delivering a convincing performance at the mute keyboard. Finally, the distraught producers went to Gelman. It was decided to engage a local pianist who bore a startling resemblance to the actor. Costumed and made up, it was he whose fingers were filmed at the piano.

After another such "performance," for the film *Humoresque,* music personnel congratulated themselves on recording a unique violin solo. An actor held the violin under his chin, while one violinist supplied the fingertips and a second supplied the bowings. These motions were photographed in synchronization to a prerecorded duet for violin and piano. (The audience, of course, saw only the actor and his accompanist.) After the recording, Oscar Levant quipped, "Why don't the five of us make a concert tour?"

The results of all this legerdemain were quite convincing. Stars of musical films were often asked to play the piano at parties. They had trouble convincing even their friends that the fingers flashing across the screen in their latest film really belonged to Harold Gelman.

Opera in Films

Composers have also had to write for films requiring original operatic compositions. A unique example was Oscar Levant's contribution to *Charlie Chan at the Opera.* The tale concerns an opera singer, wrongly believed dead, who returns to run amok at the San Francisco opera, plotting a murder onstage. Boris Karloff, wearing one of Lawrence Tibbett's opera costumes, played the villain. Levant asked Schoenberg's advice about operatic composition, but when Schoenberg replied simply, "Study 'Fidelio,' " Levant turned to his imagination. He not only provided a solo for Karloff's character, but an aria for a soprano and a military march as well.

Bernard Herrmann's operatic sequence in *Citizen Kane* has already been discussed. Another approach occurs in *Everybody Does It.* This film featured Paul Douglas as a man who discovers that his voice can shatter glass, but whose nerves shatter instead when he embarks upon an operatic adventure. Mario Castelnuovo-Tedesco (whose opera "The Merchant of Venice" was later to win an international competition) provided "Fatima and Solimano," in a lyrical Italian style, for the operatic scene. Another example is *The Phantom of the Opera,* which has been filmed several times. The remake starring Nelson Eddy contained original operatic passages in French and Russian idioms.

From the beginning, producers realized that the great operas and film were related but not necessarily compatible. Richard Strauss went to the Dresden State Opera House to conduct a filmed performance of "Der Rosenkavalier" but gave up after rehearsal and turned to a professional film music director. The idea of filmed opera continued to stimulate producers in Europe, particularly Italy and Russia. In 1951 Thomas Schippers conducted the Symphony Orchestra of Rome Radio Italiana in a performance of Menotti's musical drama "The Medium." That same year in England, Michael Powell and Emeric Pressburger produced a version of *The Tales of Hoffmann,* with Sir Thomas Beecham conducting the Royal Philharmonic and the Sadler's Wells Chorus. Two years later, an Italian production, *The Golden Coach,* presented music from the works of Antonio Vivaldi. Another notable film was Franz Aller's production of Humperdinck's *Hansel and Gretel* in 1954.

Music and Animation

Along with other photographic techniques, animation improved at an almost unbelievable pace during the 1940s. Walt Disney produced the first full-length animated feature in 1937, when his studio released *Snow White and the Seven Dwarfs,* an animated operetta complete with an overture based on the songs featured in the film. The score, written by Leigh Harline and Paul J. Smith, boasted such eminently singable tunes as "Heigh-Ho, Heigh-Ho," "Someday My Prince Will Come," and "Whistle While You Work." Though *Snow White* was regarded with suspicion by investors, it proved to be a bonanza, proving that the Disney vision of a long and successful future for full-length animated features was entirely justified.

Three years later came one of the most unusual collaborations between musicians and artists in the history of cinema —*Fantasia*. The score consisted of concert performances of Bach's "Toccata and Fugue in D Minor" (arranged for orchestra by Leopold Stokowski), Tchaikovsky's "Nutcracker Suite," Dukas' "The Sorcerer's Apprentice," Stravinsky's "Rite of Spring," Beethoven's "Pastoral Symphony," Ponchielli's "Dance of the Hours" (from the opera "La Gioconda"), Moussorgsky's "Night on Bald Mountain," and an orchestral arrangement of Schubert's "Ave Maria."

Disney wanted to showcase *Fantasia* on a wide screen, with the music heard in double dimensional sound. But European money shortages resulting from World War II cut off funds, and he had to design the film for a regulation-size screen. Investors thought that the film should be cut, but Disney disagreed.

Stokowski had expressed a desire to work with Disney, and the idea of recording Dukas' famous tone poem as the musical foundation for an animated version of the story particularly appealed to him. The tale relates the experiences of an apprentice magician whose spell over a broomstick turns into a nightmare of renegade brooms and buckets of water. The Disney version stars Mickey Mouse as the apprentice.

Stokowski conducted all the music for *Fantasia*. Abstract images accompany Bach's "Toccata and Fugue." The "Nutcracker Suite" as used in the film consists of the last six out of the original eight movements; they serve as background for a nature ballet danced by various plants and flowers. (The Chinese dance, for example, is performed by a group of mushrooms.) The "Rite of Spring" became a prehistoric panorama of volcanoes, trilobites, and dinosaurs. Beethoven's Sixth Symphony is performed as accompaniment to a classical fantasy set on the slopes of Mount Olympus, while Ponchielli's well-worn melodies take on new life in an outlandish ballet in which the premiere danseuse is a pink hippopotamus, her partner an alligator, and the ensemble a graceful company of ostriches and elephants. Moussorgsky's "Night on Bald Mountain" takes place in a primitive, macabre world full of witches, demons, and evil spirits; ultimately the forces of light triumph as the sequence merges into a choral adaptation of "Ave Maria."

Not all critics raved about this ambitious effort. Some found the film too abstract, while others thought the presence of Mickey Mouse and the concoction of various "plots" for each sequence were an arbitrary interference with the music of the masters. Conductors were no more unanimous than usual. Stokowski, needless to say, praised "the colorful and imaginative genius of Disney." George Szell, the formidable conductor of the Cleveland Orchestra, attended a screening of *Fantasia* but walked out half-way through.

One of the more curious aspects of *Fantasia* was the relationship between the Disney studio and Igor Stravinsky, the only living composer who could evaluate the treatment of his music in the film. Stravinsky said that the studio offered him $5,000 but also informed him that it would use his music without his permission if he refused to grant it. Since Stravinsky's early works were copyrighted in Russia, and since the Russian copyrights were not valid in the United States, the studio was within its legal rights. Stravinsky ultimately had his photograph taken with Walt Disney for publicity for *Fantasia*. But he objected to alterations in orchestration, including horn glissandos played an octave higher than written. The Disney studio said that Stravinsky had approved cuts and changes in his score, having visited the studio in person. Stravinsky riposted that he had been in the hospital in Europe at the time and could not have given his approval. In any event, Stravinsky in later years was less than enthusiastic over this interpretation of his work.

Disney continued to produce animated features throughout the 1940s, including *Pinocchio, Bambi, Saludos Amigos, The Three Caballeros,* and *Make Mine Music.* The last-named included an animated interpretation of Prokofiev's "Peter and the Wolf."

Another interesting experiment during this period also linked animation and classical music. Walter Lantz, an animator and producer, developed a series of cartoon shorts in which animals were the stars. All the action was accompanied by classical music, played as written, but the animals (i.e., a beaver using his tail as a percussion instrument) provided the humor. Lantz subsequently became famous as the creator of Woody Woodpecker; his wife, Grace Stafford, a noted radio actress, recorded the bird's unforgettable voice behind the scenes.

UPA also commissioned notable cartoon music, especially that by such composers as David Raksin and Gail Kubik. Although small and unusual ensembles for feature motion pictures are even now often heralded as revolutionary, Raksin and Kubik were using them years ago to perform their cartoon scores. Raksin's choice of instruments is a classic example of a composer's turning the economic restrictions of film scoring to his advantage. In his music for *The Unicorn in the Garden,* he introduced such unusual wind instruments as the alto recorder and the soprano saxophone. For *Madeline,* he employed an ensemble consisting of flute, oboe, clarinet, bassoon, violin, viola, cello, and harp.

In scoring *The Unicorn in the Garden,* a cartoon version of a James Thurber story, Raksin indulged in what he terms "the luxury of a six-piece orchestra." He decided to write for what might more accurately be described as a chamber ensemble after he noted that the animator had planned a florid and, as it were, baroque unicorn. The three string players were joined by two wind soloists, one doubling clarinet and recorder, the other (coincidentally, Albert

Raksin, the composer's brother) doubling soprano saxophone and bass clarinet. The harpsichordist was André Previn.

Raksin's score for this film has a decidedly neoclassic quality. He has long been an admirer of Hindemith, and, like the famed contrapuntalist, he likes canons, fugatos, and all types of polyphonic development. This music is gentler, with more of a whimsical touch, than accompaniments he has written for scenes of greater dramatic intensity. Raksin does not "Mickey Mouse," believing that such an approach can be heavy-handed at times. Instead he prefers to "catch" pieces of individual action *en passant,* allowing the music to grow organically as it parallels the animation.

Raksin's music makes a subtle commentary on Thurber's characters. Consider the early scenes of the cartoon. The clarinet and saxophone play spirited polyphony as the husband informs his wife, "There's a unicorn in the garden"—he pauses—"eating roses." The wife's skepticism is accompanied by a clarinet solo as she informs him, "The unicorn is a mythical beast."

When the unicorn appears, a solo alto recorder, in high register, plays a whimsical tune with a mock-martial air. As the husband runs through the garden, clarinet and saxophone join the strings and harpsichord in a spirited chase. Accompanied by a clarinet solo, he announces, "The unicorn ate a lily." The wife in turn, backed by a rather shrill soprano saxophone, observes that her spouse is losing his mind. The man's lines continue with clarinet accompaniment, the woman's with a saxophone; their argument is paralleled by the two woodwinds.

The wife's motifs tend to be brittle and unsympathetic, like the lady herself. The music becomes more chromatic and less consonant when she speaks to policemen and to the doctor. At the cartoon's climax, the doctor asks the husband if he really told his wife that he saw a unicorn. The man replies, without musical accompaniment, "The unicorn is a mythical beast." Then comes the unicorn's theme, played by the recorder, as the doctor comments, "That's all I wanted to know." The husband's final sense of ironic amusement is captured by a semimartial accompaniment in harpsichord and strings.

Raksin's use of instruments, of consonance and dissonance, and of timing add another dimension to this cartoon. Thurber wrote to him: "I am not a music maker, but I enjoyed your score, and remember with affection the recorder that spoke up when the unicorn appeared. It sounded exactly right for unicorns." A composer who can write music for unicorns has certainly done an ideal job!

In scoring animated cartoons, composers often have to incorporate or otherwise contend with a never-ending cacaphony of sound-effects. A unique score that avoided overdependence on these devices was the one accompanying the now-classic short, *Gerald McBoing Boing* (1951). Gerald, a creation of the celebrated children's author, Dr. Seuss, is a little boy who cannot speak words but can only make sounds. At first his parents are dismayed by his handicap, but when Gerald becomes famous after appearing on the radio, they and his friends completely change their attitude toward him.

Composer Gail Kubik decided to exploit the percussion section of the orchestra, offsetting it against the more melodic instruments just as Gerald is offset against the talking humans capable of normal conversation. (In a concert piece based on *Gerald McBoing Boing,* Kubik used a full-scale concerto for percussion instruments.) As always, his style is brittle, crisp, occasionally dissonant, and markedly rhythmic. The main title is scored for piano, viola, cello, trumpet, horn, bassoon, clarinet, oboe, and flute. For Dr. Malone, who is consulted by the boy's parents,

Kubik developed a matter-of-fact motif scored for flute, oboe, and bassoon. When the little boy is unhappy, he is accompanied by a plaintive oboe. Music of mock grandeur opens the radio program on which Gerald appears; his solo performance over the air is a virtuoso statement for sound-effects.

Many of the techniques that became standard for all motion picture scores were developed by specialists in the cartoon medium. Carl Stalling, Oliver Wallace, Scott Bradley, and Paul Smith were pioneers in refining and developing the musical accompaniments used in animated cartoons. (As mentioned earlier, Stalling and Bradley were responsible for introducing the technique of the click-track to film scoring.) Bradley's techniques exemplified the best cartoon scores of the day. He recalls beginning his career in the old Walt Disney studio, which was "about the size of two living rooms." In the earliest cartoons, musical accompaniments, derived from popular music, relied heavily on bouncy tunes with a steady, energetic quality. The music was highly symmetrical, like the cartoons themselves. Bradley recognized the need for a more sophisticated approach. An insight into his taste and musical outlook may be gained from a memo he once sent Ingolf Dahl, who had approached him about a magazine interview.

"METRO GOLDWYN MAYER. INTER-OFFICE COMMUNICATION TO: Dahl. SUBJECT: Dis-a and data-a- FROM: Bradley. Born . . . Russelville, Arkansas (but not an "Arkie" I hasten to add) . . . Studied piano, private instruction . . . organ and harmony with the English organist Horton Corbett . . . Otherwise entirely self taught in composition and orchestration . . . fed large doses of Bach, which I absorbed and asked for more. Conductor at KHJ and KNX in early thirties . . . entered the non-sacred realm of pictures in 1932 and started cartoon composing in 1934 with Harmon-Isking Co. . . . Joined MGM in 1937 . . . have so far been able to hide from them the fact that I'm not much of a composer. Personal: dislike bridge, slacks and mannish dress on women, all chromatic and diatonic scales, whether written by Beethoven or Bradley. Also, crowds and most people (and especially biographers). Favorite composers: Brahms, Stravinsky, Hindemith, Bartok. This will be boring to most everyone, so cut it as short as you wish. Signed: Scott."

Bradley's experiments with cartoon scoring led to the development of prescored cartoons. In *Dance of the Weed* (1941), for example, his music was recorded; animators then developed a cartoon in synchronization with it. Bradley went a step further with his "Cartoonia Suite," a musical fairy tale originally written as a concert work for a narrator and orchestra. The four movements—"Once Upon a Time," "The Calico Dragon," "Fleas," and "The Brave Little Knight"—were deemed appropriate for the cartoon idiom and subsequently used in underscoring.

Bradley became accustomed to composing with a detail sheet, which has room for a description of the cartoon in terms of camera, action, and sound. The action is measured in frames of film, which are indicated above the measures of music. A composer can thus synchronize a specific chord with a specific frame of film, and concurrently, with a specific piece of action. Bradley would decide on a certain metronomic speed and determine the metric unit of the time signature. The click-track would be prepared accordingly and Bradley, working in conjunction with the music editor, would then write his music on the detail sheet.

Cartoon scores by Bradley boast a harmonic bite and tension appropriate for a composer intrigued by unique methods of structural organization (and a devotee of Bach). In one film, *The Cat that Hated People* (1948), Bradley developed a twelve-tone row for piccolo and oboe, representing Jerry the mouse, while the bassoon played the row in retrograde as a theme for Jerry's nemesis, Tom the cat.

Novelty was also achieved by introducing the classical music Bradley loved. For one cartoon, he provided the famous "Cat Concerto" (1947), an arrangement for two pianos of Liszt's "Second Hungarian Rhapsody." The work was brilliantly recorded by John Crown and Arthur Schutts, the studio pianist at that time, and performed on the screen by one animated cat. José Iturbi, then active at MGM, happened to visit the dubbing room while the engineers were working on the "Cat Concerto." Struck by the incredible virtuosity of the performance, he asked who the pianist was. The engineers told him only that the artist was someone soon to be heard by all, leaving him to wonder how one person could play passages that seemed to (and did) require at least twenty fingers.

Bradley was so prolific during his years at MGM that the studio's music supervisor, Harold Gelman, remarks, "The sun never sets on the British Empire or a Scott Bradley score." Because of widespread international syndication of the studio's cartoons, at any time during the day, any day of the year, someone somewhere is probably listening to a Scott Bradley cartoon score.

Animals in Live Action Sequences

Closely related to animated features in their correlation between music and action are the Disney True Life Adventure films. The first of these, a thirty-minute feature entitled *Seal Island,* was released in 1948 and won an Academy Award. Since that time, the series has included such popular favorites as *Beaver Valley, The Olympic Elk, Nature's Half Acre, Water Birds, Bear Country, Prowlers of the Everglades, The Living Desert, The Vanishing Prairie, The African Lion,* and *Secrets of Life.*

The series won a number of Academy Awards and other honors. Much of their popularity can be credited to outstanding photography. The "stars" were a variety of remarkable wild animals, photographed in their natural habitats and often emerging as individual personalities in a struggle for survival. Music was another essential in the success of the films. All of them, except for *Seal Island,* were scored by Paul J. Smith, whose work merits serious study and evaluation. Noteworthy was his use of individual motifs and orchestral color in the intimate close-ups of animals.

Smith often used individual themes and instruments to crystallize an animal's personality. For example, in *Water Birds,* the comical spoonbill is accompanied by a clarinet solo, the avocet by an oboe. For the finale—a kind of ballet sequence in which dozens of water birds coast and glide over the water—Smith provided a complete orchestral transcription of Liszt's "Second Hungarian Rhapsody." The accents of the music are coordinated with the splashes of the soaring, dipping birds. (To assure complete synchronization, parts of the film had to be edited to fit the music.) In *The Living Desert,* a hesitating bass clarinet represents the slow, plodding desert tortoise, while a busy clarinet whistles background music for the millipede. Impressed by their energetic activity, the ingenious Smith wrote a square dance for the scorpions. A circus march seemed appropriate for the otters in *Beaver Valley;* the tune became so popular that it was arranged for the U.C.L.A. marching band, which plays it regularly at football games. This same film demonstrated Smith's sense of humor in dealing with animal characters. In one memorable sequence, a group of frogs, literally "natural comedians," perform against a straight rendition of the Sextet from "Lucia."

Theme Songs in Films

One element responsible for stimulating the public's interest in film music was the theme song. It was often used at the opening and closing of a film for identification purposes. Producers sometimes even asked composers to incorporate in their scores melodies written by other songwriters—requests that usually did not improve producer-composer relations. Instrumental scores that depended too much on songs lost much of their punch, for there was a temptation to use the theme song as general background music instead of providing a real musical complement to the dramatic action.

Occasionally the theme song was an integral part of the plot. One such instance was "Laura," which emerged from the film of the same name in 1944 as a milestone in Hollywood's musical history. Because the melody became so popular, listeners often forgot that it did not initially serve as a love theme. One of the film's principal characters is a detective, portrayed by Dana Andrews, who finds himself falling in love with the memory of a girl whose murder he is investigating. As he stands in her apartment, he is captivated by her portrait, the environment in which she lived, and her favorite music. The theme is used to evoke the feeling of Laura, not to underscore the meeting between the principal characters or as a love theme. (Raksin regarded the use of "Laura" as a love theme in the television remake —with which he was not associated—as artistically invalid.)

Laura was supposed to be a collaboration between Otto Preminger and Rouben Mamoulian, but Preminger eventually took over the directing assignment entirely. Studio rumors described the film as a picture in trouble. Although several composers announced their intention to refuse the scoring assignment, David Raksin agreed to accept the job.

Preminger had originally chosen Gershwin's "Summertime" as a theme, but when Ira Gershwin would not approve, he selected Duke Ellington's "Sophisticated Lady." Raksin felt that the melody was wrong, and naturally wanted to work with his own material. Finally Preminger agreed to let him write an original theme, but insisted that he do it in one weekend. A gifted, facile songwriter, Raksin had no difficulty in turning out one melody after another, but none of them satisfied him. He stopped working for a while, then suddenly got a new idea and quickly notated it. When he took it to the studio the following Monday, his colleagues in the music department were enthusiastic about its haunting, ethereal quality. (One colleague did suggest that the second eight measures were too similar to the first, so Raksin changed them somewhat.) This song, of course, was the one used in the film. Some melodic motifs from it were adapted for the underscoring. Everyone from the sound technicians to the studio messengers left the scoring stage whistling "Laura."

Reactions to the theme song of *Laura* were little short of frenzied. Mail poured into the studio: fan letters from prominent citizens and celebrities, requests for autographs. One group of college girls wrote that they had performed the song twenty-five times in succession. "Laura," one of the first screen melodies to achieve international acclaim, remains one of the most popular melodies ever to come from a composer's pen, in or out of Hollywood.

A hit tune is popularly imagined to be a film composer's dream, but it can be a mixed blessing. Raksin was delighted with the success of his melody, but soon tired of the producer's inevitable question when greeting him with a new assignment: "Can you write me another 'Laura'?" Understandably, no composer relishes being restricted or typecast because of identification with one specific work.

During the 1940s, theme songs were often extracted from motion pictures. Studios hired lyricists to provide words for instrumental themes; with luck, their songs might make the Hit Parade. Some composers' work lent itself better than others' to this type of exploitation. Victor Young produced at least one potential song in nearly every film he scored. The music of composers with a background in concert music

Lili, Bronislau Kaper

rather than Broadway or Tin Pan Alley was usually less suitable. In any case, a theme song was initially regarded only as one element that could on occasion play a role in a background score. No one in the 1940s foresaw the ultimate consequences of songwriting in relation to motion pictures. These did not develop until after Dimitri Tiomkin's phenomenally successful *High Noon* theme, with its indelible influence on composers of the 1950s and 1960s.

Source Music

Source music is music that is introduced into a scene through a source visible to the audience, or to which film characters refer. It may come from a radio or a television set, a jukebox, a pianist playing, a dance band, or someone practicing a musical instrument.

An early example of a score that relied heavily on source music was Franz Waxman's *A Place in the Sun;* music sources ranged from a radio to a large society dance orchestra. George Duning created an unusual combination of source music and composed music in his score for *Picnic,* using the popular song "Moonglow" plus his own love theme.

Some European composers feel that Americans use too much music in their films. Paul Misraki observes: "Modern filmmakers feel that *silence* has turned out to be the best background available; and whenever silence turns out to be dull, the only way out is to pretend the radio is on somewhere, providing smooth dance music or modern rhythms. In France, traditional background music is now called 'musique à l'américaine,' because so many Hollywood productions still stick to the 'classical' or 'conventional' formulas." Latter-day trends in Hollywood, however, are neither classical nor conventional. With the growing tendency to use simple pop or rock tunes, actual scoring of any sort is frequently nonexistent.

A recent American film score that made sensitive and tasteful use of source music was that for *Ship of Fools* (1965) by Ernest Gold. When he was asked by Stanley Kramer to write the music, Gold saw that the assignment might pose unusual challenges. The action takes place aboard a German passenger freighter. The script called for a small musical ensemble to entertain the passengers at mealtime and play for dancing. Gold decided that this source music could serve as the score for the entire film.

Gold tailored his score for the modest resources of the three-piece ensemble of violin, cello, and piano. Although the size of the group precluded colorful orchestration, unusually inventive melodic material compensated for this lack. The nostalgic music was in the style of Lehár and Kalman. The Viennese waltzes, polkas, tangos, and other dance pieces were all composed in an evocative, sentimental fashion, sounding very much like melodies from musical shows or operettas popular in Germany during the period. The music also set the moods for various scenes. When Glocken, the dwarf, and Lowenthal, the traveling salesman, reminisce about days gone by, the shipboard musicians play a sentimental dance piece, a combination of waltz and tango. A shipboard party is accompanied by a whirling Viennese waltz, which captures the reckless abandon of the foolish travelers.

For scenes in which the small ensemble did not appear, Gold composed poignant and expressive music. In the best traditions of film music, it intensified the drama taking place on the screen. Gold later arranged the whole score for symphony, and it was recorded by the Boston Pops Orchestra.

Ballet and Motion Picture Music

As motion pictures expanded in size and scope, one element introduced with increasing frequency was ballet, incorporated into films through a variety of methods. In some instances, films utilized classical or contemporary ballet music written for concert performance. More often, however, motion picture composers provided original ballet music. Two films notable for such sequences were *Spectre of the Rose* (1946) by George Antheil, and *The Red Shoes* (1948), with a complete ballet by Brian Easdale.

Spectre of the Rose was a choreographic interpretation of Carl Maria von Weber's "Invitation to the Dance." Antheil chose not to rely on Weber's score but instead composed his own. The essential mood of the film is one of impending tragedy, a mood captured by Antheil in a series of tragic waltzes. *The Red Shoes* tells the story of a dance troupe. The film's highlight is a short sequence of an original ballet, written by Easdale, in close collaboration with the director and choreographer.

In retrospect, much of the significant dance music in Hollywood films of this period was written for a series of MGM musicals that began with *Good News* (1947), *Easter Parade* (1948), and *The Pirate* (1948). Although ballet sequences in such films became increasingly elaborate, they functioned primarily as adjuncts to the plot, rather than as independent elements. When a director could call upon Gene Kelly or Donald O'Connor or Fred Astaire, an emphasis on modern dance was inevitable. In 1951 Gershwin's "An American in Paris" was used as the basis for an extended ballet sequence in the motion picture of the same name. The music was rearranged in five parts: "Busy Paris," "The Flower Market," "The Gay Whirl," "Tempo Blues," and "Finale." All of the thematic material was derived from the original Gershwin composition, but some themes were lengthened and juxtaposed differently. Sets were inspired by impressionist and post-impressionist painters, including Dufy, Manet, Monet, Utrillo, and Toulouse-Lautrec.

Another motion picture with extensive ballet music was *Lili* (1953), which featured an outstanding group of dance sequences composed by Bronislau Kaper. Although Kaper had maintained his interest in concert music, he also wrote popular songs, and excelled in film scores of continental wit and charm. *Lili* called for these qualities. The film tells the story of a lonely, timid girl working with a traveling carnival in France. She is befriended by a group of talking puppets, who seem to be her only friends.

Kaper's score featured not only a lilting tune, "Hi-Lili, Hi-Lo," irresistible in its innocence and naiveté, but also a number of memorable ballet sequences. The first was developed for Lili's rival, a sophisticated, predatory femme fatale played by Zsa Zsa Gabor. This jazz ballet begins with lush strings tinged with a blues quality. The jazz passages, scored for saxophone ensemble, are directly related to the dance style of the big-band era. The second ballet features dancers representing the various puppets, each symbolized by instruments expressive of his character, the whole scene accompanied by a lively series of variations on "Hi-Lili, Hi-Lo." A French accordion adds a delicate, folk-music quality to the theme, which Lili sings. Harp glissandos lead into a romantic version of the tune, this time in rhapsodic, lyrical style. The strings again become the key to the orchestra's expression. The ballet is a virtual dance-rhapsody based on the theme song. The melody itself was recorded more than 150 times, and Kaper won an Oscar for his efforts.

Occasionally, composers have had to write music to synchronize with a dance sequence already filmed. One such work was "Ring Around the Rosy," a ballet written by André Previn for *Invitation to the Dance* (1956).

It was inevitable that the film music industry would one day produce its own prodigy: such was André Previn. Born in Berlin but reared in Beverly Hills, Previn burst upon the musical scene with unique éclat. His career was to be blessed by fortuitous timing, with trends in film music unusually receptive to the particular styles that suited his talents.

An accomplished classical pianist, Previn was fascinated by American jazz. He boasted a ferocious keyboard technique, and was recognized as a remarkably facile jazz musician whose ambition was to play longer runs than Art Tatum. His formal musical education included seven years' study of composition with Mario Castelnuovo-Tedesco, before and after his studio work at MGM. (Previn's ties with the film industry were not accidental; his cousin, Charles Previn, had been head of Universal's music department in the 1930s.) A critic once described Previn's piano style as "suave, elegant, and personally detached." The same might be said of his film music, which is unsentimental, sophisticated, and of consummate virtuosity.

Previn takes a sardonic view of Hollywood. (He once described his departure from the mainstream of film scoring as a desire to avoid writing "The Low-Down, Fall-of-the-Roman-Empire Blues.") He is at his best in nontraditional styles, and his "Ring Around the Rosy" won him considerable acclaim. Previn's evaluation of his own film music since becoming a full-time symphony conductor has been exceedingly harsh. But one cannot deny that he left an indelible mark on film scoring.

Invitation to the Dance was directed by Gene Kelly. He commissioned Previn to provide music for dance scenes that had already been shot using temporary soundtracks. Every change of meter and tempo was measured according to timing sheets and click-track charts, which, said Previn, resembled the Manhattan telephone directory. His final score combined symphonic and jazz textures, and incorporated variations on a nursery theme, dynamic rhythm, and expressive blues motifs.

"Ring Around the Rosy" consists of a number of vignettes centering on a bracelet that travels from one pair of lovers to another until it returns to its original owner. The ballet is divided into eleven sections, beginning with an overture built around variations on the well-known children's tune. For a frantic cocktail party sequence in which people drink and talk at such a fast pace that they communicate nothing at all, Previn wrote dissonant music emphasizing Gershwin-style piano solos. In another scene, an artist tries to give the bracelet to his model, a ballerina more interested in food than romance. Previn's waltz for piccolo, violin, and tuba, combining awkward sounds and extreme ranges of the orchestra, underscores the clumsiness of the artist's attempts at romance. For a nightclub scene, Previn turned to the jazz scoring for which he is well known: a big-band orchestra calling for eight brasses, five saxophones, four rhythm instruments, and, naturally, a solo improvisational piano. When the scene shifts back to the cocktail party, Previn returns to his original frantic jazz, this time with a lyrical counter-theme for a reunited husband and wife.

For another sequence in *Invitation to the Dance,* the well-known French composer Jacques Ibert was invited to write a circus ballet. In this tale, a clown is torn between his love for a beautiful equestrienne and his jealousy of the high-wire artist whom she loves but has quarreled with. Trying to prove that he is as skilled as the acrobat, the clown attempts to walk the high wire but falls and dies, whereupon the girl and the acrobat are reconciled. Ibert's ballet for the film opens with a spirited scherzo for the acrobats and a comedic vaudeville dance for the clowns. The love duet is cast in a Gallic, impressionist mold, arranged for tender strings and emphasizing long melodic leaps. Because the music is slow, these leaps have a romantic, "sighing" quality that corresponds to the choreography.

The music becomes more dissonant and violent as the lovers quarrel and the clown attempts to intervene, suffering his tragic fate.

Jazz

While it might be said that the dominant American influence on film scoring in the early 1940s was the music of Aaron Copland, by the end of the decade its place had been taken by jazz. In the early days of film scoring, the characteristic harmonies and rhythms of jazz still appeared in a symphonic context, as in the concert music of Stravinsky and Milhaud. Later, however, many composers began to rely on the instrumentation of the jazz band. An important factor in the flowering of the jazz idiom was the subject matter of motion pictures in general. Although producers continued to turn out glamorous costume dramas, they were simultaneously filming more stories about war, crime, violence, and life in the modern city. Jazz seemed more closely attuned to these subjects than any other musical style. Only later did composers apply its rhythms to motion pictures with lighter themes and to comedy.

The landmark score for jazz in films was that composed by Alex North for *A Streetcar Named Desire* (1951), directed by Elia Kazan and starring Vivien Leigh as Blanche and Marlon Brando as Stanley. North had worked actively in New York theater, writing incidental and background music for major stage productions, as well as ballets for Martha Graham, Hanya Holm, and the Ballet Theater.

Streetcar, based on the play by Tennessee Williams, is set in New Orleans, so North turned to the musical styles associated with the city: jazz, ragtime, and blues. He also developed an interesting variation of the leitmotif technique. Instead of themes for individual characters, he employed themes in the form of "mental statements" for the conflicts between characters. The music thus reflected inner tensions rather than commenting upon specific actions. Another unusual element was a sort of *idée fixe* in the form of a little dance tune associated with the death of Blanche's husband. When she speaks of his suicide, the dance theme is superimposed over the other music in the scene.

North scored for small combinations of instruments wherever possible in order to relate the source music in the background (from the Four Deuces café) to the underscoring. He also experimented with writing *against* a scene, so that the music would express a character's feeling no matter what the outward action. For instance, Blanche constantly tries to project an image of extreme gentility, but North's music for scenes between her and Stanley are blues solos for clarinet, trumpet, or saxophone. (One film composer has referred to the saxophone as "the easy mark" of the orchestra; its wailing quality has traditionally been associated with characters like Blanche.) More lyrical music does occur in the latter part of the film—for scenes between Stanley and Stella and especially in the famous sequence when Stella walks down the stairs to her waiting husband. For, although North likes dissonance, it is dissonance as an outgrowth of linear counterpoint and the development of musical ideas.

In contrast to the driving, vigorous music for *Streetcar,* North's main title in *Death of a Salesman* (1951) begins with a flute solo. This was revolutionary in Hollywood, where symphonic main titles had been the order of the day.

Another film directed by Kazan and starring Brando that featured innovative, jazz-influenced music was *On the Waterfront* (1954), scored by Leonard Bernstein. The subject—a basically sensitive man caught up in a brutally harsh world—lent itself very well to jazz treatment. Bernstein combined the rhythms of jazz with the dynamic power of a full symphony orchestra.

A Streetcar Named Desire, Alex North

The composer approached the film almost as he would an opera, and most of its themes lean toward complexity. The main title begins with a canon; a violent fugato for three voices, scored for percussion, accompanies the murders in the story; the love theme is introduced by a flute solo over a harp background. This poignant melody is marked by wide leaps and a blues feeling. There are other lonely, quiet passages that seem to be seeking harmonic resolution. And one theme, heard initially as a saxophone solo, appears throughout the film as a sort of all-purpose motif. But a number of harsh, dissonant, and highly rhythmic sequences are used to provide musical background for scenes of violence on the New York docks.

In fact, the music for *On the Waterfront* was one of the least lyrical and more violent scores of its time. Not only are there three murder sequences, but Terry (Brando) is a target of scorn facing the wrath of his neighbors because of his cooperation with the law. Even the pigeons he raises are the subjects of violence. For the scene in which Terry finds that they have been killed, Bernstein combines his love theme with the main "waterfront theme." Variations of his violence motif accompany the flight sequences. A high point of the picture is the final sequence, in which Terry, after a brutal fight with a corrupt union boss, takes the first step toward freedom; he walks up to the loading dock to claim his rights as a man and as a union member. Bernstein begins the sequence with muted strings, then introduces his "waterfront motif" on the vibraphone. As Terry stops, dazed after the beating he has taken, the brass enters slowly; they join in an ascending melody while the percussion and basses set the tempo for Terry's slow march to freedom. When he finally reaches his goal and the shipping executive says "Let's go to work," the brass continue to play with a blues quality, but now the tempo is a broad march, a statement of victory. The orchestral climax is a series of full chords based on the "waterfront motif."

Bernstein, who had not worked in motion pictures before, was unprepared for some of the ways of screen folk. Concentrating on his musical ideas, he planned elaborate counterpoint and fugal developments to accompanying specific scenes in specific ways. To accompany one love scene, for instance, he wrote music that would start softly and build toward an intense high point of full orchestral eloquence. In dubbing sessions, however, Kazan decided that he had to emphasize an indispensable element of the plot—a grunt by Brando. So Bernstein's music was allowed to reach its high point only to be cut off so that the grunt, unaccompanied, could punctuate the soundtrack. Bernstein was more surprised than pleased. It was his first exposure to the standard Hollywood treatment of composers' works as subordinate to the wishes of producers and directors.

In any case, Bernstein's unsentimental, pulsating score for *On the Waterfront* was widely praised. He later used a similar approach in his theater composition, including the ballets in his musical "West Side Story."

One of the earliest motion picture features to include a long sequence scored with the instrumentation of a jazz band was *The Man With The Golden Arm* (1955). The composer, Elmer Bernstein, used a unique combination of symphonic and jazz elements for this film, based on Nelson Algren's novel about a drug addict. Bernstein objected to describing the music as a "jazz score," preferring to consider it a motion picture that incorporated elements of jazz wherever desirable. He was assisted in planning these sequences by two experienced jazz musicians, Shorty Rogers and Shelley Manne, and by orchestrator Fred Steiner. Bernstein avoided an elaborate leitmotif treatment and concentrated instead on creating a basic musical atmosphere. Most characteristic of the picture's style is the main title, which begins with a long rhythmic ostinato of triplet figures in the saxophones and trombones. A countermelody comes from the strings, woodwinds, and horns. The syncopated jazz melody, harmonized in four-part voicings, is played by four trumpets in a very high register. For a long chase, Bernstein composed an extremely percussive sequence for piano, bass, and drums, which consisted of alternating measures of 3/4 and 4/4 to create a basic time stream of seven.

Typically, Hollywood turned a fresh idea into a cliché almost overnight. Filmmakers made an instant identification between films about drug addiction and "jazz scores," an association that lasted for some time. Bernstein himself continued to use jazz elements in his scores, including those for *Kings Go Forth, Some Came Running,* and *A Walk on the Wild Side.*

As the foregoing discussion indicates, many jazz devices have been borrowed by composers who are not normally identified with the form. On the other hand, a number of arranger-performers who *are* regularly associated with improvisation have also been interested in the screen. In 1956 John Lewis, pianist-leader of the Modern Jazz Quartet, was asked to score the French film *Sait-On Jamais* (One Never Knows). Lewis said at the time: "Jazz is often thought to be limited in expression. It is used for 'incidental music' or when a situation in drama or film calls for jazz, but rarely in a more universal way apart from an explicit jazz context. Here it has to be able to run the whole gamut of emotions and carry the story from beginning to end."

The film, released in the United States as *No Sun in Venice,* received a complete jazz treatment. The three principal characters were represented by a triple fugue, "Three Windows," with subjects stated by the vibraharp, bass, and piano. Upon the second theme Lewis developed "Cortege," music for a funeral procession written in a "cool jazz" style. A composition based on blues material accompanies a scene in which a young man tries to win a girl with a rose.

Lewis said he strove to create a Venetian atmosphere, but drew upon his own background as well. The funeral procession music, for instance, was influenced by his memories of funerals in New Orleans, with their combination of sad and happy music.

In contrast to Lewis's cool-jazz, chamber-music appoach, Johnny Mandel favored big-band orchestration. His score for *I Want to Live* (1958)—the story of a woman who is executed for murder—was recorded by an all-star jazz ensemble. For the sequence in which the heroine surrenders to the police, Mandel employed five drummers. (Drums represent the police throughout the film.) This high point featured Shelley Manne (standard drums), Larry Bunker (rhythm logs, cowbells, and claves), Mel Lewis (scratcher and cowbells), Milt Holland (chromatic drums, cowbells, and Chinese and Burmese gongs), and Latin specialist Mike Pecheco (bongos and conga drums). Mandel originally objected to writing music for the gas-chamber sequence, but changed his mind, scoring it for high woodwinds, including the piccolo, in their lowest register. (Mandel later turned to the soft, muted, slow sounds of cool jazz in *The Sandpiper*.)

Duke Ellington's big-band music permeated the film *Anatomy of a Murder* (1959). His personnel included familiar jazz soloists of the Ellington orchestra, with emphasis on saxophone and brass ensembles, and the blues style identified with his other big band compositions.

One of Ellington's first encounters with the world of precise timing and stopwatches involved a television pilot based on *The Asphalt Jungle*. Ellington, having accepted the scoring assignment from MGM, then departed for Las Vegas, where his band was featured at a major hotel. Three days later, he telephoned the studio. Though he was one of the most famous jazz composers in the country, he wasn't used to working with film synchronization, and he needed help. Harold Gelman went to Las Vegas armed with detailed timing sheets and expertise in the mathematics of breakdowns and click-tracks. The two men went over Ellington's material in detail, sometimes meeting for a session after the band had finished its last show at 4 A.M.

The recording session was held when Ellington's band had time off, and they piled into a bus for Los Angeles. As recording got under way, Ellington was still uncomfortable synchronizing his music with the visual images. His solution was simple: he discarded the formal score and called his band into a jam session. Experienced improvisers, they jammed on his material, finished the session in a day, and breezed back to Las Vegas. The music, after editing, was then dubbed into the film.

Jazz figured in several other film scores of the period. Kenyon Hopkins used it, often tempered with strings, in his music for *The Fugitive Kind, The Hustler,* and *Lilith.* Leith Stevens also demonstrated jazz influences in his score for *The Wild One.* Miles Davis naturally used jazz in *Ascension in the Elevator.*

Historical Films

Historical films have always provided challenges to composers, who face the problem of writing original music with a period flavor. The 1940s and 1950s witnessed a spate of costume dramas, few more eagerly awaited or more skillfully done than Fox's *Forever Amber* (1947), scored by David Raksin.

Although some composers have turned to film work by accident, Raksin's interest in the medium came naturally. His father, a composer and conductor, had directed theater orchestras during the silent film era. Raksin emerged from his native Philadelphia as a successful arranger with experience in both dance bands and radio orchestras. After his initial visit to Hollywood and his association with Charlie Chaplin on *Modern Times*, he remained there as an active and articulate composer of screen scores. Raksin is known for his ability to express himself with great skill in both words and notes. A man of sharp wit with a predeliction for puns, he is unfailingly lucid in describing the genesis and development of his motion picture sequences. He takes his work seriously, and the high quality of his scores may be traced in part to their overall continuity of thematic and musical development.

When he first received the scoring assignment for *Forever Amber,* Raksin considered the possibility of composing an authentic accompaniment in seventeenth-century English style. Although Henry Purcell's music came after the Restoration period, when Amber's adventures occurred, Raksin felt that a Purcellian touch might be appropriate. After seeing a screening of the film, however, he changed his mind and decided to concentrate on the dramatic impact of the picture. Although he still wanted to preserve the style and tone of the period, the first order of business was composing music that would be expressive enough to convey the characters' emotions to a contemporary audience.

Raksin's recollections about writing the score for *Amber* provide useful insights into the conditions under which Hollywood composers work. He spent two and a half weeks devoting his days to searching for themes, his nights to reading the novel on which the film was based (the latter, he reports, was the more fatiguing experience of the two). Before starting to compose, he worked out a detailed plan for theme placement, keys and colors, and the technical continuity required to progress from one reel to another.

Although the music in *Forever Amber* is both highly dramatic and quite exemplary of Raksin's own style, the themes and variations do bear a relationship to music of the period. The orchestration includes instruments of the period, such as the oboe d'amore and the lute. The composer suggests that his approach is similar to that of Prokofiev, who acknowledged his respect for tradition in his "Classical Symphony" without actually writing antiquated music. One of Raksin's themes consists of a short phrase over a bass ostinato. The melody represents Amber, while the repeated scale in the bass is the cantus firmus of a scherzo sequence (dubbed a "quasicaglia" by the composer, who maintains that it is neither a passacaglia nor a basso ostinato, while combining the worst features of both). These small thematic units are subjected to dozens of variations, ranging from restatement as a chorale to a wildly energetic scherzo. Many of the sequences are polyphonic in character, although no one knows whether the producer realized that the score was full of counterpoint. ("More canons than a Balkan uprising," quips Raksin.) Even the main title is polyphonic, consisting of thirty-two variations on a ground bass. At no time, however, did the composer allow his polyphony to become academic or pedantic.

Raksin's polished theatrical instinct provided music that was both tuneful and intensely expressive. Visits to the theater or the royal court provided an opportunity for the composer's commentaries on the pomp of the time. There is a spirited fanfare called "The King's Mistress" and some sensitive melodic writing in "The Wench."

Raksin called the overture "Anachron Overture," another example of his wit and style as a punster. "Anacreon" is the title of a composition by Cherubini; "anachronistic" is Raksin's wry description of his own approach to period music. (Incidentally, the lyrics to "The Star Spangled Banner" were set to a melody originally titled "Anacreon in Heaven.")

Forever Amber also contains numerous action sequences, from a scene of danger and stealth at a robbers' den in Whitefriars to the raging fury of the great fire of London.

Throughout, Raksin's music adds color and a feeling of time and places, and provides a subtle commentary on the feelings of the men and women of Restoration England.

In the early 1950s, the major revolution affecting the film industry, and especially historical pictures, was photographic. Audiences were soon to be watching films shown on wide screens and photographed in a variety of new processes: Todd A-O, Vistavision, Cinemascope, Cinerama, and even "3-D" (which required special glasses). These techniques called for films of epic proportions, often with epic budgets to match, and historical or costume dramas filled the bill. They were in some ways a composer's dream. An epic could require an hour or two of music, written for and rescored by the best symphonic orchestra available. Some of the results made film music history.

An outstanding composer for historical films was Miklos Rozsa, who scored *Quo Vadis* in 1951. His research was extensive, in accord with an increasing emphasis on historical accuracy in music for this type of film. Commenting on his approach to *Quo Vadis,* Rozsa wrote: "A motion picture with historical background always presents interesting problems to the composer. There have been innumerable other historical pictures produced before *Quo Vadis,* and they were all alike in their negligent attitude toward the stylistic accuracy of their music. When *Quo Vadis* was assigned to me, I decided to be stylistically, absolutely correct."

Rozsa's research led him to investigate Roman instruments. Drawings were prepared, based on statues found in museums in the Vatican and in Naples, and Italian craftsmen constructed replicas. These appeared in the film, but were not actually played. For the score itself, Rozsa simulated the sound of the old instruments with modern orchestration. The clairschach, a small Scottish harp, substituted for the lyre; various combinations of cornets, trumpets, and trombones replaced the buccinas (curved horns); the unusual timbre of the bass flute was combined with that of the English horn to duplicate the sound of the aulos. Practically nothing is known about Roman music, except that the Romans adopted Greek theory and instruments. Rozsa based some of his thematic elements on Greek materials. All the hymns in the film were performed as they had been long ago, in unison and unharmonized. Themes were often built on modal scales and harmonized in parallel fourths and fifths, reinforcing the feeling of antiquity.

Rozsa's approach to a historical film was decidedly realistic. Unlike a romantic opera, a film cannot get away with rubber swords and offstage menaces; the audience must be unaware that action taking place on the screen is staged. The opening prelude is Rozsa's setting, arranged for choral ensemble, of the words "Quo Vadis Domine?" Other melodies reflect the character of the film's principals: a gentle, modal theme for Lygia; a confident, ruthless march for Marcus Vicinius; a motif from "The Hymn to the Sun," played by full brass, when Rome burns; a four-chord motif for high strings to accompany the conversation between the Lord and St. Peter.

Rozsa became identified with the historical film, and scored several other period pieces during the next few years. His approach was of a universally high standard. It is interesting to compare the films to see how this remarkable composer adapted his own style to fit a variety of periods and places.

In *Ivanhoe* (1952), Rozsa based some themes on music of the French troubadours and trouvères. The love theme for Lady Rowena and Ivanhoe is an adaptation of an old popular song from northern France, from a manuscript found in the Royal Library of Brussels. *Plymouth Adventure* was released the same year. Rozsa recalled from his research that the Pilgrims had a music book aboard the Mayflower, the Henry Ainsworth Psalter. From it he took the 136th Psalm, a vigorous melody often described as "the Huguenot Marseillaise." Arranged for chorus and orchestra, this became the main title of the film. Other themes were inspired by the style of seventeenth-century English lutenists.

In his next film, *Julius Caesar* (1953), Rozsa decided against an authentic Roman approach. Use of the Shakespearean text created a special difficulty: Roman music would have been incongruous in an Elizabethan drama, while Elizabethan music would have jarred with the Roman costumes and settings. Rozsa aimed instead to create a score appropriate for a universal drama about the eternal problems of man. He developed three main themes: one for Caesar and Anthony, the ruthless, ambitious men of Rome; a brooding melody for Brutus; and a determined, straightforward theme for Cassius. A highly unusual sequence accompanies the death of Brutus. The martial theme identified with Antony and Octavius, and scored for winds and brass, is offset against the more lyrical melody identified with Brutus, played by the strings. The march theme is heard through the right speaker (the film uses stereophonic sound), the Brutus theme through the center and left speakers. Ultimately, with the death of Brutus, the march theme fades and the strings dominate the scene as the Brutus theme takes over completely.

Rozsa's next historical work, *Lust For Life* (1956), was a filmed biography of Vincent van Gogh based on Irving Stone's novel. Written by Norman Corwin, produced by John Houseman, and directed by Vincente Minnelli, the film combined an unusual array of production talent. Though Van Gogh himself admired Wagner and Liszt, Rozsa, seeing in his paintings an anticipation of musical impressionism, drew upon the music of the French impressionists for inspiration. (He did not, however, imitate the style of Debussy's "Prelude to the Afternoon of a Faun.") It was eminently appropriate for the film, and ranged from dramatic intensity to tenderness to comedy (for the pompous postman Roulin, one of Van Gogh's favorite subjects).

Rozsa's music for *Ben Hur* (1959), which won him the Academy Award, was the longest film score ever composed. It required nine months of effort and is regarded by many critics as one of the best film scores of all time. *Ben Hur* boasts a wealth of themes: a carol-like tune for the first Christmas, ruthless marches for the Roman soldiers, a haunting love melody, an eerie background for the lepers searching for Christ, and a prelude to the spectacular chariot race. An alleluia arranged for choir, based on the Christ theme, accompanies the reunion of Ben Hur, his mother and sister, and Esther. There is even the sound of an organ in the scene in which Christ appears.

Rozsa scored several other period epics, including *King of Kings* (1961), *Sodom and Gomorrah* (1962), and *El Cid* (1961). For *El Cid,* Rozsa turned to the *cantigas* of the twelfth century, casting his themes in both Castilian and Moorish molds. The music is full of Spanish color, scored for strings and guitars. A pipe organ begins the final scene, which describes the legend of El Cid that lived on in Spain after his death. The score also contains one of the screen's most glorious love themes. It must be emphasized that Rozsa's occasional use of authentic themes as a point of departure does not render him an arranger; the scores are completely his own, and each one contains as much original material as a full-scale symphony or tone poem.

Other composers writing major scores for historical epics during the 1950s included Alfred Newman, Bernard Herrmann, and Alex North. For *David and Bathsheba* (1951), Newman composed a tone poem, "The Twenty-Third Psalm." It begins with a French horn solo accompanied

Ben Hur, Miklos Rozsa

by harp. Gradually other instruments are added until the entire ensemble plays in a full crescendo. The rhythms of the music correspond to the text of the psalm, as if the orchestra itself were reciting the words.

Newman always had a capacity for surprises in his scores, never basing his ideas on established traditions but rather on his own unique sense of the dramatic needs of a film. An example from *The Robe* (1953) is the scene where Demetrius witnesses a Palm Sunday procession. Newman avoided the expected serious treatment and instead wrote a spirited, almost dancelike accompaniment, with cymbals and sleighbells augmenting the voices. The mood is one of exultant joy. *The Robe* also contained a remarkable musical sequence in which a wordless chorus and symphony orchestra accompany the crucifixion scene. A slow march begins the scene. The voices enter in fugal imitation, with flutes, clarinets, and horns making successive entries along with them. Music for the vocal ensemble is treated in an improvisatory style based on modal scales. The strings and brass, however, play majestic, awe-inspiring chords. The effect is one of unearthly majesty, ideally appropriate for the scene. Finally orchestra and choir dissolve as the sounds of a rainstorm dominate the soundtrack.

Newman also used a wordless chorus in *The Egyptian* (1954), on which he collaborated with Bernard Herrmann. The two did not actually write sequences together; because of deadlines, each scored some of the scenes in the film, working closely to coordinate their approaches. In addition to composing considerable music of lyrical depth, Newman wrote a hymn, "How Beautiful Art Thou," based on lyrics from an ancient Egyptian prose-poem.

Alex North took a different approach to the costume drama. After a long period of writing jazz-oriented scores for Southern, Faulkner-style films, he was assigned to write the music for *Spartacus* (1960). For this epic about a

Roman slave rebellion, North decided to use modern musical techniques, casting his themes in a barbaric, ruthless mold. The music for *Spartacus* is driving and percussive. Until the thirteenth reel, the beginning of the love story between Spartacus and the slave girl Varinia, no violins are heard. Sequences in 5/8 meter accompany the preparations of the slave armies. Another unusual touch is the use of a French electronic instrument resembling a miniature piano, the Ondioline. Played with one hand, it produces sounds reminiscent of woodwinds, percussion, and mandolin.

North also composed the music for *Cleopatra* (1963), the last of the great Hollywood epics. Throughout the score, he emphasizes not Cleopatra's beauty, but her ruthless ambition. The famous scene in which she sails from Egypt to meet Antony is accompanied by an inevitable march-like theme scored for percussive strings, guitars, harps, and mandolin. Her triumphant entrance into Rome is scored only for woodwinds and percussion. The music adds a new dimension to the character of the famous Egyptian queen.

Notable scores for period pieces were also produced by Franz Waxman, who did *The Silver Chalice* (1955), *The Story of Ruth* (1960), and *Taras Bulba* (1962). Waxman, dealing with diverse historical elements in *The Silver Chalice,* employed the eighteenth-century "Dresden theme"— also quoted by Mendelssohn and Wagner—an authentic religious motif, and a polyphonic style. He also included an extract from Bach's "St. John Passion." In *The Story of Ruth,* Waxman incorporated modal scales as a means of establishing a feeling of antiquity. In *Taras Bulba,* he drew upon his travels in Russia as a source of inspiration. He was familiar with Ukrainian folk music, and wrote some appropriately barbarous music for the throbbing accompaniment to ride and chase sequences.

George Antheil always had an affinity for Spanish music. He had for instance composed a ballet, "Capital of the World," based on a bullfighting story by Hemingway. When he scored *The Pride and the Passion* (1957), he decided to do something unusual. Because the film dealt with the adventures of a group of Spaniards in the Napoleonic era, Antheil emphasized Spanish characteristics in every element of his score. The main theme, identified with the great gun, is developed for brass using Spanish scales and rhythms; a theme representing the anti-Napoleonic uprising is developed into a bolero; the love melodies, including a serenade for two Spanish lovers, is cast in a Castilian mold; a knife fight is scored as a farruca; a procession scene includes actual Spanish procession music. The result is an authentic and dynamic score.

Ben Hur
Miklos Rozsa

The Red Shoes
Brian Easdale

High Noon
Dimitri Tiomkin

A Streetcar Named Desire
Alex North

Lust for Life
Miklos Rozsa

Tom and Jerry
Scott Bradley

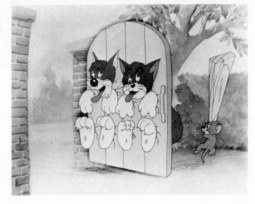

CHAPTER VI

Outstanding Scores
of the 1950s

Although an increasing number of composers turned to jazz and related musical styles during the 1950s, not every motion picture lent itself to this sort of treatment. The result was the beginning of a division, in both musical and cinematic styles, that has persisted up to the present day. A number of composers continued to write film music as it had been known for many years, fulfilling a variety of dramatic functions. Others turned to jazz orchestration, pop music, and a scoring idiom that represented a total departure from the past. To divide lists of composers into neat categories or schools may be easy for a critic, but it doesn't do his subjects justice. Therefore, we shall simply look at some of the major scores of the 1950s and early 1960s.

In the 1950s, the most prominent director of suspense films—as earlier—was Alfred Hitchcock. In this period the English master began an association with Bernard Herrmann that produced some of the most memorable film music of all time.

Herrmann's first Hitchcock score, *The Trouble With Harry* (1956), embraced elements of comedy as well as suspense. Although the film was not particularly successful, Herrmann's sardonic and satirical music was. The opening contains a three-note comic woodwind figure and a repeated-note motif for the horns. The short, rhythmic figures are the ideal accompaniment for a villain who moves on tiptoe rather than relying on brute force. The film also contains one of Herrmann's most haunting melodies, a modal theme for woodwind solo against string accompaniment, with the nostalgic gentleness of an English folksong. That same year Herrmann scored *The Man Who Knew Too Much,* the high point of which is an assassination attempt in Royal Albert Hall. (The gunman times his shot to coincide with the cymbal crash at the musical climax in Arthur Benjamin's "Storm Clouds Cantata.") Herrmann provided the underscoring music and also appeared in the film himself as a conductor.

When Herrmann turned to the score for Hitchcock's *Vertigo* (1958), he produced a masterpiece. The central figure is a detective, Scottie Ferguson (played by James Stewart). The very idea of vertigo stimulated the prelude. The opening is based on a series of broken chords, alternating the strings and an ensemble of harps, celesta, and percussion. This delicate beginning builds to a theme in the strings scored for full orchestra. A repetition of broken chords produces the feeling of revolving, which matches the dizzy feelings experienced by the main character. Scottie has a dream about Madeleine, a girl whom he is following, and Carlotta, a Spanish ancestor whom Madeleine believes has taken possession of her soul. Herrmann accompanies the nightmare sequence with an orchestral collage of Spanish rhythms, complete with castanets and tambourine, in habañera style. The nightmare culminates in passages of frenzied strings leading to overwhelming intensity. The love scene in *Vertigo* is one of the most totally romantic examples of orchestral scoring. It begins with slow, ethereal violins while Scottie anticipates Madeleine's appearance. As the scene continues, the strings whisper and then begin a cascade of tremolo figures, culminating in a statement of the theme scored for full orchestra. The scene contains little spoken dialogue; with Herrmann's music, little was needed.

Herrmann's next Hitchcock score was *North by Northwest* (1959). It opens with a stunning orchestral fandango accompanying the visual main title; the antiphonal interplay between strings, winds, and percussion culminates in a swirling, twisting orchestral glissando. Herrmann scored the chase scenes in *North by Northwest* with some of his favorite devices: pedal points, ostinatos, and sequential figures for winds and strings. There is also a tender love theme, and a return to the fandango rhythm for the famous sequence on Mount Rushmore.

Herrmann's score for *Psycho* (1960) is a classic. Typically, when most Hollywood composers were producing scores emphasizing brass and jazz ensembles, he turned to an all-string orchestra. Because the film was shot in black and white, Herrmann decided to use a "black and white" sound effect. The opening is full of nervous figures for the strings, expanding gradually into a driving, tense prelude. Herrmann wrote perhaps the most terrifying musical sequence in history to accompany one of the screen's most brutal murders. It is an astonishing example of realism, with the slashing sound of the murderer's knife echoed by glissandos in the highest registers of the strings.

Herrmann's score for *Marnie* (1964) is more similar to *Vertigo*. It is scored for a symphonic orchestra, and contains impassioned themes of great lyricism. A dazzling orchestral scherzo accompanies the foxhunting sequence, which is blended with *Marnie's* main musical idea.

Detailed analysis of Herrmann's music is challenging and sometimes difficult. In many respects he is one of the screen's few impressionist composers. He does not decorate his scores with intricate counterpoint or novelty effects. His music is emotional and direct. Like Debussy—whom he considers to be the major composer of the twentieth century —Herrmann prefers to create a musical tapestry based on orchestral colors. His scores often do contain rich, full melodies (frequently overlooked), but it is his sense of instrumentation and harmonic shading that enables him to get inside a scene. Because he adds music with an extremely careful touch, his scoring often blends with the picture to such an extent that audiences are unaware of it.

Herrmann's scores for Hitchcock's films are almost universally regarded by critics as classics of scoring for suspense. The two men worked closely together, with Hitchcock consulting Herrmann about his musical plans long before final editing was completed. The director often adjusted his cutting accordingly. As a result, many of Hitchcock's most suspenseful moments are directly derived from musical effects—the chilling shrillness of the strings that accompany the murder in *Psycho,* the cymbal crash as an assassin's signal in *The Man Who Knew Too Much,* and the sudden alternation of various instruments in the long chases in *North by Northwest.* Herrmann has described music as a key element in Hitchcock's nutcracker of suspense, and film critics have universally agreed.

Considerable public attention during the early 1950s was accorded the scores of Franz Waxman, who won Oscars in successive years for his music for *Sunset Boulevard* (1950) and *A Place in the Sun* (1951). Waxman used subtle orchestration in both. In *Sunset Boulevard,* Norma Desmond, an aging former silent-film star, leads a bizarre existence nourished by pathetic delusions of grandeur. In a high point of the film she descends the staircase of her home to face a murder charge, still believing that the men awaiting her herald her long-anticipated return to stardom; a solo violin plays an ironic and subtle tango accompaniment.

A Place in the Sun, based on Theodore Dreiser's novel "An American Tragedy," relates the experiences of a poor young man torn between his feelings for a girl with a similar background and his infatuation with a beautiful socialite, a dilemma that leads him to murder. Waxman's love theme, an elegant melody, begins with a three-note pick-up, an ascending series of notes symbolizing the young man, who looks up to the girl he idolizes. Waxman arranged the love theme for a sophisticated orchestral texture, auditioning a hundred saxophone soloists before finally making a choice. In a chase sequence, a stunning orchestral fugato, beginning with solo woodwinds, builds up to a frenzied development.

Waxman's problems began when the director of *A Place in the Sun,* George Stevens, decided that he liked the temporary music track better than some of Waxman's sequences. (At that time, studio music departments often prepared a "temp-track," an accompaniment that could be used with the film until the actual score was written; the music was drawn from other cues preserved in the studio music libraries.) The two did not reach agreement over the proposed changes, and Stevens then asked Victor Young and Daniele Amfitheatrof to rescore the disputed scenes. Since Young did not want the job, Amfitheatrof's music eventually replaced Waxman's in several sequences.

Waxman demonstrated a unique ability to write for varied settings. He composed outstanding suspense scores for *My Cousin Rachel* and *Rear Window.* His wide range was further demonstrated by his music for *Peyton Place, Sayonara, Taras Bulba, The Spirit of St. Louis, The Nun's Story,* and *Hemingway's Adventures of a Young Man.* In *Peyton Place,* Waxman tried to capture the feeling of New England by developing simple and straightforward themes. For a hilltop sequence in which two young people kiss for the first time, he wrote the familiar Peyton Place theme.

It is young, optimistic, and innocent, in contrast to the more sophisticated melodies in other sections of the score. In *Sayonara,* Waxman experimented with Japanese motifs and Oriental instruments. (He also included, as instructed, a title song by Irving Berlin.)

Waxman's score for *The Spirit of St. Louis* (1957) was among his major film achievements. Highly inventive "airplane" music, scored for percussive xylophones, cymbals, and pizzicato strings, accompanies the building of Lindbergh's plane. High strings create the feeling of a plane in flight, while the drama is heightened by a variety of themes and motifs related to the areas over which Lindbergh flies.

Waxman's music for *The Nun's Story* (1959) won the enthusiasm of director Fred Zinnemann in spite of the fact that he had originally wanted no music at all. The film is a serious portrait of a young girl who becomes a nun, only to find that she is plagued by doubts. Waxman's opening main title is based on a stunning set of chime effects scored for full orchestra with emphasis on the high strings. The composer's only twelve-tone film sequence is used in a scene that takes place in an asylum. The main theme is scored for strings and used in variation form in scenes expressing the girl's yearning to be a nun. Sensitive narration sequences are underscored with a halo of gentle, high strings. The final scene, in which Sister Luke leaves the convent and returns to a life away from the religious order, is accompanied by a solo chime.

For *Hemingway's Adventures of a Young Man* (1962), Waxman's music ranged from a lush Italian love theme to impressionistic woodwind solos set against strings, echoing the bird songs in the Michigan woods. He also wrote dissonant battle music.

Alex North, who had burst upon the Hollywood musical scene with such impact after his jazz score for *A Streetcar*

Peyton Place, Franz Waxman

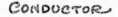

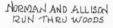

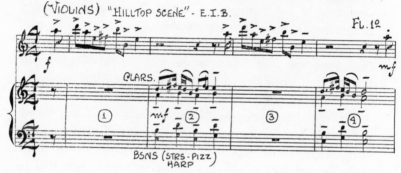

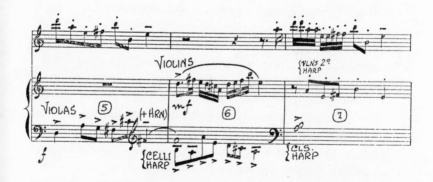

Named Desire, continued as a major creative force throughout the 1950s and 1960s. Composers are often typecast in
Hollywood. During these years, most producers seemed to
think of North as someone ideally suited to score either costume pictures or jazz-oriented films in rural settings. This was
unfair to the versatile North, who has a unique way of
marking any style he approaches, from jazz to Italian folk
music, with his own unique brand of melodic design and
rhythmic impulse.

North was a fortunate choice for the film *Viva Zapata*
(1952). He had lived in Mexico for over two years, had
studied with the composer Silvestre Revueltas, and had a
deep personal understanding of Mexican music and people.
He had always displayed a flair for percussion, and his use
of xylophones and other similar instruments highlighted
the opening main title, full of Mexican rhythms and dissonant brass chords. A delicate flute solo in the Aeolian
mode accompanies one death scene. In another scene, when
word of Zapata's capture is passed from one loyal peasant
to another, North begins a bolero-style composition with
timbales and bongos, adding a marimba and then strings
and winds. For a scene between Zapata and his wife, an
oboe d'amore plays a Mexican-style, folk-like melody over
strumming mandolins, guitars, and marimbas. North's
music was more majestic for the conclusion of the film and
the death of Zapata.

Another of North's major scores during this period was
that for *The Rose Tattoo* (1955), which made use of both
folk and jazz traditions. The opening main title is based
on a Sicilian folk tune, its orchestration incorporating mandolins and children's voices. (North carefully distinguished
between Sicilian and Neapolitan folk music, noting Moorish influence upon the former.) The jazz sequences accompanied prostitutes who appeared in the film. North also
wrote a tuneful sequence entitled "Bacio," scored for cello

solo over a gentle accompaniment by the other strings.

North likes to provide surprises in his scores. One example occurs in his music for *The Bad Seed* (1956). In the main title, North introduces a piano as a little girl is shown practicing. Then its tuneful, bright sounds are virtually chased off the soundtrack by a dazzling array of nervous, dissonant, violent orchestral figures, representing the fear and horror that accompany the discovery of the child's true character.

He approached *The Rainmaker* (discussed in detail in Chapter VIII) as if it were a musical, choosing locations for music as if he were choosing settings for songs in a musical. *Four Girls in Town* (1956) provided an unusual opportunity for the composer. He wrote a stunning jazz piece, "Rhapsody for Four Girls in Town," as a totally developed composition. The work was first recorded with André Previn as piano soloist and Ray Linn playing lead trumpet. Then themes from the work were adapted for the underscoring of the film. The rhapsody itself is cast in ternary form, with a breezy jazz opening for piano and snapping, dissonant brass chords, a lyrical middle section in ballad style, and a recapitulation.

North's jazz style extended to film adaptations of William Faulkner's *The Long, Hot Summer* (1958) and *The Sound and the Fury* (1959). The familiar North trademarks are ever-present; tense dissonance, sparse orchestration, cross rhythms, jazz figures, and an abundance of percussion. North often builds tension on the screen with short, terse musical punctuation. But his lyrical melodies, including his love theme for *The Sound and the Fury*, are gentle and introspective, with full harmonies—often in ninth, eleventh, and thirteenth chords—that always carry an air of sophistication.

Among North's other major scores during these years were *Les Miserables* (1952), *The Member of the Wedding*

(1953), *The Bachelor Party* (1957), and *The Wonderful Country* (1959). His output during the 1960s included music for *Spartacus* (1960), *Cleopatra* (1963), *The Agony and the Ecstasy* (1965), and *Who's Afraid of Virginia Woolf?* (1966)—the last-named also treated in detail in Chapter VIII.

Hugo Friedhofer continued, as earlier, to write with a romantic but unsentimental spirit, a sense of humor and wit, and a consistent degree of high musical craftsmanship. His tender and completely expressive music relied on the sound of high strings identified with the Fox studios, but his voicings and chord progressions were not so lush as those of Alfred Newman.

In *The Sun Also Rises* (1957) Friedhofer incorporated a variety of musical themes and ideas. The film, based on Hemingway's famous novel, depicts the rambling, unhappy lives of the "lost generation" roaming the capitals of Europe. The opening main title begins with a verbal quotation from Hemingway. Friedhofer leads into the narration, "One generation passes away, and another generation comes," with a harp glissando, progressing to high string chords. Then he introduces an intense, spirited main theme, stated alternately by the strings and brass. Cole Porter's "You Do Something to Me" adds poignancy to the nostalgic memories of Jake Barnes and his ill-fated love affair with Lady Brett Ashley; Friedhofer does not "plug" the song, but develops it as a legitimate theme. His music for the film is also inspired by other sources: Dixieland and jazz combos in 1920s style, the sounds of Bal Musette cafés, and fiery marches identified with the running of the bulls at Pamplona. In the final sequence, Friedhofer returns to his original main title motif, developing the melodies as the strings ascend, leading to high, ethereal string chords. The narrator's voice enters again, and restates the quote, ending with the title of the film, "the sun also rises."

In *Boy on a Dolphin* (1957), Friedhofer adopted a Greek style, using Greek instruments and elements of Greek folk music. In his own words, the music was romantic, exotic, and impressionistic. A vivid sequence contains a vocalise performed by Marni Nixon. Her ethereal arpeggio figures are arranged over a veritable wave of underwater harp glissandos and string tremolos. The voice in this instance acts as an orchestral instrument. The effect is to create an atmosphere of mystery and unseen beauty associated with the deep waters of the Mediterranean. Although the wordless chorus had been employed by Alfred Newman and others, Friedhofer's use of a single voice, without words, was most unusual. (One of the few similar instances is the main title of the film *Secret of the Incas,* which features a solo vocalise by Yma Sumac based on a Peruvian melody composed by her husband, Moises Vivanco. The melody evokes the mood of the high Peruvian Andes.)

Friedhofer, discussing his music for *Boy on a Dolphin,* took the occasion to express his views about the nature of the art in general. A film score with the complexities of a Brahms symphony, he indicated, probably would not be a good film score. On the other hand, Friedhofer does not advocate the totally unobtrusive score that consists primarily of "mood music." He believes film music should maintain its own integrity of line, functioning as a frame or connective tissue and even, on occasion, as the chief actor in the dramatic presentation.

Friedhofer's score for *The Young Lions* (1958) is in a different style. This motion picture dramatizes the experiences of three men, two Americans and one European, especially the effects of World War II on their lives. A haunting love theme is arranged for strings and solo winds, while the main title is a stirring march with brass fanfares and snare drum figures. In a North African sequence, suspense is achieved through the use of high, sustained pedal points, held by the strings over menacingly dissonant brass chords.

One of Friedhofer's most dynamic scores was that for Marlon Brando's ill-fated Western, *One-Eyed Jacks* (1961). The critics were less than laudatory about Brando's film, but they liked Friedhofer's music. The story takes place in California and Mexico in the 1880s. Friedhofer's score is unique for several reasons. First of all, he has always believed that scores about Mexico should sound Mexican and not Spanish—a subtle distinction, but one that means a good deal to a man of his craftsmanship. Also, the music, although decidedly appropriate, does not sound "Western" in the expected sense. There are no cowboy tunes or other melodies associated with Westerns (and hackneyed through overabundance of plagal cadences). In one sequence, a search taking place outdoors, the scene begins with brass, then turns to a string ostinato interrupted by an occasional figure for flute. Then the ostinato returns. It stops and permits the brass to take over; the strings relentlessly return again and again, finally in pizzicato figures. Friedhofer's love themes are often arranged for a lush string orchestra, and *One-Eyed Jacks* is no exception. His music, here as elsewhere, sounds less sentimental than that of Steiner or Korngold, primarily because he depends more than they do on added seventh and ninth chords, and on a harmonic vocabulary that incorporates modal scales and dissonances.

Many of the pioneers of motion picture music remained active during the 1950s and 1960s. Max Steiner wrote music for *Band of Angels, Marjorie Morningstar,* and *John Paul Jones.* He continued to prefer the large symphonic orchestra and use of leitmotifs. Alfred Newman scored *Anastasia, A Certain Smile, The Diary of Anne Frank,* and *The Greatest Story Ever Told.* Although he occasionally used title songs in his scores, they always served as bases for thematic development, as in the famous recognition scene in *Anastasia*. Newman continued to exploit the high strings registers.

Bronislau Kaper's scores ranged from costume romances *(The Swan)* to epics *(Mutiny on the Bounty)* to period pieces with exotic orchestrations *(Lord Jim)*. In *The Swan*, he produced a score of continental charm and nostalgic sentiment like that for *Lili*. Another versatile composer was Dimitri Tiomkin, who did Westerns *(Giant, The Alamo)*, dramas *(The Old Man and the Sea)*, epics *(The Fall of the Roman Empire)*, and suspense features *(36 Hours)*. Victor Young's lyrical approach characterized *Samson and Delilah, The Quiet Man*, and, one of his most outstanding efforts, *The Brave One*. Together with William Lava's stirring accompaniment for *The Littlest Outlaw*, this symphonically orchestrated score featuring a Mexican setting was one of the most intensive and expressive examples of underscoring for films about children and animals.

George Duning became one of the most active composers in Hollywood during the 1950s. Born in Richmond, Indiana, he studied at the Cincinnati Conservatory and with Mario Castelnuovo-Tedesco. Before turning to films, he was a dance band arranger and noted musical director in radio.

One of Hollywood's most unusual film music episodes occurred when Duning was asked to write the score for *Picnic* (1956), based on William Inge's play of the same name. He was given the assignment more than six months before scoring—in itself unusual, as a composer is normally called in at the last minute. Although he was busily completing scores for other films, Duning devoted considerable thought to *Picnic*. A native of the Midwest, he strongly identified with the region and the characters in the story. His score included a *Picnic* love theme, a tender and romantic melody.

In a key scene, the two central figures (portrayed in the film by William Holden and Kim Novak) realize that they are in love while dancing together. In the play, the scene was accompanied by a recording of a small rhythm ensemble performing the popular song "Moonglow." In the film, plans initially called for another song, the rights to which were owned by Columbia Pictures. But the director of the film, Joshua Logan, who had also directed the play, was superstitious about theatrical traditions, and insisted that "Moonglow" be used for luck. The studio arranged to purchase the rights to the song, which were controlled by a New York publisher, Mills Music, Inc. When he actually saw Novak and Holden dancing to "Moonglow," however, Logan decided that the sequence needed an additional musical touch. He asked Duning to superimpose his own love theme on "Moonglow." "At that point," declared the enthusiastic Logan, "I want to hear the *Picnic* love theme played by all the violins in our orchestra." The composer demurred, pointing out that if the two themes were played simultaneously, the clashes of various harmonies would produce sharp dissonances. But Logan insisted. Here Duning's training in counterpoint stood him in good stead, enabling him to arrange his *Picnic* theme so that it could indeed be heard simultaneously with "Moonglow." In the midst of the dance, Holden and Novak draw closer together and gaze into each other's eyes. As their attraction increases, the *Picnic* love theme enters quietly, played by the strings, and soars above the rhythm section playing "Moonglow." (Logan brushed aside all objections to the use of the big orchestra, even though the small rhythm group had been photographed accompanying the dance.)

Reaction to the *Picnic*-"Moonglow" combination was wildly enthusiastic. The score was cited by the Composers Guild of America, in cooperation with Down Beat Magazine, as "the best original underscore for a nonmusical film."

Released on record, it spent over three months on the Hit Parade. One reaction to the theme, however, was decidedly negative. Mills Music sued Duning and Columbia Pictures, insisting that the now famous love theme was merely an obbligato on the song they had copyrighted. Duning and the studio filed depositions in reply and called in as experts two musicologists from Columbia University, who insisted that the *Picnic* love theme was a separate musical entity. Ultimately, the judge recognized that the combination of the two themes was the result of some fine musical craftsmanship by Duning, and threw the case out of court.

But the composer's experiences with *Picnic* were still not over. When Steve Allen heard the theme at a screening in New York, he became so excited about it that he wrote lyrics, and the melody became a hit song. (Duning knew nothing about the adaptation until a studio executive asked him to explain how Steve Allen had gotten involved with the theme.) The recorded versions were so successful that Allen later set lyrics to other Duning melodies, although the two never actually collaborated on these songs.

Duning went on to enjoy an active and successful career in Hollywood. His scores have ranged from highly melodic accompaniments *(Me and the Colonel)* to dance-band styles *(Bell, Book and Candle)* to vigorous Western works, occasionally influenced by the music of Aaron Copland. His other films have included *From Here to Eternity, The World of Suzie Wong,* and *The Devil at Four O'Clock.*

Jerome Moross was responsible for a Western score in 1958, *The Big Country*—a new wide-screen epic—that instantly became a model for others. Moross had an extensive background in motion pictures, having been associated with Copland when the latter first became interested in films. A native New Yorker, Moross rose to fame writing music for the stage and for radio during the 1930s. His serious works include a symphony, an opera, chamber music, and compositions for ballet; his unusual musical, "The Golden Apple," was widely praised.

Moross, a highly skilled orchestrator, has absorbed some of the musical idioms developed by Copland, though infusing them with a harmonic and melodic style all his own. The main title of *The Big Country* is a vigorous overture scored for full orchestra, beginning with a furiously whirling figuration for strings and winds and resolving quickly into an original Western melody. Like Copland, Moross is fond of cross-rhythms and irregular phrasing. A charming Western waltz preserves 3/4 time and crisp orchestration while maintaining the harmonic flavor of a cowboy tune. A thunderous finale is built by developing a brisk, syncopated figure scored for the timpani. The sudden starts and stops and asymmetrical melodic figures capture a sort of Western awkwardness that lends depth and power to the film.

Moross tends to avoid a lush orchestral sound. When he does write for a symphonic combination, he often uses it to create antiphonal effects and brilliant orchestral colors. He also likes dance forms. This preference could be attributed to the frequency of dance in motion pictures themselves, but it seems more likely that a composer of such noted ballets as "Frankie and Johnny" recognizes dance rhythms as a device that can be exploited thoroughly by an imaginative film composer. His score for *The Sharkfighters* includes a rhythmic habañera and danzon. *The Cardinal* features several period dances, including a foxtrot and a Viennese waltz, the latter scored for a salon ensemble.

Proud Rebel (1958) received a treatment somewhat similar to *The Big Country,* although the more personal story called for a more intimate accompaniment than the panoramic chases and outdoor ranch processions of the latter. When Moross chooses to be lyrical, as in the "Romanza" from *Proud Rebel,* he often does so with folk tunes harmonized in pure triads. The effect is one of tenderness without undue sentimentality.

Moross's score for *The War Lord* (1965) was arranged for full symphonic orchestra. Here he turns to a modal harmonic vocabulary. Delicate flute and English horn solos over string tremolos portray the medieval countryside. The film contains a rather lush love theme; significantly, it is developed from chord progressions that are arranged over a polyphonic accompaniment, a highly ornamental scale line played by the lower strings.

David Raksin produced a remarkable score for *Carrie* (1952), the film adaptation of Dreiser's novel, "Sister Carrie." Because *Carrie* was a period piece, the composer determined that its accompaniment should be the 1950s equivalent of a silent film score. He had watched his father conduct theater orchestras at Saturday matinees, and he wanted to achieve the same "chromo" flavor.

The main theme is a lyrical melody that derives much of its expressive quality from wide, harmonically resolved melodic leaps of varying proportions. When played softly, it has a yearning, rather brooding quality. But in moments of extreme tension—for example, accompanying the flight of George Hurstwood, Carrie's lover—it is converted to a relentless, unhappy melody. It leads inevitably toward its own musical resolution and, visually, toward Hurstwood's tragic end. In the tender love scenes, the music softens the character of Hurstwood; we feel empathy with this man who has given up everything for love, only to find that it leads to his destruction.

The finale of *Carrie* is divided into four sections. It begins with a long arioso passage for strings followed by an English horn quotation of the main theme played gently and expressively. Agitated chromatic polyphony leads to another statement of the theme, this time with the "flight sequence" accompaniment, a relentless ostinato of afterbeat chords. Winds and strings alternate polyphonically and are developed further, leading the listener to a restatement of the *Carrie* theme, this time as a dirge; the music provides the ideal accompaniment for the tragic figure of Hurstwood on his last walk. The final statement of the theme is sounded by a horn over a timpani roll. Woodwinds enter in an interlude accompanying the dialogue. Then a soaring melodic statement of the main theme, again by the violins, builds toward a brass fanfare.

Raksin's experience with *Carrie* was not a happy one. He wrote the four final sections for the film as a carefully detailed accompaniment, developing his thematic material with skill and sensitivity. The degree to which the music brightened and darkened, the accompaniment was tense or calm, the melodic motifs swelled and faded—all derived directly from the emotional pulse of the final sequence, in which Hurstwood, who had suffered one catastrophe after another, finally met his fate.

The composer did not anticipate the intervention of studio executives, who ruled that the extended final sequence should be drastically shortened. Raksin was not allowed to instruct the editor so that his music could be cut properly to make adjustments, and his musical tapestry was sliced to ribbons. If a composer has worked meticulously on shading every bar, it is impossible for a production executive to cut and paste sequences together; unfortunately, this is exactly what happened. Said Raksin: "If there is a composer who can equal the dexterity with which a minor executive mutilates the form and context relationship of music to story, I have never met him." He did credit studio music cutter Bill Stinson, one of Hollywood's most experienced, with saving the music from another scene—Hurstwood's flight from his wife to Carrie—after editing shortened it and again threatened the score.

John Green (known as Johnny Green for many years)

became a familiar figure in Hollywood music circles in the 1940s. He had emerged from Harvard with an economics degree, but was drawn to music while still in school, working as an arranger for the relatively unknown bandleader Guy Lombardo and collaborating with Carmen Lombardo and Gus Kahn on a hit song, "Coquette." Green continued his career as a successful songwriter and bandleader in New York, turning out such popular tunes as "Body and Soul" for Gertrude Lawrence. Associated with Jack Benny and Fred Astaire on radio, he served as musical director for a number of radio programs. He also conducted Broadway musicals, and his work as musical director of Richard Rodgers's "By Jupiter" led to his joining the staff of MGM.

Green moved to Hollywood in 1942, where he became active as a musical director of film musicals; *Easter Parade* won him an Oscar. He later became general musical director at MGM, dividing his time among composing, conducting, and administrative duties. Green has a reputation as a dapper raconteur and sports as a trademark a white carnation in his lapel. A mercurial figure, he maintains a busy schedule of activities outside the studio, often communicating with colleagues from a telephone in his car.

Green's major original score of the 1950s was for the epic *Raintree County* (1957), a Civil War story. Green wanted an unusual effect to symbolize the raintree, the legendary tree that seems to elude Johnny Shawnessy, the picture's principal character. A toy glockenspiel with brass tubes was played alternately by two percussionists. Although almost inaudible on stage, the sound was subjected to amplification and reverberation treatment in an echo chamber. Engineers recorded this raintree motif separately on an individual channel, which could then be added to the other music in dubbing. The result was a unique, shimmering, bell-like sound that evoked the mysterious aura of golden sunlight identified with the tree.

Green decided that a title song, which the studio wanted, could be included in the score if it had a folk quality. This same feeling pervades the thirteen separate themes he wrote for various characters, each theme treated with considerable melodic and polyphonic extension. A specific orchestral sound of little bells, produced by Greek finger cymbals, is identified with the madness of Susanna, a mysterious girl with whom Johnny is in love. The mad theme is divided into two subjects, the first representing the illness itself, the second, subjected to fugal development, associated with Susanna's dolls. When Johnny and Susanna destroy the dolls, the musical accompaniment is a waltz-like variation on the mad theme. Green also provided both happy and sad love melodies for Johnny and Susanna and themes for the love story between Johnny and his childhood sweetheart, Johnny's son, and the Raintree swamp. A brash character, Flash Perkins, is characterized by a banjo, while the Raintree swamp is identified with a harmonica.

Although women have participated in almost every other facet of filmmaking, they have few music scores to their credit. Ann Ronell (the wife of producer Lester Cowan) contributed music to *The Story of G.I. Joe* in 1945, for which music credits were divided among Ronell, Louis Applebaum, and Louis Forbes. Ronell also composed music for *One Touch of Venus,* the Marx Brothers film *Love Happy,* and *Main Street to Broadway*.

Another woman composer was Elizabeth Firestone, whose grandmother had written the theme for the Firestone radio broadcasts and who had both popular songs and concert music to her credit in 1949, when she made her debut as a screen composer with the score for *Once More, My Darling*. Orchestrators were Frank Skinner, an experienced film composer in his own right, and David Tamkin. Since Ronell's first efforts were co-credited, Firestone has a strong claim to being the first American women to score a major

American feature. (Women composers had already become active in England and Europe.) Firestone completed one other score, for *That Man From Tangier* (1953).

English and Continental Film Music

In the 1950s, as earlier, English and European composers produced some excellent scores for motion pictures. One of the most prolific was Malcolm Arnold, an English composer who has divided his time between film scoring and concert music, particularly symphonies, ballets, and chamber music. He won an Academy Award for his score for *The Bridge on the River Kwai* (1957), although it gained public attention chiefly because of the composer's inclusion of the "Colonel Bogey March." Arnold exhibits a remarkable clarity in orchestration, perhaps because he is a former trumpet soloist, with a background as a symphony musician. His music, like Friedhofer's, is romantic and expressive, dependent on long, lyrical, melodic lines. He is fond of brass fanfares in his opening titles—as what trumpet virtuoso would not be? Harmonically, Arnold also likes modal scales and progressions of ninth chords. For dramatic effect, he often writes tremolo figures, not just as a means of creating suspense but also as a technique for adding shimmering vibrancy to individual scenes.

Arnold's scores for *Inn of the Sixth Happiness, The Roots of Heaven, The Lion, Nine Hours to Rama,* and *The Heroes of Telemark* are examples of his style. Although each one is highly individual, all display a stylistic consistency. Arnold seldom turns either to complex polyphony or dissonance, instead employing orchestral color and a breathless tremolo to build suspense.

Music for *The Lion* contains an Arnold favorite, a short, descending two-note motif for brass choir. The opening scene of *Nine Hours to Rama* is a driving sequence scored for full orchestra, with the addition of sitars. *Inn of the Sixth Happiness* is an example of Arnold at his best. It opens with an overture, including brass fanfares that swell and grow from the softest depths of the orchestra. The melody is stated by solo violins. (Arnold prefers single-line melodies for violins rather than chordal arrangements, with the result that his strings always maintain a crisp, clean sound.) Dramatic scenes such as the meeting between Gladys and Linnan, the initial appearance of the mandarin, and the passing of Jeannie Lawson, are tastefully scored with tremolos and melodic development of short motifs based on the main themes.

William Alwyn, one of England's most experienced film composers, wrote an intense and exciting accompaniment for *Shake Hands With the Devil* (1959), a picture dealing with the Irish rebellion in the early twentieth century. Alwyn's approach was essentially symphonic, and a large orchestra was ideal in providing atmosphere and underscoring the emotional complexities always present in this story of divided loyalties. The music ranges from the stormy to the tender. The main title begins with a violent five-note motif for woodwinds, played over a brass fanfare and leading to a main theme, an Irish melody arranged almost like a funeral march. For the Black and Tans, Alwyn wrote a wild sequence of brass flourishes and string tremolos. A love scene takes place against a haunting theme reminiscent of an Irish folk tune, somber and brooding, scored for woodwinds and strings. The composer turned to a solo violin for extended lyricism in characterizing Sean Lenihan, the leader of the Irish Republican Army who finds it impossible to give up the power he has maintained in the underground. For Kitty Brady, a young Irish woman who works with the underground leaders, Alwyn developed a Delius-style figure as she walks by the sea.

Alwyn's music is rarely lush. Like many English com-

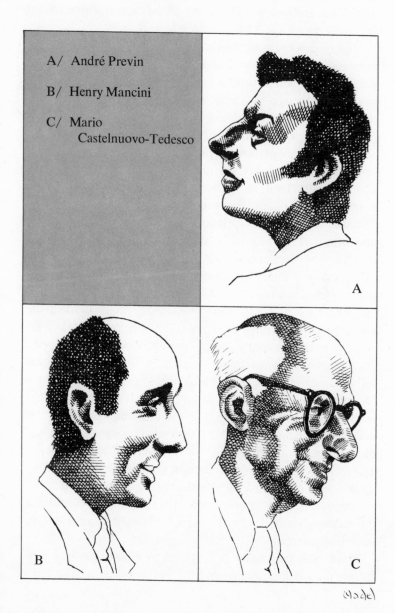

A/ André Previn

B/ Henry Mancini

C/ Mario
    Castelnuovo-Tedesco

posers, he uses an abundance of solo winds, especially oboes, over strings. Violins often serve as melodic instruments, but he prefers the creation of orchestral sound effects to the development of thematic material.

Highly coloristic orchestration and the inventive use of thematic materials also highlighted other English pictures during these years. Mischa Spoliansky combined medieval instruments with a decidedly contemporary approach in his score for the Otto Preminger production of *Saint Joan* (1957). In the opening title he introduced panpipes, an ancient instrument which he felt suggested the peasant origins of Joan of Arc. In one sequence, the king dreams that he meets Saint Joan and the other principal characters years after his death. For this Spoliansky wrote a "Dream Minuet" scored for harpsichord, celesta, harp, vibraphone, and strings. This delicate, witty music has a medieval grace that lends a distinct touch of irony to the scene; a quality of unreality is achieved through an accompaniment of light string tremolos and a bell-like orchestration. The formal, haughty pace of royal court music adds humor, since the entire meeting is only a dream. The siege of Orleans includes an unexpectedly lyrical march, one of the screen's least bombastic, which culminates in a stirring passage for full orchestra emphasizing cascading strings. For the coronation of King Charles in Reims Cathedral, the composer wrote a virtuoso toccatina for solo organ. Performed on a powerful cathedral organ, the music creates an effect of majestic authenticity. Spoliansky turned to wide leaps and frenzied chord progressions in the strings in portraying the voice of conscience of Joan's executioners. Significantly, he did not rely heavily on dissonance; in this context, a diminished seventh chord suspended over a root seems sufficiently tense.

Philip Sainton, noted in England as a distinguished performer and composer, scored his first motion picture with a symphonic score for John Huston's *Moby Dick* (1956). Sainton had enjoyed a long musical career as principal violinist with leading orchestras in England and as a composer of tone poems, including "Two Sea Pictures" and "The Island." Huston became acquainted with Sainton's work when the latter transcribed a friend's musical sketches for full orchestra.

Sainton had never read Melville's novel when he started work on the film, but developed his themes after studying the book. He worked closely with Huston, whose musical requirements ranged from intensification of a visual scene to subjective underscoring. The score runs the gamut from impressionistic sea paintings to music of raging fury. The main themes are carefully developed. When Ahab's crew exults after discovering a school of whales, the background is joyous carnival music built on old French hunting-calls and using open notes of the French horn. For the obsessive Ahab, the composer wrote a vigorous percussive theme, continually returning after chromatic departures to the same tonal center. Whale-hunting scenes were written as chases for full orchestra, with emphasis on brass. A menacing theme for the lowest tessitura of the orchestra represented the white whale, Moby Dick.

Elizabeth Luytens, one of the few women to become prominent as a film composer, was acclaimed for scores she wrote in association with England's famous Crown Film Unit during World War II. After the war she divided her time between serious music and film music. Her motion picture credits include *A String of Beads, The Boy Kumasenu, El Dorado,* and *World Without End.*

An English composer noted for his symphonic and operatic works is Richard Rodney Bennett. Although he is capable of considerable dissonance, his film scores exhibit a more tonal approach to the harmonic spectrum. His scores have included such important films as *The Devil's Disciple,*

Billy Liar, Far From the Madding Crowd, Secret Ceremony, Nicholas and Alexandra, Lady Caroline Lamb, and *Murder on the Orient Express. Far From the Madding Crowd* has a quiet, brooding score, often featuring haunting folk melodies written for oboe, flute, English horn, and a string accompaniment. For a storm sequence, he turned to virtuoso effects for strings, highly impressionistic orchestration, and dissonant variation on his themes.

In *Nicholas and Alexandra,* Bennett employed soft, pastoral harmonic colors, somewhat in the manner of Delius. Although he often calls for high strings, he shuns excessive doubling, preferring an introspective, sustained style in which woodwind motifs dart in and out of a string background. He has an inclination toward serial writing and wide melodic leaps bordering the atonal harmonic colors, a tendency that becomes clear in scenes of great stress or emotional tension.

Italian film scores of the 1950s tended to be opulent, highly romantic, and full of lyrical themes not unlike opera arias. One exception to this rule was the music of Giovanni Fusco, who wrote scores for chamber ensembles. His works included accompaniments for many films directed by Antonioni, and for Resnais' *Hiroshima Mon Amour.* Among his best-known scores were those for *Red Desert* and *La Guerre est Finie.*

Mario Nascimbene is a lyrical composer who prefers symphonic orchestrations stressing long, expressive melodic lines. Lilting tunes characterized *The Barefoot Contessa.* He also did epics, among them *The Vikings,* and *Scent of Mystery,* an experimental film in which various scents related to the action taking place on the screen were released in the theater. Nascimbene, who has composed symphonic, ballet, and chamber music, has written over a hundred film scores for Italian, American, French, and British productions. One of his most important scores, in the tradition of Steiner and Newman, was his musical accompaniment to David O. Selznick's *A Farewell to Arms* (1957). Nascimbene composed leitmotifs with broad, sweeping lyricism. His main title was a somber, dissonant dirge. He used an out-of-tune barroom piano and nostalgic harmonica solos to contrast the grim realities of war with the sentimental reminiscences of peacetime.

Alessandro Cicognini wrote lush arrangements of Italian popular songs for such films as *It Started in Naples,* approaching Viennese motifs similarly in *A Breath of Scandal.* His expressive music for *Indiscretion of an American Wife* is representative of his best work, emphasizing development of long, lyrical lines and string orchestration.

Another Italian melodist actively engaged in motion pictures since the 1940s is Nino Rota. After studying at the Milan Conservatory, the Academy of Santa Cecilia in Rome, and the Curtis Institute, Rota turned to the screen. His best-known scores include those for *Anna, La Strada,* and several Fellini productions; his music for *La Dolce Vita, Boccaccio '70,* and *Juliet of the Spirits* is full of tuneful dance melodies with an Italian flavor. He has also scored epics, among them *War and Peace* and *Waterloo.* For the former, he produced a thoroughly expressive symphonic score in a style similar to that of Nascimbene in *A Farewell to Arms.* Rota was an unlikely choice for wide commercial acclaim in an era of electric guitars. Nonetheless, his theme song from Zeffirelli's *Romeo and Juliet* became an enormous commercial success, and Rota soon drew a choice scoring assignment, *The Godfather.*

Angelo Lavagnino scored numerous Italian films; for *The Naked Maja* he wrote some stirring dance music including boleros in the tradition of nineteenth-century Spain. Renzo Rossellini and Roman Vlad both became active in the 1940s. Vlad is somewhat of an exception among Italian composers. He employed serialism and considerable dissonance in his score for the 1955 production of *Romeo and Juliet,* including a twelve-tone variation on Juliet's theme for the poisoning scene.

In more recent years, many important films have been scored in Europe, where American popular influences have combined with European styles. Ennio Morricone has specialized in "spaghetti Westerns," adventure films, and costume dramas. His scores have included those for *Guns for San Sebastian, The Battle of Algiers* (with G. Pontecorvo), *A Fistful of Dollars,* and *The Good, the Bad and the Ugly.* Morricone's trademark is his employment of unusual sound effects, including the human voice. His scores contain long pedal points and show the influence of current trends in pop music, including the use of electric guitars.

Mikis Theodorakis has composed the music for a number of important films, especially those dealing with his native Greece. They include *Zorba the Greek, Z,* and *State of Siege.* Georges Delerue is a French composer fond of impressionist shadings, with gentle woodwind solos played against string backgrounds. His scores include *Day of the Jackal, King of Hearts, The Pumpkin Eater,* and *Interlude.*

Younger Composers in Hollywood

Among the younger composers who came to prominence in the 1950s were men who, compared with the older generation, leaned toward more jazz and dissonance, and preferred brass and winds to strings.

André Previn is equally accomplished in both jazz and classical idioms, and many of his scores can be placed in one category or the other. His music does not represent a major break with film scoring traditions. On the contrary, though he was more inclined to turn out a tune than some symphonic colleagues (and it might be recorded by a muted trombone instead of a violin), basically his scores combined the worlds he knew during these years: the jazz combo, the dance band, and the symphony orchestra. For *The Subterraneans* (1960) Previn wrote a main title sequence in a cool jazz style. He also appeared in the film as a pianist, improvising in his own manner, which has been shaped by such masters as Bud Powell and Art Tatum.

Previn's more traditional work has absorbed the influences of Hindemith, Shostakovich, and Copland, not to mention the intensive orchestration lessons of Castelnuovo-Tedesco. One film in this style was *Elmer Gantry* (1960), based on the novel by Sinclair Lewis. Set in the 1920s, it is a scathing attack on religious quackery. At its heart lies the complex character of Gantry, a combination of gifted preacher, traveling salesman, and scheming opportunist. Previn's music, like Lewis's book, was written with Middle America in mind. Wailing, blues-style brass solos and clusters of high strings give it a folk quality reminiscent of *Our Town* and *The Best Years of Our Lives*. The music is dominated by a sharp, syncopated, rhythmic figure traded back and forth between the percussion section and the rest of the orchestra. The main theme captures the personality of Gantry, fast-talking and driven by a compelling zeal to fulfill his appetites and ambitions. Intense, brooding themes also accompany him; in addition the score boasts revival hymns and popular tunes of the period.

In another symphonic work, the score for *The Four Horsemen of the Apocalypse* (1962), Previn wrote harsh, dissonant music, intense polytonal clusters for strings, and a throbbing timpani ostinato. Much of the dissonance and tension accompanied the ominous shadows of the four horsemen, whose allegorical images haunt the central characters of the film. Previn did something quite unusual at the end of the main title: he cut off the entire orchestra, leaving only a cloud of dissonant high strings, which gradually resolve into a pure triad. The effect is one of transition from the extreme violence of war to the calm of peace.

Previn's lighter scores show another side of his personality. His music for Billy Wilder's *Irma la Douce* (1963) ranges from racy cancans to romantic melodies for accordion and strings. He likes to open his scores with a horn motif emphasizing the interval of the fourth; using such a motif, Previn wrote one of his most unusual main titles, that for *Dead Ringer* (1964). In this film, a murder mystery starring Bette Davis, a poor twin murders her wealthy sister and takes her place. The main title is scored for harpsichord, which, like the mansion of the wealthy sister, exudes a feeling of antiquated mystery.

Elmer Bernstein has had an unusual career in Hollywood. In some respects, he began as a successor to Victor Young, writing the score for the DeMille epic *The Ten Commandments* when Young's illness prevented him from doing so. He also scored other epics, including *The Buccaneer*. His style was often like that of Young, but after he turned to jazz in *The Man With the Golden Arm*, there have been, in effect, many Elmer Bernsteins. Experiments in jazz would be followed by lush string sequences for such historical-religious epics as *The Miracle*, while a love theme for *From the Terrace* was written in the style of a piano concerto. Two widely praised Bernstein scores were those for *To Kill a Mockingbird* and *Birdman of Alcatraz* (both 1962). For the former, Bernstein wrote a haunting, misty main title. It begins with a single-line melody, innocent and folk-like, on the piano, followed by a gentle flute solo playing over an impressionistic background of harp and strings. The principal theme is subsequently introduced by a piano accompanied only by the bell-like tones of a vibraphone. *Birdman of Alcatraz* contains delicately orchestrated bird-call effects for the woodwinds, used in the scenes where the prisoner, Robert Stroud (Burt Lancaster), discovers the wonders of nature.

Leonard Rosenman went to Hollywood under unusual circumstances. One of his piano students in New York was a young man named James Dean, and when the latter went to Hollywood to star in *East of Eden,* he suggested his teacher (and close friend) as a possible composer. Rosenman, who considers himself primarily a serious writer of concert music, regarded the film medium with reserve. Typically, when Kazan invited him to score the film, he suggested, "Why don't you approach Aaron Copland?" As it turned out, Rosenman did go to Hollywood and did turn to the screen for his livelihood.

Having studied with Schoenberg, Rosenman is a devotee of the twelve-tone serial school, and reacted negatively to the nineteenth-century romantic style popular in Hollywood in the early days. He likes to write polyphonically, and prepared an individual theme for each principal character in *East of Eden.* For the dramatic scenes he planned development sequences combining various motifs extracted from themes and arranged in linear relationships. Kazan objected to the composer's atonality, so the two men worked out a compromise. Rosenman wrote tonal music for scenes involving children, and was permitted to write dissonances for the adult conflicts. Ironically, the main title of *East of Eden* is triadic and thoroughly tonal. Notable sequences in the film include a delicate dance to accompany Cal's discovery that he can cover his father's business losses, and a nocturne for high strings played when Cal climbs into Abra's bedroom window to ask her to prepare a surprise birthday party for his father.

Rosenman's next picture, *Rebel Without a Cause,* also a James Dean film, received a similar treatment. Rosenman composed tense music for the fight in which two young men battle each other with switchblades. Dissonant music for high strings accompanies a scene in which Dean visits a planetarium and imagines the end of the world. Rosenman also wrote the music for *Cobweb,* a film about a mental institution. For this he composed what is often regarded as the first completely twelve-tone film score.

Rosenman prefers writing film music that "does not direct itself exclusively toward the popular subculture." A nonconformist in many ways, he admires the trend toward lean, sparse orchestration. For example, instead of scoring a bustling city scene with a Gershwin-style cacophony, he suggests another approach: "It seems to me that a composer with more of a sense of modern dramaturgy, more of a sense of mid-twentieth-century imagination, might elect to have the sound effects played down. He might introduce something which would not be immediately perceptible through seeing the image on the screen—perhaps, that the city is a lonely place, in counterpoint to this very busy kind of setting." Rosenman goes on to observe: "He might employ, for instance, a saxophone, a very lonely kind of sound. Therefore, music would have entered into the plot, and told the audience something about the picture that they could not have otherwise seen for themselves. In other words, the music would act as a catalyst to manipulate the audience's perception of the image."

Jerry Goldsmith, like Rosenman, is identified as a modernist. He cultivates an eclectic style, drawing upon dissonant serious music, jazz, and, more recently, pop music. He learned the basic techniques of film scoring in California, where he studied with Mario Castelnuovo-Tedesco and Miklos Rozsa. His film music embodies various styles, from atonal dissonance *(Freud)* to lyrical romanticism *(The Blue Max).* In the latter, he displayed a Newman-style penchant for high strings and rich melodies. In *Stagecoach,* he turned to triadic folk harmonies, sparsely voiced orchestration, and numerous solo passages for trumpet, banjo, and harmonica. He also used the solo harmonica in his score for *Lilies of the Field,* written in a similar style. Goldsmith's scores include those for *The Prize, In Harm's Way, Von Ryan's Express, A Patch of Blue, The Sand Pebbles, The Hour of the Sun, Planet of the Apes,* and *Patton.*

Goldsmith's score for *Planet of the Apes* (1968), notably avant-garde for Hollywood, is not unlike Webern's concert works. It consists entirely of sound effects produced by orchestral instruments, with no melodies in the traditional sense. Instead, the composer uses clusters of dissonant chords, complex nonmelodic rhythmic passages, and percussive atonality.

For *Patton* (1970), Goldsmith wrote a main title beginning with an organ prelude. It is interrupted by martial figures played by the brass and treated electronically so as to provide an echo effect. Then the full orchestra plays a march. The score alternates between furiously tense passages in martial rhythms and quiet sequences for high strings, often sustaining long pedal points. In the hospital scene, the searching melodic line for strings and folk-quality woodwind progressions are reminiscent of Bernstein's music for the rooftop scene in *On the Waterfront.*

John Williams, a native of New York who studied at Juilliard, also worked with Castelnuovo-Tedesco. He is an accomplished pianist, equally at home in serious music or jazz improvisation, and, as a musical director for film musicals, draws upon extensive experience as a television composer. His versatile scoring may call for jazz combos, dance bands, or traditional symphonic combinations. He also writes serious music, and his concert works have been performed by many American symphony orchestras. He has been praised for his work as arranger-musical director of *Goodbye, Mr. Chips* and *Fiddler on the Roof.*

Although he is often identified with jazz, Williams has excelled in his screen accompaniments for Westerns *(The Rare Breed)* and films requiring a folksy exuberance *(The Reivers).* The latter, a filmed adaptation of a work by William Faulkner, is set in turn-of-the-century Mississippi, its central figure a 12-year-old boy who takes his first automobile ride with a pair of adult friends and in the process finds out what life is all about. Williams's music, here essentially traditional, plays an essential role. It creates an atmosphere of innocence through the use of high strings and the clean, clear harmonic style of Stephen Foster. Both the banjo and harmonica figure prominently. One critic described the score as one that sounded as if it were written and conducted with a fishing rod in country air.

Ernest Gold is a dedicated melodist. Like Steiner a native of Vienna, he writes music that reflects an expressive and emotional approach to the screen. Gold studied piano and composition in Austria before moving to New York. Turning to song writing, he produced several successes, including "They Started Something," featured on Kate Smith's radio programs, and "Practice Makes Perfect," which stayed on the Hit Parade for seventeen weeks. His interests also extended to serious music, and he wrote a symphony, a piano concerto, and chamber music.

In Hollywood, Gold's music did not follow fads or fashions and failed to receive the attention of those critics who admired bizarre orchestration for its own sake. His career received considerable impetus from the phenomenal success of his theme music for *Exodus* (1960), but he had already scored many other important films. Gold's film music is full of lyrical themes. Typical is the haunting impressionist melody, like a gentle berceuse, composed for *Inherit the Wind,* and the nostalgic Viennese theme for *Judgment at Nuremberg.*

For *Too Much, Too Soon* (1958), Gold's score boasted long, lyrical melodies, written, according to his own description, in the traditional style of the Steiner scores of the 1930s. Gold has never "plugged" songs. In his scores for such films as *The Young Philadelphians* and *A Child is*

Waiting he favors poignant, occasionally sentimental melodic ideas. But he develops these motifs with great imagination, and he can write music of tension and striking power whenever the need arises. His approach, consistently thematic and melodic, relies heavily on the string orchestra.

In his score for *On the Beach* (1959), Gold employed as a main theme the familiar Australian tune "Waltzing Matilda." He introduces it in the main title as the atomic submarine surfaces in Melbourne harbor. *On the Beach* also contains one of Gold's most expressive melodies, beautifully scored for strings and woodwinds. For a sequence depicting the deserted city of San Francisco, a constant high pedal point in the strings offsets a two-note motif in the high woodwinds, repeated against a melodic theme in the strings. A love scene receives a lush string treatment. To underscore a sailboat race, "Waltzing Matilda" is arranged for winds over an accompaniment of strings playing in perpetual motion. Light strings, played spiccato, add a martial note when a pretty girl arrives on board ship.

Although he is not regarded as a jazz composer, Gold wrote some spirited, finger-snapping pieces for *Pressure Point* (1962). He emphasized a syncopated jazz clarinet and saxophones, playing a quasi-improvisational set of solos over the steady beat of a snare drum. The main theme is developed through a variety of musical devices, including augmentation and diminution, eventually surfacing as a tuneful but relentless exclamation in the jazz idiom.

Laurence Rosenthal, a versatile composer, has divided his time between films and the theater. A pupil of both Howard Hanson and Nadia Boulanger, he gained early recognition for his music for theater productions (among them "Becket" and "Dylan"), ballets, and stage musicals. His screen scores for *A Raisin in the Sun* and *Requiem for a Heavyweight* also won critical acclaim. Rosenthal's approach to film scoring might be characterized as neo-impressionist. He is capable of extreme lyricism but often prefers to establish a mood through harmonic shading, misty progressions of sustained chords, ostinatos, and highly coloristic orchestration. His scores are always surprising and imaginative.

When Rosenthal scored *Hotel Paradiso* (1966), he turned to a salon orchestra of fifteen different instruments. The result is one of the screen's most tasteful—and least-known—comedy scores, full of Gallic wit and nineteenth-century abandon. Satirical French waltzes, sentimental tunes, and a sparkling chase benefit from clear, crisp orchestration ideal for this continental farce.

In *The Comedians* (1967), Rosenthal employed Haitian instruments and created suspense through long pedal points and the use of bongo drums. His main title is striking: Haitian percussion instruments play bell-like ostinato figures and string tremolos lead to a children's chorus chanting "Duvalier, President of Haiti, President for Life." The children themselves seem innocent enough, but Rosenthal's menacing orchestral background adds ominous overtones.

Rosenthal has thought a good deal about the use of thematic material in a film score. "The whole idea of themes was derived from the Wagnerian concept of the leitmotif. I think it is impossible to make a generalization. In some films, the leitmotif might work very well. It always has to be treated skillfully and in a subtle manner. Otherwise it can become nonsense. If every time 'X' appears, we hear 'X's theme,' the technique can be hopelessly naive. I've used that device, but more and more, I try to develop themes which have a certain integral relationship with one another, instead of each one being an emblem in the sense that each represents a specific character. The music becomes an element of emotional color in a film which can relate to other areas of the motion picture."

For Rosenthal, thematic development has its limitations as a screen device. "Some films shouldn't have themes at all.

Certain films seem to resist use of thematic material, because they require an atmospheric background, while any kind of thematic use would be completey wrong. Truffaut used a jaunty boulevard tune in *400 Blows,* and it was played sympathetically, ironically, and in various tempi. The European films have occasionally featured the use of a pop tune which is permitted to ride roughshod over the entire film. Any one of these devices, including playing a theme to death, can be a dreadful idea if overdone. A certain amount of repetition has artistic validity. People go to see a movie, not a concert. Their focus is visual, and music must enter through a side door. Reemphasis of thematic material makes the listener aware of what the composer is trying to do. The composer who scrupulously avoids repeating anything renders his music vulnerable to the accusation that it is an unnoticeable, gray color. In order to create a subliminal response in the average film viewer, a certain amount of repetition is valid."

Lalo Schifrin is an Argentine-born composer with an extensive jazz background. Trained in Paris, where he divided his time between French serious composers and nightclubs featuring American jazz, he brings to films an eclectic style. He regards himself as a composer in the avant-garde tradition of Olivier Messaien and Pierre Boulez. But his jazz background (including experience as an arranger for Dizzy Gillespie) and an interest in Latin-American percussion instruments and rhythms also figure in his work.

Schifrin draws an analogy between the relationship of music and film and the relationship between two contrapuntal lines. "Music must contribute to the audiovisual counterpoint. What does the second line of a two-part counterpoint contribute? Actually, both lines are of great importance to each other. Some people feel that music for a film should only help the action and help the mood. That's one extreme of opinion. The other is that music should be so important in commercial films that it doesn't matter whether you help it or not as long as you get a good theme that will sell and help commercial promotion of the picture. Music should be present, but it shouldn't be so unobtrusive that we are completely unaware of its presence. At the same time, it should not be overwhelming. Rather, the music should be in balance with the film as balance exists between two lines, one visual and the other aural."

Schifrin's scores are usually harmonically complex and dissonant and written for unusual ensembles. Occasionally they display the influences of jazz and the bossa nova. His credits include *The Cincinnati Kid, Blindfold, Cool Hand Luke,* and *The Fox.*

Another extremely versatile composer-arranger, Nelson Riddle, is comfortable in and out of the jazz medium. Like so many others, he studied formal composition and orchestration with Castelnuovo-Tedesco, and enjoyed many years of experience as a dance-band arranger. His prolific pen has turned out a steady stream of arrangements for big bands accompanying Frank Sinatra's recordings. He has worked as arranger, orchestrator, and musical director for film musicals, and did scores for *Come Blow Your Horn, Lolita,* and *Paris When It Sizzles.* His style is influenced by his natural inclination toward swinging jazz written for big-band combinations.

Influences of pop music and big-band arrangements may also be found in the scores of Percy Faith, Frank DeVol, and Broadway songwriter Cy Coleman. All three men have stressed exaggeration in their comedy scores. Faith used an old-time movie tack piano (a standard instrument with tack-covered strings) in a mock battle sequence between a devil and an angel in *I'd Rather Be Rich.* Cy Coleman used the tack piano, playing silent film hurry music, in *The Art of Love.* In recent years, dance-band effects have been popular for comedy as well as for drama.

New York Musicians

Although motion picture scoring in the United States has generally been identified with Hollywood, several composers have managed to pursue careers in film music while basing themselves in New York. In general, their New York work involves either serious concert music or orchestration or composition for the Broadway stage.

One such composer is David Amram, whose creative activities are augmented by his career as a conductor-performer, and who is adept at both serious music and jazz. Amram, a rugged individualist, disagrees with many established Hollywood procedures, and describes his approach in this way: "First I read the script to decide whether or not I wish to write music for it. Ninety-five percent of the time the answer is no before I even see the script; by avoiding becoming a millionaire I have a chance of being an honest composer. When I do occasionally compose for a film, it is something with which I can feel proud to be associated. Then I watch the filming to make certain that it is what the script said it would be. I talk to the director. If it happens that he is already involved in the next film he will direct, I decline to write the music for this film, because I realize that the final decisions regarding the music will be left in other hands than the director's by the time I've finished composing. Next, I make certain in my contract that no other music can be used in the film without my permission. This is to avoid having a title song written by someone else or fragments of others' music inserted where the production people feel that something more 'popular' or 'known' will increase the box-office power of the film. If this provision isn't clear in the contract, I refuse to accept it."

Obviously, this is not a typical attitude, but Amram has been a nonconformist in many respects. He first gained recognition as a composer of incidental music for stage plays in New York. His works included over thirty scores for Shakespeare productions, plays both on and off Broadway, and two operas. His musical style is eclectic; he draws inspiration from several sources. Like Leonard Bernstein, whom he greatly admires, he maintains considerable interest in both serious and popular music.

Amram's music for *Splendor in the Grass* (1961) called for a principal theme that was brooding and folk-like. He often employs an Elizabethan style in his writing for strings, but adds "blue notes" and other devices acquired during his years as a jazz musician. Much of Amram's other film music is derived from jazz. The accompaniment to *The Young Savages* (1961) includes numerous jazz pieces, a main title duet between harmonica and guitar, and a march written on a base of five notes articulated first by five tuned tympani and developed by the orchestra. A gentle, baroque-style piece for strings serves as the main theme. Amram used the strings to simulate police sirens, and a solo trumpet to highlight a Puerto Rican funeral march, adding the organ in a requiem scene. For suspense sequences, he employed long, high pedals in the strings and violent syncopation figures played by the bongo drums. The accompaniment to a love scene between Burt Lancaster and Dina Merrill is another poignant piece for strings. Amram also played the piano in a series of jazz ensemble pieces used in the film; they were scored as well for tenor saxophone, bass, and drums, with occasional additions of alto saxophone and harmonica.

Amram's music for *The Arrangement* (1969) included a delicate work for oboe and strings. The composer is fond of harmonizing in thirds and sixths, and, though his music can be highly tonal, it is never lush. His string counterpoint usually involves the development of long, melodic lines, invariably influenced by jazz. One sequence is treated in a highly unusual manner, with a chamber music accompaniment; "Sunny Days" is written in an almost Mozartean harmonic vein.

Amram describes his aesthetic approach to films in these terms: "I watch screenings of the film as many times as possible in order to get a feeling for each scene and character, and only then do I begin to write. I try to construct the fabric of the music so that it relates to the film as well as existing independently, and I try to use it only where I think it is necessary, only when the extra dimension it lends will actually enhance. And, rather than take one melody and grind it out in seventy-four different ways (which may help the subsequent record sales but usually means rotten music or needless repetition), I write to suit the moment of the film it will underscore."

Frank Lewin is an unusual combination: a composer who is also an accomplished sound engineer. He was trained in New York and at the Yale University School of Music, where he studied with Hindemith. His works have included symphonic and chamber music, song cycles based on poems of Blake and Thomas Nashe, a cantata composed for and performed at the White House, a requiem mass in memory of Robert Kennedy, and works for the operatic stage. He has also written theater music and scored the television series "The Defenders." In addition, Lewin worked as a professional sound engineer for a number of years, and has made an intensive study of electronic recording techniques.

Lewin's film music has been written primarily for the many industrial and documentary films that are produced on the East Coast. He provided the music for the Academy-Award-winning documentary *A Year Towards Tomorrow*. Although essentially emotional rather than cerebral, he is not a devotee of leitmotifs, and works often with chamber music combinations to achieve both light comedy and serious drama. One documentary, *Paintings in the White House: A Close-up,* uses a collage of musical vignettes from America's past, Ives-like quotations of railroad and frontier melodies, trolley waltzes, and march tunes. His unobtrusive music frequently relies on long sustained chords or unusual sound effects, occasionally produced through manipulation in the mixing room. Recently he has begun to experiment with the Moog synthesizer and with combining various tracks to produce music that cannot be achieved on the sound stage.

Another composer who has worked actively in New York is Elliot Kaplan. After studying at Yale and in Paris with Nadia Boulanger, Kaplan divided his time between serious music and commercial work. One of his most ambitious undertakings was the music accompaniment to the film adaptation of James Joyce's *Finnegans Wake*. Kaplan's approach to the film evolved after a careful analysis of Joyce's complex work. The book itself contains many references, often subtle or implied, to various pieces of music. Kaplan decided to write an original score in which many musical references could be interpolated; there are twenty-six in all, including popular tunes of the years during which Joyce lived, Irish folk songs, an Irish march composed by Kaplan, and patriotic, concert, and operatic compositions.

Kaplan composed a virtual musical tapestry, woven in and out of the Joyce dialogue with a skillfully orchestrated score. Musical quotations are often enveloped in a background of high strings; the tuneful musical allusions are appropriately arranged for banjo and accordion. Woodwind solos are eager and breathless, with melodic motifs for strings and harp darting in and out of the accompaniment. Kaplan alternates between tongue-in-cheek mock heroics (quoting the "William Tell" overture on a single trumpet) and delicate, sensitive underscoring. The main theme, Kaplan's original march, is developed during the film but not played entirely until Finn has awakened from his dream to face reality.

Gerald Fried began his career as an oboe soloist with symphony and chamber ensembles, turning to film scoring

Laura, David Raksin

by accident. His scores range from jazz-oriented works *(Dino)* to more traditional approaches. He based his music for *One Potato, Two Potato* partially upon a children's tune, using it to reflect both youthful innocence and tragic irony when the youthful illusions of childhood are shattered.

Electronic Scores

Electronic sounds have been popular with some film composers since Honegger's use of the Ondes Martenot in *L'Idée* and Rozsa's scoring for theremin in *Spellbound*. Use of the theremin, by the way, created a need for the first time for two-channel recording. Paul G. Neal, musical engineer for *Spellbound,* described the procedure: "The theremin was placed on the sound stage, in such a way that no one was sitting behind the player with a loud instrument. He was cued in regularly by the conductor, just like any ordinary instrument. I watched his microphone, to make sure that the instrument was recorded in proper balance with the rest of the orchestra."

Some films have been "scored" entirely with electronic sounds. Louis and Bebe Barron experimented with the development of sounds produced by electronic circuits. They called these sounds "electronic tonalities" and used them in short experimental films produced by Ian Hugo and Walter Lewisohn for various European cinema festivals. They designed and constructed electronic circuits which, when properly controlled, would react predictably to various predetermined stimuli. The sound activity was then recorded on magnetic tape and translated into audible form. This was their procedure for the electronic accompaniment to the science fiction feature *Forbidden Planet* (1956). As might be expected, electronic sounds have been identified primarily with horror or science fiction films.

One of the most unusual mechanical alterations of recorded sound occurs in David Raksin's score for *Laura*. So much attention has (deservedly) been focused on the haunting theme song of this motion picture that even most film music enthusiasts have been unaware of the manipulation involved.

Raksin discovered a device invented by a studio sound engineer, Harry Leonard, employing off-center bearings (called Lenatone bearings after Leonard). Its original purpose was to provide a quaver in the voice of Gregory Peck, then a young actor portraying an elderly man in *The Keys of the Kingdom*. Raksin found that the device could provide a remarkable musical effect simulating vibrato. He had experimented with recording piano chords and having the microphone pick up, not the chords themselves, but their overtones. The microphone could be opened and closed by an engineer, who would also combine the overtone-chords with the regular soundtrack. The off-center Lenatone bearings were placed on sound dummies, which were sound projectors.

The composer chose the chords that supported the main theme used in the scene, and had them recorded on A and B tracks; they were permitted to overlap and combined in alternation with the previously recorded regular musical soundtrack. The A and B tracks containing overtone-chords were played on sound dummies that had been treated with the Lenatone bearings.

Urban Thielmann played the chords on the piano. After they were subjected to the Lenatone quaver, they achieved the mysterious echo quality desired by the composer. At his signal, they were added to the soundtrack containing the rest of the music. Thus the normal orchestral score was punctuated and augmented by these "Lenatone" chords, with their own unique electronic quaver.

Otto Luening and Vladimir Ussachevsky, active in the Columbia-Princeton Electronic Music Center, used electronic devices in their film accompaniments. Luening worked with Orson Welles on *King Lear,* Ussachevsky on the filmed adaptation of Jean Paul Sartre's *No Exit.* Lalo Schifrin added electronic sounds to his regular orchestral soundtrack in *The Fox.* And Harry Sukman's symphonic orchestrations for *Around the World Under the Sea* were augmented by electronic sounds produced in the studio of Paul Beaver, who specializes in research and experiments with the Moog synthesizer.

The Moog synthesizer, an instrument with a piano-style keyboard but unrelated to keyboard pitches, can be used to produce a variety of sounds, and composers have made it a fashionable device. As a rule, however, electronic sounds, except to underline elements of horror (nightmares in *Spellbound,* eels in *Around the World Under the Sea)* or suggest the eeriness of outer space (as in *The Day the Earth Stood Still*) have shown only a limited capability in expressing the full range of human emotions.

Frank Lewin, in his computer-image film, *Pixillation,* provided a score that was originally recorded by a keyboard player performing against a click-track, on six tracks: (1) harpsichord recorded at 7½ ips and played back at 15, to create music that exceeds the range of the instrument and is faster than can be played normally; (2) harpsichord at normal speed; (3) celesta; (4) ondioline—an electronic keyboard instrument capable of changing tone colors rapidly, recorded at 7½ and played back at 15; (5) and (6) ondioline at normal speed. The score was based on permutations of a twelve-tone row, and everything in it was derived from movements, colors, textures, and the mood of the images.

Why such a complex combination? Lewin did not want to use a traditional soundtrack for this totally abstract film, and he decided to approach the computer-generated images mathematically. He recalled Hindemith's advice that a composer must make everything conscious that he puts down on paper. Lewin at first regarded this observation with skepticism because he prefers music that is emotionally communicative; now, however, he says Hindemith is absolutely correct. "Music must evoke an emotional rather than a cerebral response. (In concert music, the ideal response may be a mixture of the two, but you do not have that luxury—especially the time spans—in films.) But to do this with control, a composer should be able to call himself to account at any moment, to have a reason for every note he puts down. This is especially true when he is working in as concentrated a medium as film."

Laura
David Raksin

The Swan
Bronislau Kaper

North by Northwest
Bernard Herrmann

Lili
Bronislau Kaper

Anastasia
Alfred Newman

The Nun's Story
Franz Waxman

CHAPTER VII

The Emergence of Pop Music

Until the recent rise of pop music, few motion picture scores received much attention from the general public. Most of them fulfilled their function only in relation to the specific films for which they were written. There were a few notable exceptions. In 1942 excerpts of Miklos Rozsa's music for *Rudyard Kipling's Jungle Book* were made available on a commercial recording. Also released were *The Song of Bernadette* (Alfred Newman), *For Whom the Bell Tolls* (Victor Young), *Spellbound* (Rozsa) and *Duel in the Sun* (Dimitri Tiomkin). These, however, were the exceptions rather than the rule. Most film scores remained in studio music libraries.

In 1949 Anton Karas introduced the zither in his score for *The Third Man*, a theme that became tremendously popular. Paul Misraki, who scored many European films, observed: "The commercial success of *The Third Man* theme induced the producers (for non-aesthetic reasons) to gamble on the publicity given by odd main themes played by all sorts of unusual intruments, even percussion solos, not to mention accordion, harmonica, whistling, etc."

During the following decade, more and more commercial soundtrack recordings were made available to the public. Commercial success went to several songs that had appeared originally in motion pictures, most particularly Dimitri Tiomkin's theme from *High Noon*. By the mid-1950s, the composer of a musical score for an important film (artistically or financially) could be assured of consideration for commercial recording. In spite of these changes, though, the environment did not seem likely to spawn a giant industry of hustlers, promoters, con artists, and manipulators. The events that gave impetus to this revolution, popularly described as the "new sound," occurred in an unexpected way.

In 1959 a television producer named Blake Edwards decided to engage a jazz composer to score his television series, "Peter Gunn." Jazz scores were hardly unknown in Hollywood. Edwards, however, chose a man whose record albums would change the face of the film music industry forever. His name was Henry Mancini.

Mancini, a former pianist and arranger with the Glenn Miller orchestra, was an unlikely figure to start a revolution anywhere. He had contributed to over a hundred films as a staff composer and arranger at Universal. Some critics have speculated about the changes in his style, but an examination of his early scores reveals a consistent stylistic direction. His was not a new face in Hollywood, but even the best film composers seldom achieved star status, unless they were also virtuoso performers like André Previn.

Mancini's score for "Peter Gunn" was totally jazz-oriented. The fast sequences were big-band arrangements; romantic ballads were in the idiom of cool jazz, as typified by Miles Davis. The music was nominated for an Emmy award. More important, it was released commercially in a record that sold over a million copies and was voted Album of the Year by the National Academy of Recording Arts and Sciences. Mancini had been discovered. No one seemed more surprised about all this than Mancini himself, who returned from television scoring to the film medium as its best-known composer.

Producers were quick to jump on the bandwagon. From a business standpoint, they reached two conclusions. First, they decided that film scores could sell records. Second, they determined that these records should be oriented as much as possible toward pop music. So they made a concerted effort to find composers who would provide, not dramatic underscoring, but commercially viable pop pieces that could be exploited on records. The entrance of record company executives into the film music field changed it forever. For the first time, a key element in evaluating the worth of a score was totally divorced from the motion picture itself: Could the score sell records?

So much attention has been focused on Mancini's commercial success that people tend to forget his original reasons for using jazz in the "Peter Gunn" series. It was an adventure show about the exploits of a dectective (Craig Stevens) who frequented jazz clubs. A low-key, underplayed tension dominated every scene. Record producers decided that it was the jazz or pop sound itself that had commercialized the Peter Gunn score. Since this sound had proven exploitable, the record men insisted on jazz or pop scores for other films. Unfortunately, many of these pictures had nothing to do with detectives who visited waterfront jazz clubs. The die, however, was cast. For better or worse, pop scores were a force with which every composer had to reckon.

Mancini's orchestra was essentially a jazz band augmented by strings. He liked brass and saxophone ensembles, swinging jam sessions, and blues sequences. The piccolo and bass flute were used for comedy cues, a departure from the traditional idea that jazz was appropriate only for scenes of violence. Mancini's approach was essentially a departure from symphonic scoring in the direction of dance band arranging. Latin dances or ballads accompanied by a steady rhythm section were among his trademarks. In fact, the sound of a jazz rhythm section, drums, and pizzicato "walking bass" became standard Hollywood fare, ultimately imitated by almost every Hollywood orchestrator. Mancini also liked to end his jazz phrases with a short, downward glissando that trailed off without resolution.

Ultimately, much of Mancini's success depended upon his record albums, which consisted of lyrical tunes plus a variety of pop pieces arranged for dance band or jazz combinations. *Breakfast at Tiffany's* was typical. Although the score consisted primarily of jazz sequences, the song "Moon River" was what listeners remembered. *Breakfast at Tiffany's* won the Oscar as the best score of 1961, defeating such stalwart competition as the symphonic masterpiece *El Cid,* one of Miklos Rosza's best efforts. One composer, whose work was nominated but failed to win, put it this way: "I know what happened. Everyone looked at the ballot and said, 'Moon River' was a great score." (This inability to distinguish between a song and a score would plague the industry for years.) Mancini was established as a major name in Hollywood, to such an extent that shortly afterward, record producers publicized an album of his with the following slogan: "The Place—Paris; The Movie—Great! The Music—Mancini! "

Musicians had long been dealing with temperamental producers, and at first the emphasis on scores that could produce hit records seemed to be nothing out of the ordinary. Gradually, though, the people who had written most of Hollywood's best film scores for thirty years found themselves in a professional dilemma. "Song plugging" had become the order of the day, and producers were turning away from composers of serious orchestral music. The ideal composer, according to the new norm in Hollywood, was one who could produce a hit tune and sell not only the film but thousands of records as well.

Beginning in the mid-1960s, producers began hiring as their musical advisers a number of persons with backgrounds in songwriting. (Songwriters had worked in the studios in earlier decades, but as tunesmiths, not scorers.) The popular music industry had changed radically over the previous decade, with rock and roll dominating the market. Unfortunately, much of this music did not lend itself well to films. Harmonically primitive and rhythmically dependent upon a constant, throbbing beat, it lacked the capacity to adjust to a variety of moods, so essential to screen scoring. Many of its performers could not even read music. Still, producers saw nothing strange about contracting with inexperienced musicians to "compose" a film score that would actually be written by studio orchestrators or ghost-writers. The name of a well-known rock and roll performer could sell records. The Beatles went to Hollywood, and record producers began demanding "sounds" in their scores. They instructed composers to write "something with a beat."

Composers adept at producing commercially exploitable records seemed to fall into two categories—those who wrote rich melodic themes that could be played over and over, and those who depended on a hard, driving beat, generally derived from rock music. In the first category were Maurice Jarre, Francis Lai, and Michel Legrand. Jarre's music for *Lawrence of Arabia* and *Dr. Zhivago* won him two Oscars. His melody from *Dr. Zhivago*, "Lara's Theme," is the prototype of what producers sought. In the second category were men like John Barry, who came to wide public attention after he scored the James Bond films, combining Mancini-style jazz with English-style rock.

Barry's accompaniment to *Born Free* was typical of the new pop scores that were delighting producers and record company executives. It was accompanied by one single theme repeated over and over. At the end, the audience walked out of the theater whistling "Born Free." "Can you write something the kids can whistle?" became the standard question a producer asked a composer. If the answer were no, the producer in all likelihood would look for another composer, someone who could write another "Lara's Theme" or "Born Free."

The Consequences of Commercialism

Music had traditionally served certain basic functions in motion pictures. In order to do so, it was carefully timed and edited, with the composer allowing for high and low points in orchestral color and texture. Leitmotifs and themes were tailored and developed to brighten or darken, always coordinated carefully with the second-by-second action. Pop music cannot be evaluated in the same terms because its basic purpose is not to score a film, but to sell records. A score consisting of a single pop theme is not, by definition, really a score. It is unrelated to the aesthetic and emotional demands of motion pictures. It may, in fact, seriously damage a film. Loud voices or amplified noise in a soundtrack are a jarring intrusion, drawing the viewer's attention away from the screen so that he or she may be conscious of little more than the producer's taste in music.

The influx of pop writers upset a lot of apple carts. Some distinguished pioneers in the film music field were distressed. In England, where producers were following the Hollywood trend, composer Benjamin Frankel commented unhappily: "There is a growing and pernicious tendency to decorate a film score with a theme which will lend itself to commercial plugging. No doubt this is good for the business side of things, but it has nothing to do with the art or craft." Leighton Lucas, another English film composer, noted: "I deplore the tendency to turn film music into a pop parade. I see no artistic justification in the propagation of film songs in serious pictures. It is *de rigueur* in a musical comedy film, but one does feel that serious background music should consist of something more profound than ear-tickling. I also dislike the modern tendency to overuse the brass. Screaming trumpets can be exciting at a climax, but nowadays one's ears are permanently assailed." Malcolm Arnold also complained about the influence of record producers.

Roy Webb, a pioneer Hollywood film composer, had this to say: "I think you can hurt a motion picture a great deal by making audiences conscious of the music, unless you want them to be aware of it for a particular reason. If someone is singing a song, you should hear that and be conscious of it. But if it's what you call mood music, that's another thing entirely. Mood music is something we've been arguing about and developing for years. Much of the music used on television today makes it impossible for me to hear what the people are talking about. When composers score in this manner, I don't think it's good."

Leonard Rosenman, ironically a (self-defined) modernist who had regarded much traditional film music as old-fashioned, was not pleased with the new trend either: "One finds the use of some popular songs simply marvelous in films. The best example I know is one of the best popular songs ever written, which happens to be 'Laura' by David Raksin. The song transcended the film, and the illusion was terrific. I don't mind tunes, and have written them myself. But when you produce a film and spend seven or eight million dollars and then get a songwriter to write the score of the film, you're spending seven or eight million dollars to publicize a song, and it is completely unnecessary. You suddenly have a group of Tin Pan Alley songwriters who are saddled with a terrible problem. They don't know what to do with the dramatic sections of the film, and have to play a popular tune over and over again ad nauseam."

The Academy of Motion Picture Arts and Sciences entered an era of flux. In 1967 the award for best score went to Elmer Bernstein, not for a dramatic score—although he had been nominated for these many times—but for his work in a film musical, *Thoroughly Modern Millie*. A subsequent Oscar was awarded to Francis Lai for his accompaniment to *Love Story,* which consisted primarily of a single piano theme. Controversy at the Academy centered on the question, when is a score not a score? New and bizarre locutions developed: for example, the "song score" versus the "non-score."

Long-standing associations between composers and producers began to break down. One was that between Bernard Herrmann and Alfred Hitchcock. The reason? Hitchcock insisted (presumably at the urging of studio executives) that Herrmann's score for *Torn Curtain* be exploitable. Herrmann did write a score for *Torn Curtain,* but it was passed over in favor of music by John Addison. Otto Preminger, previously associated with David Raksin and Ernest Gold, turned to a folksinger named Harry Nilsson. Some of Hollywood's most distinguished composers found themselves without work. One veteran Oscar-winner was dismissed from his studio contract because his record albums had been outsold by another studio composer. The head of the music department of one of Hollywood's largest studios indicated that he could not find a job for his oldest friend, a man whom he considered to be "the most talented in town." More than a few Hollywood musicians stifled their objections to the new trends in order to hold on to their jobs. Praising the "new sound" publicly, they admitted cynically in private that they now regarded film scoring as a way to make money, nothing more.

Bernard Herrmann resigned his membership in the Academy, declaring that he wanted to be judged by his peers, not by his inferiors. Bronislau Kaper expressed distress over the sudden influx of rock groups and their attempts to "score" films: "They say, 'We like the new sound,' but the sound of the rock and roll groups is the sound of a song being repeated over and over again. They sing and record, but can't even write a lead sheet." Max Steiner, in response to a question about the "new sound," replied simply, "I just don't understand."

Studio music departments underwent drastic change. Producers often hired a group of performers to come to a sound stage, watch a film for the first time, and then improvise themes that could be inserted. Such complexities as relationships between film and music were quickly dispensed with, usually at the insistence of the producer. (Pop singer Bobby Goldsboro praised the new trend because the film composer could write anything he pleased; the music didn't have to have any connection with the film.) Credits became jumbled. *Goodbye, Columbus*, for instance, was released with this single notation: "Music by The Association." More often than not, there are no actual scores, simply the contents of record albums.

One veteran composer described a recording session at which some musicians, obviously under the influence of drugs or alcohol, were brought into a studio, told to plug in their electric guitars and amplifiers, and "score" a film. On another occasion, an experienced studio vocal soloist arrived at a recording session to find the conductor (dressed as a railroad engineer) running about the stage giving each section of a chorus a set of nonsense syllables to sing. Each section sang as he pointed to them, and thus the "score" was completed. Timings, orchestration, color, and melodic development were totally eliminated.

Harold Gelman describes some of the situations studio music departments may now have to contend with. "A producer goes to a night club, and says 'I want that group!' He may listen to a record and say, 'Get me all the records that these people have made.' The music department has no choice but to search for the records." Gelman goes on to observe: "These people constitute a completely new threat to the musical world in many ways. They may know nothing about scoring a picture. In their world it's almost a deterrent now to read music. It used to be that you had to be a trained musician. But these pop stars have been successful on the rock circuit. They play what they call 'head music.' We call them 'hummers,' because if they can't play, they can hum into a tape recorder. That's as far as they go. They put it on tape, and we engage someone to take down their ideas in transcription. They have been responsible for a new breed of studio musician: the take-down artist. It has to be written down, or it can't be copyrighted. A skilled arranger transcribes the melody and it is then arranged for use in the film. It's a far cry from the days of solid professionalism that were associated with major studio music departments."

The take-down artists and orchestrators who arrange and adapt the music and often ghostwrite cues are paid for their services. But the "hummer" is the only person whose name is credited, since the purpose of hiring him is to get his name on a marketable record album. Asks George Duning: "Are we just writing for the exploitation of the film or are we trying to help the dramatic possibilities? Very few of the songs that are put in motion pictures these days make the charts. So producers hire young people, a single or a group, to write the music. They have absolutely no technique of scoring. Then older composers are brought in to patch things up." One composer with many years of experience described his last assignment: "I just ghostwrote two films last year for pop songwriters. I did the work, and they were given the music credit." The songwriters had drawn their scoring assignments because they had "composed" songs for hit records—tunes that, ironically, had also been ghostwritten.

One "hummer" arrived at a recording session and announced to an astonished orchestra that he would provide his own orchestration. He gave the violins a single-line melody and asked the other string players to make up their own parts, harmonizing the melody. The "hummer" didn't realize that, except for double or triple stops, the other strings were also limited to single lines. He assumed that the strings could vertically harmonize a melody he had hummed, and that all the supporting chords would fall magically into place. Another pop writer, slightly more knowledgeable, tried his hand at notation. What he didn't understand were some of the more basic conventions. For instance, he would write the oboe part at the top of the score on one page, at the bottom on the next.

At one studio, producers engaged Jim Webb, a successful songwriter, to score a film. When musicians arrived for their first recording session, they found miniature scores by Bach and other baroque composers waiting for them; Webb had decided to use this music as part of "his" score. The studio then refused to accept the score, declared Webb *persona non grata,* and hired a replacement. The new composer refused to accept the job unless it was completed in Europe. So the studio ended up paying a standby orchestra in Hollywood (which didn't record at all) as well as the French orchestra that ultimately recorded the new score.

Bob Dylan came to a recording session wearing a leather jacket with spangles. Recording engineers were disturbed when their sensitive microphones picked up noise from the jacket, but the producer refused to ask Dylan to remove the garment, insisting that it was "part of his creative thing."

A Time of Uncertainty

The film music industry is still in the throes of an economic and psychological depression. Composers depend for employment primarily on their associations with individual producers. Styles and approaches vary greatly, with no coherent trends discernible. Record companies are very much the dominant force in film scoring, and a host of motion pictures are accompanied by record albums. With album producers constantly looking for innovation, new styles of orchestration or electronic instruments are much sought after and widely imitated. Fads abound, not only in music. A film called *Willard* told the story of a young man with a remarkable ability to train rats. Hollywood was immediately glutted with films about animals running wild. A sequel to *Willard* brought forth more rats. Then came giant rabbits that multiplied (as they will); snakes; frogs; and even attack dogs. Suddenly the trend ceased. (The word among studio personnel was that, with its demise, a self-respecting rat couldn't even find an agent.)

Frank Lewin, the noted composer and film music analyst, suggests that cycles and trends are natural in an industry that depends on the whims of business executives: "We run in cycles and have fads. It used to be the full orchestra in the beginning, then the musical—in which the music is part of the subject—then the song motivated by the picture (as in *High Noon*), now any kind of song for commercial exploitation, frequently without any artistic validity in terms of the picture. We also had jazz, which is basically nonexpressive film music, or at least limited, since there are some situations which fit technically and still don't fit the picture."

Lewin goes on to observe: "Songs seem to be on the way

out. Jazz has given place to rock and roll. What jazz spawned, however, is what I like to call the unrelated score —some examples are a Bach piece running along with the action, or a random piece of pop music (not source music), as in *A Man and a Woman*. If you must use music in a film, the best method, it seems to me, is to work out your orchestration according to what colors the film should use, then write *very detailed* and highly expressive music where desired, music that fits both physically (cuts, climaxes where they should be, etc.) and emotionally."

Composers writing film music now come from varied backgrounds. Their appoaches vary so radically that they often seem to be living in different creative worlds. Pop song writers are too numerous to mention, their rise to stardom (and decline to oblivion) sometimes lasting no longer than a week. Former dance-band arrangers working in films include Nelson Riddle, Frank DeVol, Quincy Jones, and Lalo Schifrin. The generation of composers that rose to prominence in the 1950s is represented by several men, among them Ernest Gold, Jerry Goldsmith, Elmer Bernstein, and John Williams. Among the great names of film music still writing are David Raksin, Alex North, Miklos Rozsa, Bernard Herrmann, and Hugo Friedhofer. Henry Mancini has emerged as a television personality. Dimitri Tiomkin has turned his attention to producing films of his own, including a screen biography of Tchaikovsky. André Previn, with his impeccable sense of timing, didn't wait for the revolution. He was in the right place at the right time, as always. When the roof fell in on Hollywood's legitimate composers, Previn had departed the West Coast to pursue a career as a serious symphonic conductor.

Recent Trends

An examination of recent scoring credits yields no set patterns. Producers have used noise, allowed rock albums to be inserted in a soundtrack at deafening levels of amplification, or dispensed with music altogether. In curious contrast to the amplified pop film accompaniments are the equally commercial song-scores. Again, these are not scores as such, but variations on a single theme, often orchestrated in several different ways. Francis Lai *(Love Story)* and Michel Legrand *(Summer of '42)* are popularly identified with this approach, although Lai's *Mayerling* had considerably more thematic variation than his other scores. Controversial X-rated productions such as *Midnight Cowboy* and *Easy Rider* emphasized pop record albums and commercial sounds instead of dramatic underscoring.

Improvisational accompaniments to motion pictures have become one new fashion. Lalo Schifrin accompanied the Wolper production, *The World of Insects,* with music played by an ensemble of jazz and chamber music performers. Schifrin made notes for each sequence, but didn't actually write a score. He gave the players clusters, motifs, and twelve-tone rows, and let them improvise their own musical ideas. He also wrote an accompaniment sequence requiring two conducters. Another recent trend has been the adoption of traditional classical concert music. Thus an excerpt of a Mozart piano concerto is curiously identified as "the theme from *Elvira Madigan."* *Death in Venice* was "scored" with extracts from Mahler symphonies. *A Clockwork Orange* contained excerpts from the works of Rossini, Beethoven, Purcell, and Elgar, as well as electronic sounds. In *The Last Picture Show,* Peter Bogdanovich used pop music of the 1950s: vocal solos by Hank Williams, Eddy Arnold, Eddie Fisher, Tony Bennett, and Jo Stafford. Strangely enough, such "compiled scores" were first used during the silent film era; perhaps film scoring has come full circle.

Exceptions to the preference for pop tunes are historical epics, which still tend to receive a symphonic treatment.

Georges Delerue composed a variety of fanfares and period pieces for *Anne of the Thousand Days*. Richard Rodney Bennett's music for *Nicholas and Alexandra* is entirely symphonic. Children's films in England are other exceptions to the rule. Johnny Douglas produced a touching and rather lush accompaniment to *The Railway Children*. His work is thoroughly tonal, often martial, and dependent on scoring for strings. John Lanchberry produced a remarkable accompaniment to the children's ballet, *Tales of Beatrix Potter*. The score included symphonically orchestrated dance sequences, a tarantella for Peter Rabbit, a waltz for the mice, a frog's polka, and a concert gavotte. Lanchberry's work contained quotations of numerous traditional melodies and original themes. He cast it in a thoroughly appropriate mold of nineteenth-century ballet. Ron Goodwin is another composer who has always favored a full symphonic orchestral combination for his films, which include *Sword of Lancelot* and *Of Human Bondage*.

The Academy of Motion Picture Arts and Sciences continues to sidestep the whole question of just what a film score is. In 1972, although Nino Rota's music for *The Godfather* was originally nominated, controversy arose when the composer acknowledged that he had used some of it in an earlier film, *Fortunella*. So the Oscar went to Charlie Chaplin for his accompaniment to *Limelight*. The latter, which contained the popular "Terry's Theme," had just been released for the first time in Los Angeles, thus becoming technically eligible for the award.

Marvin Hamlisch won the 1973 Oscar for his score for *The Way We Were,* primarily because of the success of his nostalgic, darkly expressive theme song. Hamlisch won another Oscar for his music for *The Sting,* although the score consisted mainly of ragtime compositions by Scott Joplin. To a public rediscovering Joplin, the rags represented a different type of popular music in a film context.

David Copperfield, Malcolm Arnold

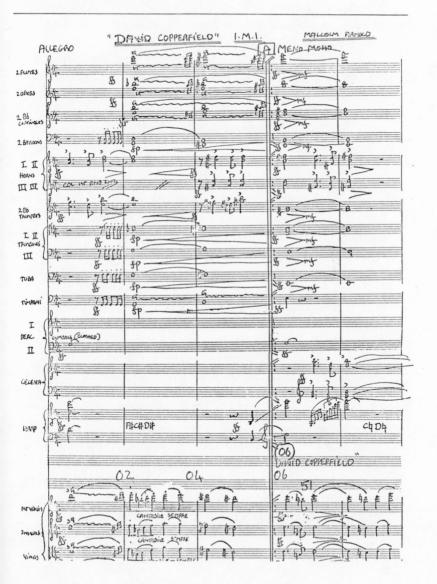

Academy Awards for such scores as *Summer of '42* and *The Way We Were* indicate a new emphasis on lyrical theme songs, in contrast to cacophonous "Top Forty" sounds. Whether or not this trend continues is open to speculation, because the ebb and flow of trends in Hollywood is always erratic and unexpected.

Producers do continue to hire composers, but demand they score a film and produce a hit record simultaneously. If they fail, their work may end up on the cutting-room floor. After Bronislau Kaper wrote the music for *The Salzburg Incident,* the producer decided that he wanted "something for the kids"; Kaper's score was dropped and replaced by rock-pop records.

Major scores by distinguished composers do receive critical praise, but little attention from the record companies. Recent important scores have included Malcolm Arnold's stunning symphonic *David Copperfield,* a lyrical work containing haunting, modal themes and gently shaded orchestration; Bernard Herrmann's *The Night Digger,* an intense and sometimes ethereal exercise in suspense; David Raksin's remarkable score for *What's the Matter With Helen?;* and Miklos Rozsa's colorfully orchestrated music for *The Golden Voyage of Sinbad.*

It is one of the classic ironies of Hollywood that the greatest interest of critics and students has focused on film music at a time when the legitimate film score has reached its lowest ebb. Motion picture buffs have organized fan clubs and musical societies to honor the men they most admire. There is a society in honor of Max Steiner's memory, and one that closely follows Miklos Rozsa's current work. Universities are beginning to offer courses in motion picture music. (Hugo Friedhofer, referring to the dissolution of studios in general and their music departments in particular, quips: "Now that the ship is sinking, the rats are all coming aboard.") In 1973, an album of musical sequences from films by Erich Wolfgang Korngold became a source of delight and discovery for those previously unfamiliar with Korngold's music. The album was the first in a series produced by George Korngold, the composer's son and a record producer at RCA. Subsequent albums have included tributes to Alfred Newman, Max Steiner, and excerpts from film scores that accompanied some of the great Humphrey Bogart and Bette Davis films. Bernard Herrmann and Miklos Rozsa have conducted recording sessions for albums based on their own scores.

The major question facing traditional composers interested in films remains: Will the industry continue to be dominated by the pop record companies and their publishers? Miklos Rozsa, one such composer, paints a gloomy picture: "We are now at the lowest abyss you can imagine. We play to the lowest common denominator. The dramatic, let alone symphonic, score is gone. My generation tried to establish the serious motion picture score with a symphonic background. I personally believe in the form of motion picture music derived from Wagner's book "Opera and Drama." He discusses the *Gesamtkunstwerk,* an all-comprising art of drama, writing, and music. What could come closer to this description than motion pictures? I believed that music could play an important part in films. Nobody goes to the cinema to listen to music, they go to see a drama. But dramatic music can be an important factor. This is all finished now; all they want is to sell a song, play a cheap tune over and over, and sell records. The high ideal of the *Gesamtkunstwerk* has gone out the window."

Film music has gone back to its very origins, Rozsa believes. The trend toward song-plugging started with *Singing Fool,* which popularized "Sonny Boy." Then the emphasis on promoting hit songs declined. Rozsa doesn't find all pop tunes objectionable. They're fine in musicals, which he regards as filmed operettas. Nor does he object to beautiful themes that are suitable for recording. But he does question the validity of Tin Pan Alley songs as the basis for film scores. "In my youth, when I was still idealistic about Hollywood, I described the responsibility of Hollywood composers to bring good music subconsciously to the public through radio. Toscanini was on radio conducting the NBC symphony at that time. The general public was not listening to Toscanini. They would turn down the radio and wait for Jack Benny. But when the same people went to see a film, they heard good music even if they didn't know it. They slowly got used to a new musical language. This educational function was fulfilled only by films. Now it is completely forgotten. If I said anything like this in a studio, they would send me out faster than I came in." Not surprisingly, Rozsa is critical of the new pop-rock performers who provide film accompaniments. Rock and roll, he says, is "the most God-awful noise mankind has invented since leaving the jungle. It is thrown into every film. They say, 'The kids like it. Play for the kids.' If the kids like sex, violence, and horror, we do not help them change their values; we are merely playing down for the dollar."

Producers today have rejected the perspective of composers like Rozsa. Perhaps the revival of interest in outstanding scores of the past will lead to a renaissance of film music. It is safe to say only that predictions about Hollywood provide no clues to the ultimate direction of film music.

The Red Pony
Aaron Copland

Rebecca
Franz Waxman

Citizen Kane
Bernard Herrmann

Who's Afraid of Virginia Woolf?
Alex North

Forever Amber
David Raksin

The Tales of Beatrix Potter
John Lanchberry

CHAPTER VIII

The Functions
of the Film Score

Music for motion pictures involves many elements not encountered in the composition of concert music. Consequently, critics need a unique set of standards in judging it. In order to formulate these standards, we must examine the various functions of film music; this is best done by considering certain key motion picture scenes that required musical underscoring. Each example illustrates not only the specific solution of a particular composer, but also a basic function of film music.

In every instance, we shall devote primary attention to the music as related to a visual context. The critic of a symphony or sonata can discuss the form and structure of a composition on a purely musical level. Form is dictated, more often than not, by the taste and musical imagination of a work's creator. But in motion pictures, music is by definition an auxiliary to the visual image. A film music sequence may be the work of an outstanding composer, but totally inappropriate for the film; another musical selection may be ideal as film accompaniment but lacking in interest when divorced from its pictorial context. The composer must constantly tailor his ideas to precisely timed images

211

that may or may not suit his own musical plans. He may labor with complex thematic development in his studio only to have his ideas disappear amidst sound effects or dialogue, or suffer from extra-musical decisions relating to camera angles and visual editing. Musicologists may assume that the best film scores are those that can be explained in formal or analytical terms. This is simply not the case. A film score can be evaluated only in relation to the motion picture it accompanies. The film composer's job is like that of an opera composer. He must, as Frank Skinner has written, "be able to understand moods in music and be able to grasp a mood in a pictorial situation."

In the early years of sound motion pictures, producers and composers used to argue about the justification for any music. Alfred Hitchcock, directing a scene of a lifeboat adrift in the ocean, intended to omit music altogether. After all, he asked rhetorically, "Where is the music coming from in the middle of the ocean?" To which David Raksin offered a quick retort: "Ask him where the camera comes from and I'll tell him where the music comes from." Why have composers used music in given sequences? For many reasons. Their efforts can be best understood if we consider what music can do for a sequence that initially contains only dialogue or silent action.

Music to Intensify or Relax the Pace of a Film

Almost any motion picture depicts events that are larger than life. The audience must be stimulated and encouraged to believe in what is taking place on the screen. Yet a theater is full of distractions. At a key moment, a viewer may be thinking about buying another box of popcorn. To prevent this from happening, he or she must respond on a more intense level than with events observed in real life.

For example, a man is shown walking across the street. If his purpose is to commit murder, menacing music puts the audience in a certain frame of mind, if only subconsciously. If he intends to offer a child an ice cream cone, the same music would be ludicrous.

Mario Castelnuovo-Tedesco composed music to intensify the drama in his score for *The Loves of Carmen* (1948). This motion picture presented a difficult challenge, since it was based on the same story that had inspired Bizet's opera. All of the characters were already associated with specific and quite memorable music. The composer met the challenge brilliantly after deciding to disregard all of Bizet's familiar melodies.

The final sequence of the film, entitled "Death and the Black Cat," begins slowly as a black cat, a symbol of death, crosses Carmen's path. The action speeds up: Don José discovers Carmen, kills her, and is executed immediately by nearby soldiers.

The composer's problem was clear. He had to write music that would underscore first the mood of foreboding and then the tragic resolution of the story. The sequence begins with a chromatic run articulated by the bass clarinet and clarinet, followed by a statement of the "fate" or "death" motif, played by the English horn. As Don José approaches Carmen, string tremolos become agitated. He pleads with her to return; the strings quickly quote another important motif, the love theme. Carmen refuses to meet Don José's demands; the oboe adds the fate motif. During Don José's final effort to persuade Carmen to leave the city with him, a sweeping scale in the violins leads to the "Carmen" theme, interrupted by trumpets proclaiming the beginning of the bullfight. Don José shouts, "For the last time, are you coming with me?" The fate motif returns, Carmen spits in his face, he stabs her, and the waiting soldiers shoot him. Once more Don José proclaims his love, again accompanied by the love theme. While the two lovers fall dying, the full orchestra proclaims the fate motif, this time as a funeral march. An enormous orchestral crescendo leads to a final exclamation of the fate motif, the black cat exits, and the film ends.

Without music, the sounds of this scene would have consisted only of performers' shouting voices. The composer created an element of agitated tension, reminding viewers of the predictions of disaster made by Carmen throughout the film. The pace of the final scene never slackens because the music keeps it going. At the same time, the audience is not expected to absorb thematic transformations. (If it did, the composer's techniques would have failed; his music must do its job subconsciously.)

Just as music can create tension, it can also relax the mood of a film. *Who's Afraid of Virginia Woolf?* was a controversial picture based on a play by Edward Albee. It concerned a casual gathering between two married couples that turned into a vicious round of screaming, accusations, and bitter truths. For the time—1966—the language was regarded as unusually harsh for the screen.

When Alex North accepted the scoring assignment, he experimented with intense dissonance in a serial score and with driving rhythmic passages in a jazz score. He rejected both of these approaches, and decided to treat the characters sympathetically. His orchestration enabled him to stress the universality of this modern story. The opening main title is scored for a unique ensemble, including C flutes, an alto flute in G, and even a bass flute. Another section is arranged for harpsichord, two harps, and a small woodwind ensemble with instruments ranging from piccolo to an E-flat contrabass clarinet.

A key sequence in *Virginia Woolf* occurs when a taunting, bitter man shatters his wife's fantasy about her son, revealing her deepest, most damaging secrets. North's accompaniment is a touching, reflective saraband, the opposite of what one might expect. Believing that no musical dissonances

could add to the atmosphere of two tortured people screaming at each other, North underplays the scene with music that
represents an emotional calm after a psychological storm.
"Since I believed in the relationship of these two people
as a romance, despite the horrible scenes exposed on the
screen, I decided that I would write something in quasi-
baroque style, which had a purity about it. It was completely removed from the terrible conflict and bitter scenes
of the screen."

For this same sequence, called "The Party's Over," North
provided a musical surprise. His unusually introspective
piece begins with a dissonant chord timed to coincide with
the wife's collapse. The initial four-bar melody, stated by
the cellos accompanied by flutes and harps, is gradually
joined by the strings. Next comes an interlude for woodwinds, a cello theme, and a mournful, pensive oboe solo.
The strings finally take over the main theme and are subsequently joined by woodwinds. For another sequence,
"Colloquy," North provided a solo for the oboe d'amore
over string accompaniment, followed by a muted string
interlude and a recapitulation of the main theme.

North talked about some of the challenges involved in
scoring scenes that stress dialogue. He said, "Since there was
no music in the play, it was a most difficult score to write.
In general, I'm against music behind dialogue. That's a
technique in itself. The music must not interfere with the
rhythm of the dialogue, or it would overpower it. I recall
writing a scene with Orson Welles in *The Long, Hot Summer*. I had to write above the range of his voice, because
Orson speaks with a kind of basso quality. You must consider the range of the voice of a particular actor, and also
write a fluid style of music so that there are no accents or
anything percussive."

North's baroque style, with its chamber-music delicacy,
succeeded in making Albee's characters seem more human

and more sympathetic. In a very real sense, his music relaxed the pace of *Who's Afraid of Virginia Woolf?*

MUSIC TO REFLECT EMOTION AND
PROVIDE ATMOSPHERIC SHADING

Composers are often called upon to try to "save" a scene. The reasons can be varied—faulty direction, poor performances by the actors, inadequate dialogue, or inept editing. A producer assumes that music can somehow rescue such a scene; often he is right. Even when a rescue operation is not called for, appropriately timed music can provide incredibly subtle shading to express emotion.

An outstanding example of the use of music to create color and an emotional response is Bernard Herrmann's score for *The Ghost and Mrs. Muir*. Though Herrmann has become identified with Hitchcock thrillers, this music demonstrates his uncanny ability to score an ethereal, sensitive romance with great delicacy.

Lucy Muir decides to take her small daughter, a housekeeper, and her few belongings to a cottage off the English coast. She finds herself falling in love with the ghost of Captain Daniel Gregg, the irascible former owner of the cottage. Although he decides to go out of her life after a year when he realizes that Mrs. Muir has no future with him, he returns much later, at the moment of her death, and the two spirits are reunited forever. *The Ghost and Mrs. Muir* might have been simply a charming and romantic story about a young widow and a sea captain, a costume piece set in the early years of this century. But Herrmann, writing one of the most inspired scores of his career, turned the film into a production of great musical significance.

In a key scene, the ghost realizes that he must let Mrs. Muir resolve her own destiny and, while she sleeps, he comes to bid her farewell. The composer had the obvious

The Ghost and Mrs. Muir, Bernard Herrmann

REEL 9 - PART 2
S·160 + 161
5080·3 5081-1

DANIEL TELLS LUCY GOOD-BYE AS SHE
SLEEPS — IT HAS ONLY BEEN A DREAM

"FAREWELL"

PROD. № A-510 — "THE GHOST AND MRS. MUIR."

COMP. FOR ORCHESTRA
BY BERNARD HERRMANN.

TWENTIETH CENTURY MUSIC CORP

LENTO

options. He could allow the scene to proceed with dialogue and no music, or he could supply an accompaniment. He chose to use music for atmospheric shading.

The scene begins with an oboe solo set against strings. High chords in the strings accompany the captain's references to Lucy Muir's life among the living and his hopes that she find fair winds to lead her to a peaceful harbor. The colors change from major to minor, progressing by thirds, as he says, "It's been a dream, Lucia." When the ghost talks about the life they might have had together had they lived at the same time—marveling at the North Cape, the fjords in the midnight sun—the music becomes more intense. He describes a scene in which the whole sea is whipped white, but suddenly the storm in the orchestra ends, resolving in a ghostly high chord for strings. As quickly as a dream, it has gone.

Herrmann's music moves in and out of this film with such subtlety that the casual listener may be unaware of its presence. It is this kind of sensitive accompaniment that measures the difference between a piece of functional film music and a masterpiece. Without the music, a fine actor is speaking his lines; with the music, the voice could belong only to a ghost.

Another example of music expressing emotion may be found in Jerome Moross's score for *The Cardinal,* which makes use of a device known as thematic analogy to establish mood. A composer develops a particular orchestral texture to be associated with a character or situation. He can then remind the audience of this mood by reintroducing the music, even if the characters are not on screen.

One of the most important scenes in *The Cardinal* portrays the struggle in the mind of a young American priest, Stephen Fermoyle, as he tries to decide whether to continue in the priesthood or leave it to marry a young Austrian girl he has met while teaching in Vienna. On a leave of absence,

Fermoyle arrives home after an evening of dancing. When he sees himself in the mirror, lavishly dressed, he becomes conscious of the difference between his present and former modes of living. He picks up his clerical garb, and is next shown entering a monastery for meditation. When he emerges from the church, dressed now as a priest, he strolls through Vienna, and accidentally sees the young woman, Ann-Marie. They do not speak, but she understands that he has decided to remain in the priesthood.

Since the scene contained little dialogue, the music had to provide atmosphere and a sense of the conflict in Fermoyle's mind. His view of himself in the mirror is accompanied by a quotation of an original Viennese waltz theme, an impassioned musical reference. As he examines his clerical garb, the mood shifts suddenly, and Moross plunges into a baroque motif identified with Fermoyle. The latter theme grows and expands when he visits his superiors in the church. As he begins his stroll around Vienna, the waltz returns, grows in intensity, and reaches a high point when he sees Ann-Marie. The waltz symbolizes secular life (as the baroque style represents the Church). Its texture is intensified along with the feelings of Fermoyle and Ann-Marie.

In *The Miracle Worker,* the most dramatic sequence occurs when young Helen Keller, though deaf and blind, realizes that words and ideas can be communicated. Composer Laurence Rosenthal could have ruined the scene with poor scoring, but instead displayed consummate sensitivity in placing and timing his music.

Helen makes her discovery as she stands by an old pump and tries to form the word "water" with her lips. Here Rosenthal uses only the clear, crisp sound of flutes. A gentle halo of strings envelops the winds as Annie Sullivan, Helen's teacher, says "yes." Helen exclaims "ground" as the strings enter gradually. Then she says "pump" as a harp glissando begins the feeling of exhilaration. Descending chord progressions accompany the overwhelming feeling of joy as Annie Sullivan shouts, "Mrs. Keller! *She knows!*" At this point, a lyrical theme swells and bursts forth from the full orchestra.

Rosenthal's main title for the film is a collage of cascading orchestral figures emphasizing the piano and vibraphone. In both of these sequences, the keyboard instruments project a dark sense of mystery, while the strings symbolize the light of discovery and joy.

Malcolm Arnold employed a similar approach in the concluding scene of *The Chalk Garden*. The high point of this film is the decision of Laurel, a young woman, to leave her domineering grandmother and return home to her mother. She makes this decision after an important encounter with Miss Madrigal, a mysterious but devoted governess, subsequently revealed to have once been convicted of murder. Although this entire final sequence is accompanied by Arnold's highly melodic main theme, he varies its speed, colors, and design according to the moods of the characters, and builds tension through falling string tremolos. When Laurel tells Miss Madrigal, "You've finally convinced me," the strings carry a sweeping melody. When she insists that she will never say good-bye to Miss Madrigal, Arnold again quotes the main theme. Laurel's grandmother invites the governess to remain at her home. But when she asks about the murder, the music—scored for timpani, flute, and strings —suddenly becomes menacing. Miss Madrigal refuses to answer and the grandmother vows to find out before she dies; Arnold then brings up the main theme, this time toward a full symphonic resolution.

Music to Provide a Composer's Comment and a New Dimension

A composer is often able to provide his own unique addition to a film score: a commentary upon a character's true motive or thoughts. For instance, a man may seem to be very happy, but appropriate music can make the audience aware that he is quite alone. A woman may rage in an absolute fury, but the right (or wrong) music can make her anger seem funny. Composers place great value upon these opportunities to add an extra dimension to a scene. It is a challenge that is exclusively theirs.

George Antheil compared orchestral accompaniments in film to those in opera. In opera, he believed, both voices and orchestra present different aspects of the same pattern. In film, however, he felt that the music should always "know" what is happening to the characters in the film, even if they themselves do not know. Thus he often chose to comment on screen action without illustrating it. Actually, in his own early operas, he experimented with scoring against the voice or the action, a technique that he regarded as perfectly applicable to cinema as well.

Gerald Fried expressed a similar idea: "The point about music that really interests me is that it can say what is not being shown on the screen. In a picture with serious intent, there are times when characters will be thinking one thing and doing another. For me the really satisfying function music can serve is to reach out to the audience and tell it that there is more going on than meets the eye." Alexander Courage agrees: "Music must supply an enormous amount of the emotional content of the film. If you view a film before the music has been added, you see immediately how much the music can help."

One of the most difficult scenes to confront a composer was the famous vision sequence in *The Song of Bernadette*. Alfred Newman rejected the obvious approaches, and chose a musical style that added tremendous significance to the emotional impact of the scene.

Bernadette, a young French girl, becomes aware of an odd change in the atmosphere at a grotto. She has stopped there after running through the countryside with some friends. The wind ceases, the air is still, and then the grotto is lit by an unworldly light. It is the brightest light Bernadette has ever seen. In its glare she sees a beautiful woman. The girl does not regard the experience as a spiritual one, but she is enraptured by the beauty of the woman.

Initially, Newman considered writing music that might be in the same style as other works built around inspiring religious experiences—the great oratorios, Wagner's grail music from "Parsifal," Schubert's "Ave Maria." After a careful study of Werfel's book, however, he decided to write the music from the standpoint of Bernadette, who claimed only to have seen a beautiful lady, not to have had a divine revelation. In other words, he would provide a commentary on the scene by expressing Bernadette's reaction to the wondrous beauty of the vision, not the majesty and power that lay behind it.

The music that opens the scene conveys the change in atmosphere at the grotto. Newman's letimotif for Bernadette is stated by high strings. The flutes play very fast chromatic scales in triads, augmented by rapid, whirling figures in the strings. The oboe's birdlike call is echoed by the bassoon as the strings create a feeling of blowing winds. Then the English horn adds another agitated exclamation. The powerful triads in the winds, a descending melodic line in the bases, and full string tremolos build tension. The strings increase in dynamics and the brass play full chords as the music soars to a magnificent B-major chord scored for full orchestra. It is at this moment that Bernadette first sees the vision.

Newman's leitmotif for Bernadette is an inspired melody identified with the vision. It is based on one of his favorite melodic devices, a rising scale line outlining alternating major and minor chords. A solo violin states the "vision" theme, while tremolos are augmented by harp glissandos.

A/ Bernard Herrmann

B/ Alex North

C/ David Raksin

(Nade)

The atmosphere is one of radiance and beauty, of wonder and delight. A chime leads to a restatement of the theme by the full orchestra over a tremolo accompaniment. (Newman's rising sequential line, one of his trademarks, was also used in the final scenes of *The Diary of Anne Frank* and in the love theme from *David and Bathsheba;* the effect is one of overwhelming optimism in the face of adverse circumstances.) Newman's gentle melodic solo is innocent and poignant in its harmonic purity. The audience does not have to imagine how Bernadette feels about the vision. Newman's music tells us.

When David Raksin scored *Al Capone,* he had to cope with numerous scenes of violence. There were many murders in the film, but the most shocking were those in which the victims were former friends of Capone. Raksin felt that his music could make these murders seem extraordinary even in a context where violence and death seemed commonplace. In one sequence, Capone's hired killers do their work to the accompaniment of a Caruso record. Here Raksin provided a remarkable musical mix, in which happy, carefree 1920s dance music and lyrical Italian opera are combined in violent distortion. This blending of musical quotations makes the insanely casual violence of the scene seem doubly brutal.

In *The Snows of Kilimanjaro,* the story unfolds in flashback, primarily through the reminiscences of a character portrayed by Gregory Peck. He describes his early days as a writer, dwelling especially on an idyllic interlude in Paris, a period in extreme contrast to the war years that followed. Bernard Herrmann provided the atmosphere with a gentle "Memory Waltz" scored for a favorite Herrmann orchestral combination, high strings and harp. It is a sentimental piece, charmingly evocative of a Paris that everyone imagines must have existed. The string orchestration creates an effect of nostalgia and dreamlike escape from the harsh realities of the world. Again, the composer provides an insight into a character's attitude, in this case underlining his feelings of yearning for the past.

In his score for *A Streetcar Named Desire,* Alex North's introduction of the little dance tune "Varsouviana" whenever Blanche thinks of her husband's suicide is another case in point. The melody is associated with their last dance together; its entrance in the score is an automatic reminder that Blanche is thinking of the past.

For *The Rainmaker,* North composed a sequence entitled "The Golden Fleece" to accompany the narration of a mythological tale by Starbuck, an adventurer. Starbuck here introduces an element of fantasy into the humdrum life of Lizzie, the woman to whom he has turned his attentions. North decided to vary his orchestration as well. The story of the golden fleece is an element of exoticism out of keeping with American small-town life, so the composer underlined it by departing from his essentially diatonic approach. He developed a waltz, a romantic dance form in itself, scored for strings, celesta, and harp. The cellos have a waltz theme of their own, which, played in a high tessitura, functions as a contrapuntal melodic line. The violins add a short two-note appoggiatura figure with a "sighing" motif. In the midst of the scene, the waltz resolves into a spirited motif identified with the hustling rainmaker, a vigorous, brash theme for timpani, bassoons, cellos, basses, and snare drums. Then there is a recapitulation of the original waltz theme. North's music serves to tell us something that is not otherwise stated about Lizzie—her astonishment at discovering a world of fantasy.

MUSIC TO PARALLEL OR UNDERSCORE ACTION

One of the basic functions of music in motion pictures has always been in relation to scenes of action. At its most primitive level, action music is the pianist's glissando when a Keystone Kop slips on a banana peel.

A composer may have only a few seconds in which to deal with an idea. Consider the detail involved in the music of a scene in *The Adventures of Don Juan,* scored by Max Steiner. While reminiscing with one of his past amours, Don Juan discovers to his horror that he has no real idea where and when he became acquainted with the lady. She is furious when she realizes this, but then determines to win his affections all over again. At this point her father and fiancé enter and confront the couple. Don Juan flees. The scene dissolves as he ponders his predicament, concluding, "Woman, thy name is trouble."

Steiner's accompaniment for this scene consists of a series of rapid-fire quotations of all the motifs identified with the various characters. The young woman's outburst of temper is accompanied by a woodwind glissando. When she exclaims, "This time you won't forget me," Steiner quotes the roguish, sauntering melody that serves as the Don Juan love theme. As the philanderer tries to disengage himself from her embrace, she calls to her father, "I'm trying to get away from him, but he's so strong." When Don Juan identifies himself, the composer quickly quotes the Don Juan hero motif. The girl pouts, "Stop being so Spanish!" Immediately, we hear a tambourine, castanets, and Castilian rhythms. Don Juan's rapid departure is accompanied by a typical Spanish march. The principal theme is stated as a lyrical melody when he contemplates his fate, and resolves in the stirring hero motif again. Hardly any of these themes lasts more than a few seconds; the entire scene is only 3½ minutes long.

Of course, not all action sequences feature rapid bursts of dialogue. Jerome Moross provided considerable excitement for feuding ranchers assembling a war party in the Western, *The Big Country.* Long sustained chords in the woodwinds and timpani lead to a driving ostinato, which derives its pulsation from an alternation of 3/4 and 6/8 measures. As the war party gathers momentum, so does the music. Antiphonal effects involving winds and strings heighten the feeling of excitement as the men on horseback ride across the land. Eventually a Western-style tune is superimposed over the ostinato. Without Moross's music, the sequence would be visually expansive, but the tremendous tension of the Western chase would not be present.

Music as an Element of Time or Location

The score is always a key element in establishing location. Even in scenes of otherwise standard action, music is second only to costumes as a means of conveying a feeling of a specific period, a sense of place, or both at once.

For *The War Lord,* Jerome Moross developed a sequence entitled "Nocturnal Procession." The music had a modal flavor and thus created a "medieval" mood. A folk-like melody, with phrase units often broken asymmetrically across the bar line, gave the listener a sense of primitive abandon.

Moross believes that the use of such elements as local color is as valid and as much fun for the creator of a film score as it is for the theater composer. "I rarely use folk themes, but I do use stylistic elements," he says. "Color is an old necessity for the composer. It has been used in the theater, in ballet, and now in films. Even in the days of the early musical theater, Gluck thought he was writing Greek music. Today we would say it was Greek in spirit. Around 1910, everyone thought that Puccini's 'Butterfly' was extremely Japanese. Now we don't think so. In its time, it was the idea of what Japanese music sounded like; the same was true of Sullivan's music for 'The Mikado.' The nineteenth-century German composers talked about 'character pieces.' There are many piano pieces by Mozkowski and Rubinstein that can be termed 'character pieces.' In the nineteenth century, they wrote pieces in what they thought was a Spanish style. Even today, we can hear works by Stravinsky in which he paraphrases what he thinks is a Chinese style. Ravel wrote Spanish music that is more French than Spanish. One of the most French pieces ever written is Debussy's 'La Soirée dans Grenade'; despite the title, it is the epitome of French music."

William Walton's sequence, "Charge and Battle" from *Henry V,* is highlighted by open-brass fanfares that we associate with the period of the film. The sound of galloping horses is conveyed through a two-note ostinato pattern in the low strings. Walton builds up the orchestration gradually, adding timpani, harp, and cascading strings to the ever-dominant brass. Eventually he incorporates a quotation of a French folk song in the pastoral accompaniment that concludes the sequence.

In the remarkable final sequence of the epic, *El Cid,* Miklos Rozsa weaves a tapestry of recapitulated themes. It begins with a majestic organ solo, then develops into a driving polyphony. Brass figures and counterpoint in the low strings are derived from the various motifs that have been exploited throughout the picture. The most lyrical recapitulation is the soaring love theme, eminently Spanish.

Walton's sequence could not possibly have taken place in Spain; Rozsa's could never have been associated with *Henry V.* The point may seem trite, but it is essential in understanding a key role that music plays in motion pictures. A jazz score, for instance, is decidedly inappropriate in a Western. An opulent accompaniment in the Viennese style would be less than ideal for a chase scene in downtown Manhattan. When composers exercise a high degree of skill, they can provide an element of local color and a sense of period that can come from no other possible source.

MUSIC AS AN ELEMENT OF COMEDY

The role of music as an element of comedy cannot be underestimated. From the earliest days of scoring, music and laughter have gone hand in hand.

Jerome Moross has criticized what he terms the "Hollywood notion that music has to accompany every comedic motion on a literal basis." Avoiding the obvious can thus make comedy scoring difficult. Yet composers have demonstrated great skill in providing musical accompaniments that do make us laugh. Prokofiev's brash and whimsical themes in *Lieutenant Kije* are wonderfully irreverent. Miklos Rozsa's characterization of the pompous postman in *Lust for Life* uses a nicely jaunty, French-style tune. Bernard Herrmann's satiric music for *The Trouble With Harry* displays a wry sense of humor. And Laurence Rosenthal's frantic chase sequences in *Hotel Paradiso* are irresistibly funny.

English composer Anthony Hopkins was asked to provide the music for a farce called *Vice Versa*. He quickly realized that it was full of sequences that cried out for an ironic treatment. He used it even with the traditional gong that accompanies the identifying emblem of J. Arthur Rank productions: in his version an opening drum roll is followed by a tiny ringing triangle. Hopkins's main title is a direct parody of silent film music, an exaggerated version of a "hurry." In another sequence, two swordsmen are interrupted in mid-duel and pursued by the police. The chase interrupts a performance of "The Merry Wives of Windsor Overture" by a military band. The band plays splendidly until the duelists and the police arrive. Then more and more wrong notes blunder forth until the roof of the bandstand collapses amidst a grand cacophony of shrill brass dissonance. It is hard to imagine how either of these sequences would have unfolded without Hopkins's skilled touch.

Other leading English film composers have also demonstrated a flair for comedy. Arnold Bax's score for *Oliver Twist* made even Fagin seem amusing. Benjamin Frankel employed a delightful effect for one scene in *The Chiltern Hundreds*. While the audience witnesses a mock debate between Conservative and Labour candidates in a local election, a musical parody offers a "debate" between the tuba (representing the Conservative candidate) and the piccolo (as Labour). Frankel's tongue-in-cheek orchestral ornamentation in a pompous style also provided a perfect background for Dame Edith Evans's portrayal of Lady Bracknell in *The Importance of Being Earnest*—a film that presented an especially difficult challenge since it consisted almost totally of dazzlingly witty conversation.

Scoring assignments for Hollywood comedies have often gone to men with backgrounds in the jazz field, especially in the dance band style. Percy Faith, confronted by a mock battle sequence between a devil and an angel in *I'd Rather Be Rich,* wrote an accompaniment using the old-time movie tack piano. The same instrument appealed to Cy Coleman, a Broadway songwriter who moved to the West Coast to score *The Art of Love.* The film deals with a pair of Americans in Paris (played by Dick Van Dyke and James Garner) who plan a suicide attempt as part of a confidence game directed at the Parisian art world. When their scheme backfires, Garner finds himself being carted off to the guillotine on a murder charge. For a scene with Van Dyke running awkwardly through the streets of Paris in an attempt to reach the execution site in time, Coleman provided a parody of silent film music for tack piano, brilliantly orchestrated by Russell Garcia. As an accompaniment to some sham heroics, the orchestra played passages that sounded like the finale of a Mozart symphony—thoroughly ironic in this context. Frank DeVol wrote a soap-opera score for a Rock Hudson-Doris Day comedy called *Send Me No Flowers.* With the scenes deliberately overacted, his romantic, pseudo-tragic music added to the fun. In recent years, Henry Mancini has used straight jazz as a comedy element, emphasizing instruments that play in extreme registers, such as the piccolo and the bass flute.

MUSIC TO PROVIDE UNITY

Composers often try to provide an element of unity through thematic development. During the 1930s, many followed the model of Korngold, who used leitmotifs extensively but did not believe in "catching" bits and pieces of action; or of Steiner, another devotee of leitmotifs who believed in "catching" everything. Alfred Newman, also fond of leitmotifs, was identified as a "mood music" composer par excellence, who concentrated on the individual characters' emotions as he developed motifs for each. (Oscar Levant once remarked that Newman's approach to a screen romance called for a "wife theme," an "other woman theme," and a "conflict theme"; to Levant, the "other woman theme" always seemed more vibrant and exciting than that for the wife.)

Occasionally a composer will try to establish unity on another level, developing thematic materials in such a way as to parallel the action or emotions on the screen. This type of unity is exceptionally difficult to achieve. What one regards as thematic development, as found in concert music, is impossible on the screen because of visual requirements. Two examples of a composer's efforts to accomplish something uniquely musical within the context of a film are scores by David Raksin, those for *Separate Tables* and *The Redeemer*.

For *Separate Tables*, Raksin had to write music for a complex scene depicting an encounter between a husband and wife after a long separation. (The husband had fled after being accused of beating his wife, and their encounter is a surprise.) At first the man seems to have the upper hand, but then the woman assumes the advantage. Raksin suggested to director Delbert Mann that the scene might be best without music, but Mann insisted that music was essential.

Raksin decided to write an extended contrapuntal sequence, beginning with a free fugato on a nine-tone row with one note deliberately repeated. His musical forms developed along with the complex emotions depicted on the screen, with structural divisions well subordinated to the filmed episode. When preview reactions to the film were mixed—possibly because the film's complex characters may have been too sophisticated for the preview audience—the producer and director blamed the film's problems on the music. Raksin refused to rewrite the sequence and left the picture, giving the producer and director the bonus of some valuable advice. He reminded them that they had had similar troubles with many of his colleagues, some of the best composers ever to write for films. When the finest composers couldn't understand the musical intentions of a producer or director, said Raksin, the executive was not making his intentions clear. (The prime difficulty stems from the fact that, as Alfred Newman observed years ago, "In Hollywood everyone knows two things—his own business and the music.")

Nothing daunted, the producer engaged Herbert Spencer, a veteran composer-orchestrator, to rewrite the music. Spencer looked at the film, described Raksin's work as a "great score," and refused. He urged Raksin to return to the film and rewrite the terrace scene. Raksin finally agreed, displaying an unusually generous attitude for a composer.

A comparison between Raksin's two versions of the terrace scene provides an interesting insight into a composer's technique. The original version was called "Verkehrte

Nacht," which might be translated as "Topsy-Turvy Night" —a pun on Schoenberg's "Verklärte Nacht" ("Transfigured Night"). It begins with a fugal entrance by the violas, followed by various announcements by the strings. After a development of the initial theme, the woodwinds state the fugato subject in inversion. An intimate, tender melody, remarkably organic in its musical growth, is derived from the counterpoint as a cello solo. Raksin allows the music to become homophonic as the husband and wife kiss. He resolves his melodic lines in a wonderfully touching deceptive cadence.

The revised version of the scene is half as long as the original. The melody is sung by a lyrical trombone, possibly because the producer wanted the sound of a sophisticated love theme. The scene emphasizes melody rather than thematic development. The tense, carefully shaded polyphonic accompaniment is gone. Even so, the music is of high quality.

Raksin enjoyed a happier experience with *The Redeemer*. This film was produced by the Family Theater, an organization affiliated with the Roman Catholic Church, and is concerned with the last days of Jesus Christ. Raksin devoted considerable time and thought to his choice of musical idioms. "Of all the music written about this subject, it seemed to me that the most eloquent of all was the music of Bach. Aside from my affinity for it, I feel that in a time such as today, when dissonance can hardly be achieved, a diminished chord over one or another root is a more excruciating sound when heard in one of the Passions of Bach than anything else. No one has ever written more eloquently than Bach did in those works." Raksin's score is thus a homage to Bach, a non-developmental approach in which freely extended arioso passages serve as accompaniment. Instead of working with leitmotifs, Raksin used long melodic phrases that he extended rather than developed.

The main theme of *The Redeemer* is tense and tragic. The music keeps pulling away from the tonal center, a continuous yearning for harmonic resolution. A touching and expressive lyrical melody based on wide leaps is identified with the appearance of Mary.

The film's most important sequence begins when the crowd shouts that Barabbas should be set free and Christ crucified. The scene is punctuated by a sharp extension of a brass chord and melodic figure for horns and trumpets. The music alternates between dissonance and resolution, between the tense, tortured agonies of the moment and the ultimate power and majesty of the central figure of the story. A canon for three English horns and three oboes over an ostinato pedal point follows Jesus as he is taken through the crowded streets to Golgotha. As he is nailed to the cross by the Roman guards, a menacing figure is established in the cellos and basses. The music snarls as the thieves grumble. An impassioned outburst of the strings leads to a high chord as Jesus says, "Father forgive them, they know not what they do." His promise to one of the thieves—"This day you will be with me in Paradise"—is punctuated by full orchestral chords. The baritone oboe sings the theme identified with Mary, one of the most poignant melodies ever heard in a screen accompaniment. Each new camera shot is accompanied by an alteration in orchestral color or texture. The full orchestra states the procession theme as a somber dirge when Christ says, "Father, into thy hands I commend my spirit."

Raksin later interpolated a theme originally written in dedication to the famed Brazilian composer, Heitor Villa-Lobos. After the Resurrection, as the disciples are talking about Jesus, Thomas is skeptical. But then they hear Christ's voice as a soft chord enters and gradually builds to a crescendo. The audience does not see the face of Jesus.

This entire sequence consists of over twenty minutes of

extended music. Raksin accomplished the unusual, composing music that stands on its own as a tribute to Bach and also achieves it specific goal in relation to the highly important detail of a film. Composers are rarely able to produce such substantial orchestral pieces without sacrificing the integrity of the motion picture score.

Madame Bovary
Miklos Rozsa

Dragonwyck
Alfred Newman

The Sea Hawk
Erich Korngold

CHAPTER IX

Ethics and Aesthetics,
Fables and Folklore

It is impossible to judge film scores without considering the circumstances under which they are written. Hollywood is a cross between an amusement park and a factory. It has glamour and glitter, but it also has a vast array of business people and technicians who function behind the scenes. The history of American film music cannot be regarded as an independent saga isolated from the colorful and sometimes bizarre life of Hollywood. The relationship of the composer to the producers and directors and the work done by highly skilled music specialists play an essential role in determining the final outcome of a film score. Musicologists like to speculate on why a composer has placed an accidental in front of a note; in the motion picture industry, the composer's sharps and flats, like everything else he does, must be approved by a variety of people, many of whom know nothing about music.

In earlier years, studios maintained their own music departments, but these exist no longer. Most scoring jobs are contracted through independent producers. Composers had unhappy experiences aplenty with major studio executives, but the trend toward independent producers has not improved matters. Bernard Herrmann, in fact, feels that he had much greater freedom working for a studio than for today's producers, many of whom, he complains, know nothing about films. Herrmann gloomily predicts that the art of film scoring may become extinct because new people in the field lack technical know-how.

The influence of record companies continues to grow in inverse proportion to the quality of film scores. By and large, these corporations regard the successful film score as one that can sell records. This criterion determines not only which scores are released to the public, but also who writes the score in the first place. Composers are arbitrarily divided into "commercial" and "non-commercial" categories—with most legitimate composers falling into the latter group. The best composers try to surmount the demands and pressures of record executives, but in a tight job market this becomes increasingly difficult. Experienced film composers privately express a desire for more artistic freedom, but as long as decisions are made by businessmen, the future seems doubtful.

The film colony is somewhat like a zoo: there are kings (and queens) of beasts, majestic and powerful; there are rabbits fearful of being fired and consequently of appearing to have any ideas whatsoever. Not to carry the analogy too far, there are both pompous and humble individuals who can be as mighty as elephants, as quick as hummingbirds, as slow as turtles, and as slippery as snakes. The world of the film composer is at once puzzling, confusing, amusing, and stimulating.

PRODUCERS

Bronislau Kaper once characterized the position of producer as the vaguest job in existence. When Walt Disney was asked to define his own function, he described it as the stimulation of ideas.

Films are produced in what is essentially a business environment. Producers talk about box office gross far more than they discuss camera angles, film aesthetics, or the judgments of motion picture critics. A movie is expected to make money; if it doesn't, its worth is automatically diminished in the eye of the executives.

The most interesting comments on the role of producers in relation to motion picture music come from the composers themselves. Unfortunately, much of what they say about their employers in private is unprintable, and they are reluctant to discuss them publicly. The basic fact of life is that the producer's authority is absolute. (Aaron Copland once described his function as that of a dictator.) It is he who selects the composer—as well as the director, the costume designer, the writer, and the principal actors. He approves the final recording of the score, and can, if he chooses, refuse to use any or all of the music the composer has written. If a producer and composer work well together, the music will be written under the best possible conditions; if they don't, it will suffer. The latter circumstance has unfortunately been the norm more often than not.

One problem is that producers often acquire a superficial familiarity with the terminology of a variety of fields. And they frequently equate their own taste with that of the public. "I don't know anything about music, but I know what I like" is the classic statement that has greeted many an unhappy composer over the years. One producer is known to evaluate film composers by asking his twelve-year-old son to watch his films when they are shown on television. Afterwards, he asks the boy if he liked the music. If the answer is no, the composer will have to look for work elsewhere. The producer justifies his method on the assumption that film music must "please the kids"; he regards his son as typical. No matter whose superficial opinions they may consult, producers like to portray themselves as laymen who see beyond technicalities and appreciate the overall impact of a film. They often characterize composers as being too involved with musical complexities. The composers' response is that producers are put off not by musical complexities but by their own ignorance.

A number of appalling tales circulate through Hollywood. One producer, for instance, was preparing to release a film set in Paris. He wanted the composer to "Frenchify" the score by doubling the French horn section, and the composer had to explain that the French horn wasn't French at all. According to one version of this story (and the incident could have occurred more than once) the composer, in a sequence involving an Englishman in Paris, concluded it with the English horn.

Shortly after release of *The Third Man,* a leading Hollywood composer was approached by a producer of the copycat variety, who insisted that he wanted the score of his next picture to feature only one instrument. The patient composer had to explain to a less-than-patient producer that writing three- and four-voice harmony and counterpoint for a single flute or clarinet is physically impossible.

Many anecdotes revolve around the great names of music. One venerable West Coast tycoon is reported to have declared: "We must use the music of Johannes Brahms in this film, and bring Brahms himself to Hollywood to conduct it." Another story concerns a producer who prided himself on his sophisticated taste. He stunned a veteran Hollywood composer when he suggested that a score be done in the style of Alban Berg's opera "Wozzeck." The composer's enthusiasm was soon dashed. When the producer, dining at his home, heard a record of "Wozzeck" he snorted, "Turn that garbage off!" It developed that he had never actually heard any of Berg's music; someone had told him that the composer's "sound" was "far-out." John Barry once dealt with a producer who insisted on a sequence scored with "something big, like Mahler." Barry replied that the producer wanted not Mahler, but power, and proceeded accordingly. When the producer gave his approval to Barry's musical solution, he commented, "That's Gustav baby, all right!" When Victor Young was scoring films for RKO, he received instructions on one film from the studio's chief executive, the formidable Howard Hughes. Although the picture was a Western, Hughes insisted that Young adapt for the main melody a theme from a Tchaikovsky symphony. Young protested, but did as told. Not long afterward, Hughes heard a radio broadcast of the symphony and called on Young to explain: "How could this happen? They're using *our* theme!"

Such anecdotes are amusing. But when a highly skilled composer finds himself at the mercy of an authoritarian producer with no musical knowledge, he may find it hard to summon up even a weak smile.

Second only to producers' ignorance as a subject for wry humor is their vanity. In the early 1930s, when studio music departments maintained staffs, composers developed specialties. One might be a "chase" specialist, expected to write the agitatos; another might be identified with pictures in which all the actors wore armor. One composer became known as a master of the main title. Why his rise to prominence? He once succeeded in synchronizing a cymbal crash with the screen appearance of the name of the producer. Apparently the latter dropped off to sleep at a preview, and was awakened by cymbals just in time to see his own name flashing before his eyes. The effect was startling. When the producer recovered, he knew he had found the ideal composer. (A distinguished musician once turned the tables on his producer by synchronizing the musical climax with the appearance, not of the producer's name, but of his own.)

Producers keep watch over each other. If they think that a particular fashion or style is politically advantageous, they will go to great lengths to achieve it. They are also slaves to novelty. When David Susskind produced a television adaptation of *Laura,* he and his colleagues discussed whether to commission a songwriter to write a new song called "Laura"—in spite of the fact that the David Raksin melody is undoubtedly the most famous of all film tunes, identified inseparably with the characters of the original film.

Most disheartening to composers is the power of producers to edit, rearrange, or cut their music. A composer's completed score may have been recorded but, after the recording session, when the producer and director discuss the music, the producer may decide to replace any or all of the composer's music without his knowledge. After Aaron Copland finished his score for *The Heiress,* he went home to New York. A studio executive then decided to replace Copland's rather dissonant main title, chose another piece, and never bothered to explain the situation to Copland. The composer, understandably furious, made a public statement disclaiming the main title. His treatment was hardly unique, but he wasn't used to standard Hollywood procedures.

George Stevens removed a number of cues by Franz Waxman from the score of *A Place in the Sun,* replacing them with excerpts by other composers, among them Victor Young. Though Waxman wanted his name removed from the credits, it was not, and he won the Academy Award. Curiously enough, the incident came full cycle when Stevens asked Waxman to rewrite cues originally composed by Victor Young for *Shane.* Another Stevens film, *The Only Game in Town,* had a rapid turnover of musicians: first Alex North, then Johnny Mandel, and finally Maurice Jarre. Another merry-go-round involved Miklos Rozsa. He gave up a chance to score the film *Judith* because of a challenging offer to write music for *The Bible*. Then director John Huston decided that he had discovered a "Japanese Beethoven" in Toshiro Mayazumi. (Huston and the producer, Dino de Laurentiis, had already rejected some cues written by Italian composer Ennio Morricone.) Huston and De Laurentiis decided to divide the score between Mayazumi and another Italian, Geoffredo Petrassi. Finally they deleted all of Petrassi's work and used only Mayazumi's music.

Producers can throw out entire scores faster than they trade in their used cars. Stanley Kubrick deleted Alex North's music for the first half of *2001* without telling the composer; only when North attended the New York premiere did he learn what had happened. A neat turnabout concerned a composer whose score was deleted in favor of a series of symphonic variations on "Pop Goes the Weasel." He was hired for another assignment when a producer, seeing his name on the screen, concluded that he had written the variations.

One of the best-known instances of a score being dropped occurred when MGM signed Heitor Villa-Lobos to write an original score for the film *Green Mansions*. Since the classic novel was set in Brazil, it seemed only natural to engage that country's most famous serious composer. Villa-Lobos arrived in California with a surprise: a huge orchestra score under his arm. He had written the music for the film without ever seeing the picture or studying timing sheets. It was a symphonic tone poem that he mistakenly thought could be used in its original form. Since this was impossible, Bronislau Kaper developed a new score, wherever possible using Villa-Lobos's original material.

Composers can deal with interference from executives in various ways. The urbane (and multilingual) Rozsa discovered one way of ignoring producers when he first arrived from Europe; he simply told them that he didn't understand English. Occasionally a composer will refuse to follow a producer's dictates. George Duning balked when asked to use an Irving Berlin song as an integral part of a proposed score for *Sayonara*. (The film was ultimately scored by Franz Waxman.) Probably the most satisfying recourse of a composer whose work has been mangled is to use the material in other ways. After Kubrick's substitution of Strauss for North in *2001*, the composer reworked the deleted material into a symphony. The subject of concert versions of film music is discussed at the end of this chapter.

DEPARTMENTS AND DEADLINES

When each studio maintained a staff of contract composers and a studio orchestra, musicians worked regularly, and composers knew they could depend on a large ensemble of fine performers. Each studio department had a director, usually a figure of considerable power and influence in the studio hierarchy. John Green (MGM) and Alfred Newman (Twentieth Century-Fox) were both composers and conductors. Newman especially exerted a strong influence on film music, not only as a composer but also as an administrator working with younger colleagues on the Fox staff. With the rise of independent producers and the demise of studio music departments, executives who nominally control a studio's musical activities have neither contract orchestras nor staffs of composers at their disposal. Assignments regarding music are left to the discretion (or indiscretion) of producers. Most production officials, in fact, are independents who check on and off the studio lots faster than guests at a hotel.

Perhaps nothing could better illustrate Hollywood's treatment of composers than reactions to the score for *Double Indemnity*. Miklos Rozsa composed music which the administrative head of the studio music department disliked from the very beginning. Conductor Irvin Talbot and the orchestra musicians liked the score, as did the producer. But since the head of the music department disapproved, Rozsa was summoned to his office after the recording session. There he informed Rozsa that this score was not motion picture music; with an absolute sneer, he delivered the ultimate insult: "This is music for Carnegie Hall." It happened that Bruno Walter had conducted a work of Rozsa's in Carnegie Hall, so the composer mentioned that perhaps the description could be taken as a compliment. The music executive was undaunted. "It wasn't meant that way," he asserted.

The executive objected particularly to the main title, which he said was appropriate for a battle, not a film with three principal characters. Rozsa suggested that since these three people were complex personalities, they merited tense, dissonant music. "Why don't you write lovely melodies?" demanded the executive. "We want to amuse our people, not bore them." Rozsa tried to explain that such an approach would be inappropriate here, but to no avail. The music executive then announced that Buddy De Silva, his superior in the studio hierarchy, would soon hear the score. "He will hate the music. He will take out this music; this is the end of your career in the studio. This will also reflect on me because I engaged you."

Nevertheless, director Billy Wilder was enthusiastic about the music, and it remained in the picture until the preview, held in Long Beach. It was clear that Rozsa had been declared *persona non grata,* for the music executive ignored him during the long ride to Long Beach and all through dinner. The preview was a success. Afterward, as the music staff was leaving the theater, De Silva approached Rozsa and the executive. The latter went to face his superior, in Rozsa's word's, "like Louis XVI walking to the guillotine." Clearly, he felt that heads were about to roll, and that his would be among them. But he had no time to apologize for engaging Rozsa. De Silva put his arm around the composer and exclaimed, "Thank you for that great score. I knew that the music would be good, but not as wonderful as this. It is exactly what the picture required — strident, dissonant music." The department head smiled and put his arm around De Silva. "Buddy," he said, "don't I always get you the right man for the job?" He never apologized to Rozsa for his behavior, nor expressed any other opinion about the music.

Each film studio maintains a library of music. At one time, every studio library contained full scores for every film it owned. It also housed conductor books—eight-line reductions of the full-size orchestral score that enabled a conductor to see at a glance the general outlines of the composer's intentions. Conductor books also provided a ready reference for studio legal departments in cases involving copyright statutes. In a recent exercise of callousness, studio executives at several of Hollywood's largest motion picture companies decreed that these books—an irreplaceable summary, note for note, of the history of film music—should be burned. In some instances, librarians have been able to rescue the music from the incinerator, and many are currently withstanding pressure from executives to carry out such orders.

One factor that hasn't changed is the deadline, which plays a crucial role in scoring. A producer normally invites a composer to see the film after it has been completed. Then the latter is told, "They want the music yesterday." (Miklos Rozsa suggests that Bach's weekly cantatas and Rossini's opera scores, produced in a few days, should serve as an inspiration to film composers.) According to Alex North, the standard procedure is to give the composer three weeks to write a score on a ten-week contract.

The pressure can be extreme. Lennie Hayton once found it necessary to prepare a cue for recording the following day.

Harold Gelman, MGM's music supervisor, offered to prepare cue sheets or provide detailed timings, but Hayton declined the offer. Instead, he watched the scene on the screen, wrote down some notations on the inside cover of a matchbook, and went home to write. Deadlines may be complicated by studio politics. One veteran screen composer complained that he had trouble meeting his deadline because the producer had given the only existing work print of the film to his girlfriend.

The ultimate dictator of decisions in film scoring is not a man but a machine—the clock. Composers of motion picture music face no deadline more important than their own individual timing sheets. The complicated devices that govern film scoring procedures have been refined over many years, and depend most heavily on the click-track. Click sheets are prepared at a composer's request. They indicate the title of a given sequence, its overall timing, and the metronomic beat and specific frame-click beat to be used.

There are three main types of click sheets. In one, the basic click sheet, the music cutter provides a sheet listing the numbers of individual clicks. A second form is available to composers who write directly on the sheet. It contains staves and bar lines. A predetermined number of clicks is assigned to each measure, so that the composer must maintain a uniform time signature throughout a given passage. The third variety of click sheet is similar to the second but without bar lines. The composer can still compose on the click sheet, but he can divide his measures into a variety of tempos.

Another aid is the footage chart, a breakdown of screen action according to footage rather than time. Footage counts are listed in one column; some composers actually score their films on these charts.

Composers have reservations about the click-track, for music written with it tends to sound metronomic. Generally, they rely on it only when absolute coordination is essential. In other words, they might use it for a fight or chase sequence, but not in a love scene. Click-track techniques are also common in scoring animated cartoons. In recent years, the emphasis on precision and coordination has declined, and most composers write to timing. A major exception is the Disney studio, where musicians composing for both animated and live-action films always write with click sheets or footage charts, never to timing. Disney composers break down films on their own Movieolas, which they keep in their offices.

Pop and rock performers have no experience with click-sheets or footage charts and, as a rule, no interest in learning about them. Their emphasis is on producing a hit record album, so they regard coordination of music and screen action as unimportant.

ORCHESTRATION

If the names of Hollywood's most prominent orchestrators were to be listed here or elsewhere, it is doubtful that any member of the filmgoing public would recognize them. Orchestrators perform their tasks in what may be best described as militant anonymity, a dubious status not of their own choosing. In essence, they are paid for doing a job for which someone else usually gets the credit.

What exactly is an orchestrator? (The query is not at all superfluous; when noted serious composers such as Mario Castelnuovo-Tedesco and Ernst Toch arrived in Hollywood, they asked the same question.) Put very simply, it is someone who assigns the elements of a composition to the instruments of the orchestra. Composers of serious concert music have always done their own orchestrating, and thus regard the idea of someone else orchestrating their material as incongruous. In Hollywood, the function of orchestrators varies depending on individual composers. Hollywood's best musicians do not need orchestrators in the sense of being unable to orchestrate themselves. Miklos Rozsa, for example, some of whose film scores have been orchestrated by Eugene Zador, orchestrated all his own concert music. But he used an orchestrator for certain film scores because of tight deadlines. The same is true of the collaborative associations between Alex North and Henry Brant or Erich Korngold and Hugo Friedhofer.

Although orchestrators are often called in primarily to help composers meet deadlines, some have played an important role in developing the actual scores. The influence of Edward B. Powell on the music of Alfred Newman, of Leo Shuken on Victor Young, and of Shuken and his partner Jack Hayes on the composers they now work with cannot be overestimated. It was Powell's style of string orchestrations, for example, that became identified so strongly with Newman and with the entire music department of Twentieth Century-Fox.

Normally a composer gives an orchestrator a sketch—an eight-line reduction of the full orchestral score—with all the instrumental parts written in the same key. (If the composition were in the key of B-flat, a B-flat clarinet part would be written in that key; since this clarinet part always has to be written a full tone higher than it sounds, the orchestrator would transpose it to the key of C.) In addition to dealing with such transpositions, the orchestrator adds and expands orchestral textures according to his own taste and imagination.

Of course it is helpful if a composer gives an orchestrator detailed instructions. After David Raksin had invited Hugo Friedhofer to orchestrate his score for *The Redeemer,* the latter was asked to write an original score for another film. Raksin's sketches were so detailed that the copyist could write out the individual parts from them. In this way Raksin was really responsible for his own orchestration. In some cases, however, a composer can be carried away by musical zeal. A colleague once complained to Dimitri Tiomkin, "Maestro, you've written piano chords that require ten fingers on each hand." Tiomkin reportedly replied, "Let the pianist pick the notes he likes best."

Some composers totally reject the idea of orchestrators. John Greenwood, a pioneer in scoring English motion pictures, advised his colleagues: "Orchestrate or arrange your own music, thus stamping your work with your own original style! Do not leave this important part of your work to someone else, who cannot know what orchestration you think of when you compose your music. Think *orchestra,* not *pianoforte.*" Bernard Herrmann is another who has no use for the whole idea of orchestrators. "It's impossible to separate composition and orchestration," he maintains. "It's the same as saying, 'I'll give you the ideas, and you write the book,' or 'I'll paint the picture, and you put in the colors.' Each instrumental part is important, and must receive the full attention of the composer." Herrmann describes many of his colleagues as men who are "not composers, but people who have orchestrators." (He himself is a master orchestrator.) He objects particularly to the idea that an orchestral score can be reduced to an eight-line sketch. He once offered $500 to any of his colleagues who could duplicate the original orchestration for Wagner's "Lohengrin" preludes based on a sketch; he found no takers.

An unfortunately large number of musicians in Hollywood today do not know how to orchestrate well. This is especially true of the current group of pop songwriters, who have no idea of how to write for instruments. Orchestrators may ghostwrite sequences for such musicians. One well known "composer" is reputed to maintain an informal staff of "orchestrators" who actually compose a good deal of his music.

Generalizations are unwise but it's safe to say that the most successful orchestrations are those done either by composers or by orchestrators who are able to carry out composers' intentions faithfully. Many of Hollywood's orchestrators are unsung heroes, undiscovered composers whose activities extend to improving and developing the work of others. Many composers began this way. Hugo Friedhofer orchestrated several films for Erich Korngold and Max Steiner before becoming identified as a composer in his own right. Ernest Gold orchestrated for George Antheil, Franz Waxman for Frederick Hollander. Today, orchestrators may first move into composing television scores and then to films, but such advancements often depend less on their musical skill than on their ability to gain producers' attention.

Miklos Rozsa's description of the orchestration problems of film composers in the United States is highly perceptive. "When I came to America," he recalls, "I was informed that I would not be allowed to conduct because I was not a member of the union. I had orchestrated *The Thief of Baghdad*. (For that, in Europe, you get more time.) I was also informed that my orchestration could not be used because I was not a member of the union. It was surprising, but they had rules and regulations. They said, 'You can get a standby conductor who gets paid for you.' Then they insisted upon a standby orchestrator. I became angry because, I said, this is my orchestration. Nothing will be redone; that is how it stands. And what has this to do with art? A composer cannot be separated from his orchestration. Finally they allowed me to do *The Thief of Baghdad* because it was done in England. I couldn't join the union; you had to be in Hollywood for one year without working. I came here under contract to do a job. It was an idiocy.

"When I did my second picture, *Lady Hamilton,* the union said I would not be allowed to orchestrate. I had to look for an orchestrator, something I had never done in my life. I was accustomed to writing the score, first in very loose sketches, then in full score. Now I had to start out writing exact sketches. The Italians call this process *spartita*—condensed score. You can learn it, and I did. I tried many orchestrators, and my scores sounded as if they had been written by someone else. I told the orchestrators, 'Don't write in anything I haven't written down.' But they said, 'We will make it sound lush.' I said, 'Don't make it lush, leave it as it is.' I finally found a man who did what I wanted with the score. With the Hollywood tempo, it is not possible to write out the full score."

Rozsa relates a conversation he had on this subject with composer Ildebrando Pizzetti. When Rozsa went to Rome in 1950, his friend Mario Castelnuovo-Tedesco suggested that he visit Pizzetti, with whom he had studied. Pizzetti was eager to hear about Hollywood, and immediately asked if it was true that composers did not orchestrate their own music 95 percent of the time. Rozsa explained that a good composer did write a complete score, but that it was condensed. How long, he asked, did it take the Italian composer to complete his recent opera, "Murder in the Cathedral"? Pizzetti answered that he had spent three years on it. Rozsa pointed out that in Hollywood a composer had only six weeks to write the same amount of music. For his own scores, three different orchestrators could notate the music in full score and it would all sound as if done by the same hand. (Rozsa recalls that it took him a whole summer to orchestrate a twenty-minute concert work. And Roland Manuel, a close friend of Ravel, told him that the French composer spent an entire year orchestrating and re-orchestrating the final dance in "Daphnis and Chloe.")

Finally Rozsa reminded Pizzetti of an experience of Stravinsky's when he first went to California. The composer was receiving no royalties on his most frequently performed works, the three early ballets. Friends suggested that he could make a lot of money by writing a film score. So when Louis B. Mayer, then the all-powerful head of MGM, invited him to his office for an interview, the composer decided to accept.

Stravinsky, ushered into the office, found the executive seated at an enormous desk. For the next half hour, Mayer talked about all the telephones on his desk, about how he could call every director or producer directly from it. Stravinsky was puzzled; he had come to talk about music, not desks. Then Mayer said, "I have been told that you are the greatest composer in the world." Stravinsky bowed. "How much money would you ask as a fee for composing a film score." Stravinsky named a huge sum, equivalent to about $100,000 today. Mayer retorted without the slightest surprise, "If you are the greatest composer in the world, you're worth the money." Stravinsky again bowed. "Now, how long would it take you to compose an hour of music?" Stravinsky paused for a moment, then replied, "One year." Mayer stood up and said, "Good-bye, Mr. Stravinsky."

In sum, Rozsa says, composers should orchestrate their own work, but since they don't have the time, orchestrators are a necessary evil. Actually, he maintains, because of the highly detailed condensed score he produces, he does orchestrate his own music. He also proofreads the full scores notated from his sketches, and makes hundreds of changes.

One cannot overemphasize the significance of orchestral color in writing good film scores. Symphonic orchestration was the mode in the 1930s, when studios maintained large contract orchestras and composers were conscious of a symphonic tradition. Also, producers of this era wanted a full accompaniment to their motion pictures, especially for the costume dramas and romantic epics that were in fashion then. A number of today's composers seem inclined to avoid a large orchestra in favor of a sparse, lean sound.

The studios have been pleased with smaller combinations

for economic reasons; clearly, it is much less expensive to score a film for twenty musicians than for a hundred.

Composers often have intensely personal ideas about orchestration—which they are even permitted to execute on occasion. They may use smaller combinations because of a desire to emphasize a certain orchestral color. Alex North, who went to Hollywood after composing incidental music for the Broadway stage, was used to theater accompaniments for small ensembles, and used them in his scores for *Death of a Salesman* and *A Streetcar Named Desire,* even though large orchestras were available. He felt that the lonely people portrayed in these films could be best portrayed through small orchestral units.

Some of the finest motion picture music has been written for small or unusual orchestral combinations. One such score was David Raksin's for *The Unicorn in the Garden* (see Chapter V). Raksin also used a bass saxophone to good comedic effect in the cartoon *Sloppy Jalopy*. William Alwyn and Malcolm Arnold are other composers who have devoted considerable attention to small ensembles. Daniele Amfitheatrof has experimented with a number of different sounds. For *Heller in Pink Tights,* he augmented a standard orchestra with such Renaissance and baroque instruments as the oboe d'amore, viola da gamba, viola d'amore, and clavichord. In *The Beginning or the End,* for a scene depicting the flight carrying the first atomic bomb to Hiroshima, he scored for strings alone—but for sixty-three players. In contrast, several of the scenes in *Letter from an Unknown Woman,* featuring extensive narration, were accompanied only by a muted string quartet underscoring the dialogue. In his score for *Trial,* he used just percussion: two pianos, one bass, and four drummers playing twelve drums. In *Paths of Glory,* Gerald Fried also employed an all-percussion orchestra. *Yangtse Incident,* scored by the English film composer Leighton Lucas, includes a midnight scene where men attempt to refloat a ship that has gone aground after fleeing gunfire. Lucas scored the sequence with a single note, F, voiced in five octaves and sustained for over two minutes. The open-voiced orchestration seemed eerily to be more silent than silence itself. As Lucas recalls, "The nocturnal photography stressed the tension and anxiety, and the complete silence was almost painful in its intensity."

Bernard Herrmann regards the symphonic combination as a mistake if used for its own sake, and his scores have emphasized a unique application of orchestral color. He made film scoring history with his famous all-string score for *Psycho*. He also used exotic orchestral effects in *The Seventh Voyage of Sinbad,* emphasizing English horns, oboes, and contrabassoons: percusive scoring for timpani and chimes to characterize the Cyclops, and a xylophone to give a macabre impression of living skeletons. Orchestral color also heightened the drama of his scores for *Journey to the Center of the Earth, Mysterious Island, Jason and the Argonauts,* and *The Three Worlds of Gulliver. The Day the Earth Stood Still* called for a large brass ensemble, primarily because of the robust, futuristic feeling he associated with outer space. His score for *Fahrenheit 451* called for strings and percussion alone.

As discussed in Chapter VIII, composers frequently create a feeling of period or location through their choice of instruments. For his score for *Lord Jim,* Bronislau Kaper went to Cambodia to research the instruments of Southeast Asia. Frank Skinner introduced similar instruments in his score for *The Ugly American,* as did Jerry Goldsmith in *The Spiral Road.* When Edward Powell orchestrated the incidental music used in the film version of *The King and I,* he established authenticity through orchestral color; a ballet sequence, "The Small House of Uncle Thomas"—scored by Alfred Newman and orchestrated by Powell—called for a complete ensemble of Siamese instruments. Lalo Schifrin used banjos, twelve-string guitars, and harmonicas in *Cool Hand Luke* to create a feeling of blues and bluegrass music.

What's the Matter With Helen? is a film whose principal characters have some bizarre emotional problems. For the main title, David Raksin scored a relentless, driving ostinato for wind instruments, emphasizing the solo saxophone. Suddenly imposed over this music is an old-fashioned ragtime piano version of the song "Goody, Goody." The piano here is intentionally shocking, and provides a momentary musical insight into the characters' private world of madness. In the final sequence, Raksin uses "Goody, Goody" again, but with two additional tracks. One duplicates the original track 4½ frames later at lower volume; the other was produced by recording the piano arrangement backwards to a click-track and then turning it around, so that in playback the musical impact falls on the end of the notes rather than the beginning. The three tracks were combined and run through a Buchla synthesizer to create what the composer refers to as the "5000-meter flesh crawl."

Various electronic instruments have recently become especially popular. Notable were some unusual orchestral effects created by Mario Nascimbene in his music for *Barabbas*. In one sequence, Barabbas sees the sun for the first time in years after serving a long sentence in the underground sulphur mines. With its blinding light, a piercing and resonant sound cluster bursts forth. It was prepared by combining the sounds produced by a large electric guitar, an electronic organ (with reverberation), a piano, and a vibraphone—all recorded at double volume. Another scene involves an eclipse of the sun. Here Nascimbene uses a high pedal point sustained by sopranos and contraltos singing a tone apart, with first and second violins doubling the voices. The composer then introduces thick, ponderous chords voiced for bass tuba, bassoon, contra-bassoon, timpani, piano, and tam-tam. These chords were recorded at half speed, and then augmented by the resonance of a gong, also recorded at half speed. (The technique of recording certain effects at half speed or double volume has added new colors to the orchestral palette of composers; such effects have been employed for humor as well as for drama.) Scenes depicting the death of Barabbas are underscored through extensive overlapping of voices in a wordless chorus.

As always in Hollywood, trends and styles change. At one time, when string ensembles were the order of the day, a quiet main title would have led to a battle with the producer. Today, those active in screen scoring remark privately that composers are afraid to use the strings to their fullest potential because "anyone walking into a recording session with a string ensemble would be regarded as old-fashioned." Electric guitars and synthesizers are the fashions now. What tomorrow will bring is anyone's guess.

CONDUCTORS

Many film composers conduct their own scores. But coordination and synchronization being so highly refined, many others would rather defer to specialists in the field. The conductor of motion picture scores must be able to control a group of musicians who have the diverse temperaments expected of professional virtuosi. He must also have razor-sharp reflexes and the capacity to adjust to split-second timings—plus the ability to draw upon these talents while conveying the music's meaning to the orchestra.

It is instructive to study the procedures of one conductor, Irvin Talbot, in preparing scores for recording. During Talbot's long career with Paramount, he conducted hundreds of musical features (often uncredited) in association with some of the finest screen composers. Among films he conducted were *Our Town* (Aaron Copland) *Peter Ibbetson* (Ernst Toch), *Lost Weekend* (Miklos Rozsa), *The*

Rainmaker and *The Rose Tattoo* (Alex North), and *One-Eyed Jacks* (Hugo Friedhofer).

Talbot would obtain a detailed cue sheet from the studio on a Friday. Over the weekend, he would study the score, making detailed notations while following his stopwatch, His wife, an accomplished pianist, would sight-read the orchestral scores and help him in the timings. At the recording session, Talbot would watch the screen, his stopwatch, the score, and the cue sheet, simultaneously transmitting signals to the orchestra with his hands. (A film music conductor needs the manual coordination of a surgeon; recording sessions can be expensive, and a misplaced cue might necessitate additional sessions.) In addition to conducting the recording sessions, Talbot supervised the activities of music cutters, training them to edit music tracks. Composers have praised his wizardry in making the musical deletions necessary to correspond to cuts in the film without altering the composer's intentions.

Experienced musical directors become so expert that they can handle assignments of staggering difficulty. Talbot recalled two instances involving dubbing that illustrate the requirements of his demanding profession.

In the film *I'll Walk Alone,* Lizabeth Scott was to sing while accompanying herself at the piano. The task fell to Irvin Talbot to coordinate and conduct a singer making a vocal track, a pianist recording a piano soundtrack, and a separate orchestral track. Another pianist trained the actress to mouth the words of the song. Then Talbot, working at a Movieola, combined all the musical tracks in precise relationship to each other. Music cutters could then print the soundtracks on film.

A remarkable example of both conducting and editing synchronization is an episode from the film *My Geisha,* which tells the story of a motion picture company shooting "Madame Butterfly" in Japan. When Paramount first planned to produce the film (in Japan), its music department was advised that there would be no scenes of Puccini music being sung. After the company had been in Japan for some time, however, it was decided that the film's star, Shirley MacLaine, would be photographed singing two arias from Puccini's score, the famous "Un Bel di Vedremo," and the finale.

A Japanese soprano, Michiko Sunahara, was hired as a vocal coach for Shirley MacLaine. She taught the American actress both arias in Japanese. When the scenes were photographed, an album recorded by Renata Tebaldi was used as a guide. Cameramen then filmed MacLaine singing in Japanese against a playback of Tebaldi singing in Italian.

After the film was edited, Franz Waxman was engaged as composer and musical director for the film. While he was busily composing original underscoring, conductor Irvin Talbot (acting as musical adviser) and music editor John C. Hammell set about the extremely difficult task of making click-tracks to the existing music that had been used on the set, the Tebaldi recording. From these click-tracks, piano tracks were made as guidelines for Michiko Sunahara, who went to Hollywood to record the final vocal tracks for the two arias. As she watched the filmed scenes of Shirley MacLaine singing, her earphones played the final piano tracks. Her fine singing, carefully edited, provided vocal tracks recorded in Japanese and matching Shirley MacLaine's lip synchronization.

In the final orchestral recording, Franz Waxman had to conduct accompaniments to fit the Sunahara vocal tracks, an exceedingly challenging assignment. The vocal tracks could not be altered, nor could they be changed to suit the shadings of the orchestral accompaniment. They could be moved forward or backward only very slightly, because they were now "in sync" with MacLaine's lip movements. The job took several days. Anyone seeing these scenes today will observe Shirley MacLaine, ostensibly singing two arias in Japanese, perfectly accompanied by an orchestra—the simplest thing imaginable!

Over the years, musical directors compiled scores from the tracks maintained in studio libraries. These "temp-tracks" were used for a film until a composer was commissioned to write a score specifically for it. Irvin Talbot assembled hundreds of such scores, arranging for cues to be edited so that transitions from one theme to another were smooth. Sometimes a producer liked the temp-track so much that he asked a composer to write music exactly like it for the film. There were also cases in which a producer had original music written but still preferred the temp-track and used it instead. In the case of very low-budget films, the same procedure might be used to provide a "stock job," employing music ("stock") already owned by the studio's publishers. In this case the studio would assign an experienced musical director who would work with skilled editors to assemble a score from music already recorded.

Challenges for the conductor continue to multiply. An example is a Lalo Schifrin score requiring two conductors. As he recalls: "I once wrote a chase sequence which called for an unusual orchestra including cymbalom, Indian sitar, tambura (a drone instrument), Portuguese guitar, and two pianists playing inside the strings. I didn't write notes, only clusters. When the chase became more intense, I selected the instrument I wanted. I used my own method of notation, employed no timings, and did the whole thing by instinct. In some sequences, a conductor directed the regular orchestra according to predetermined timings, while I conducted the aleatory orchestra according to instinct."

STUDIO MUSICIANS

The studio musician is a curious paradox: a successful person in a field he did not choose. Most musicians who record for motion pictures on a full-time basis began their careers as would-be concert virtuosi. Many have graduated from excellent conservatories in Europe. Some have appeared as soloists with great symphonies, or given solo recitals in important concert halls. A few have even conducted. But success in a concert career depends on a capricious combination of skill, luck, and politics. Thus a number of talented men and women find themselves in Hollywood—prosperous and successful, playing music that may not interest them at all.

In the days when outstanding composers were writing film scores, studio musicians found the music more stimulating. The increasing commercialization of the art, with its accompanying increase in banality, has done little to bolster their morale. Nor has it made for security. When a studio musician belonged to a contract orchestra, he could expect a steady year's employment on a salaried basis. Today he works as a free-lancer. He may earn more money, but he is dependent on a contractor, who sets up recording dates at various studios. Although a composer may have certain preferences regarding players, his is not necessarily the deciding voice. David Amram was intensely disillusioned when he first went to Hollywood and was informed by a studio contractor that his choices of musicians would disturb studio politics—in particular, the contractor's own clique of friends.

In the 1930s, especially in England, musicians had time to rehearse, but they enjoy no such luxury today. Studio musicians have to be excellent sight-readers, capable of dashing off even the most complex orchestral fireworks at first glance. Only a specialist, such as pianist Ray Turner, occasionally has the opportunity for advance preparation of a virtuoso solo or cadenza. Obviously, Hollywood musicians are good. A string section may be composed of four or five first-chair concertmasters; jazz ensembles are likely to consist of all-star soloists with backgrounds in the best dance bands dating back to the swing era. Dimitri Tiomkin once discovered a "violinist" who had spent several years in a studio orchestra playing a muted instrument incapable of producing sound; the man had drawn a steady salary but couldn't play a note. He was an exception. Studio players may be less than delighted to spend hours sight-reading repeated sixteenth-notes in an agitato, but they are invariably experts.

Like most orchestra personnel, studio musicians take a dim view of newcomers. When André Previn ascended the podium for the first time as a teenage prodigy, he asked for the traditional "A" so players could tune up. Instead, they gave his ear a test by playing B-flat. Previn, never lacking in self-confidence, remarked nonchalantly to the orchestra, "Gentlemen, will you please transpose your parts up one half-step." The orchestra stood to applaud; Previn instantly "belonged."

One veteran studio conductor has remarked that the problem with orchestras that record film scores is the same as with any orchestra: "Every musician has a baton hidden in his back pocket." Of course the musicians are not without their grievances. One veteran composer became famous only late in his career. Now he could command attention from studio executives and issue some demands of his own. For one score, he announced that the studio must contract a "legitimate harpsichordist" to play the solo harpsichord in his latest effort. (Normally a pianist can easily execute passages on the harpsichord—or the tack piano, for that matter.) The studio complied, hiring a specialist who understood the complexities of baroque notation and harpsichord ornamentation. When he arrived, he found that the harpsichord part was a single-finger melody, ironically the "plug theme" destined for instant immortality (and quicker oblivion) as the film's main theme.

MUSIC EDITORS

Music editing is one of the least-understood arts relating to motion picture music. The technical process whereby scenes are timed and synchronized with recorded music has received little publicity. The highly skilled men and women responsible for doing it must have not only mechanical facility, but also a high degree of artistry and musical taste.

The relationship between a composer and music editor actually begins before the former writes a single note of music. Composer and editor attend a screening of the film, where the composer may discuss the music with the producer or director. The music editor makes notes of such discussions, especially if they deal with cues or accents regarded as important in terms of the score. Later the editor runs the film reel by reel on a Movieola. It contains a footage counter, so that he can locate specific points on the film with mathematical precision. He can also stop or start the film at will, checking the most minute piece of action. He then compiles a detailed cue reminder or music guide which contains a brief identification of any cues that are important, along with their respective timings. The cue sheets are then compiled and typed for the convenience of the composer, the music editor, and the sound editor.

The procedure of two of Hollywood's most experienced editors—John Hammell and Patrick Moore—is exemplary of the best in music editing. After making cue sheets, they confer with the composer. They discuss click-tracks and any special elements that may be required in overlapping sound-tracks. They also determine the placement of special accents—for instance, if a man slips on a banana peel or kisses the leading lady. The editor makes notations on the timing sheets to indicate these mood changes, which become "lines" in the recording session. At this time, as the film is shown, the "line" appears as a diagonal streamer moving across the surface of the screen. It serves as a warning signal to enable the conductor to make changes to fit the mood.

The original tapes, exactly as recorded, are known as masters. But they may be altered. Although the composer determines the music for a given sequence, deletions or other changes may come later. A producer or director may want to shorten a scene to heighten suspense. A star may want to trim a sequence with which she is displeased. Obviously, turning a ten-minute scene into a two-minute episode radically alters the music. The task of making the music fit the film falls to the editor (often called a cutter).

Composers who want additional information on timings can now compute their own mathematical data. There are two technical handbooks to help them, one developed by composer Ruby Raksin, the other by music editor Carroll Knudson. Raksin's book includes a master click chart, which enables a composer to convert metronome tempos and provides detailed information on decimal equivalents of click and metronome tempos as well as on other timing devices. The master click chart is graduated from seven to thirty-four frames in increments of quarters of a frame. Knudson's volume is a bound set of charts that relate click beats, timing, footage, and metronome tempos. They are graduated from six to thirty-six frames.

Both books provide a service to the composer who may not want to depend on a music editor for immediate information. He can be more flexible in understanding his own timing procedures. And, if he wants to compose at dawn or in the middle of the night, he can draw up his own mathematical calculations and go to work immediately.

MUSIC ENGINEERS

The musical engineer, or music mixer, plays a key role in recording motion picture scores. Paul G. Neal, who directed mixing and engineering procedures for some of Hollywood's most important features, describes the mixer's functions: "A music mixer (or music engineer, as he is sometimes known in the record industry), along with his crew, has the responsibility of achieving the proper balance in orchestral recording. The medium of recording most often used is tape, subsequently transferred to 35-millimeter film or records. The music mixer must have a knowledge not only of electronics and acoustics, but also of musical values. He should be able to read and follow a score, because it's a great handicap for him to depend on a musician to indicate changes in microphone controls. He must seat the orchestra, place the microphones, and control as many as twenty-four dials for recording on individual channels."

Before a recording session, the music mixer sets up a diagram-chart for the crew, indicating placement of microphones in order to achieve orchestral balance. For instance, brasses can obliterate woodwinds if the musicians are seated in the wrong place. The mixer then sits in a sound recording booth and follows the score as it is recorded. He can, with a single motion, bring out a solo piccolo over the full orchestra simply by opening the piccolo microphone or by turning down other dials. The mixer can thus maintain complete control over the balance of a film score, balance that cannot be achieved on the recording stage itself.

Concert Performances of Film Music

Composers of motion picture scores constantly discuss how their music would fare on the concert stage. This is not idle speculation, for film scores have been arranged and adapted both for record collectors and for full-scale concert performance.

Opinions on adapting film music are lively and varied. Leonard Rosenman draws a sharp distinction between film music and what he terms "real" music. "Music for films has all the ingredients that real music has—counterpoint, orchestration, harmony, voiceleading, bass line—but it doesn't have the primary ingredient that separates music from non-music. The propulsion is not by musical ideas, but by literary ideas." He goes on to observe: "In any other art form inspired by literary ideas, such as oratorio, opera, or art song, the composer is free to manipulate the form according to the musical concept. In films, however, the composer must manipulate the music to fit the image." Gerald Fried concurs, finding most concert performances of film music lacking in interest. Robert U. Nelson, a professor of music at U.C.L.A. who has analyzed many film scores, states that "Although there are a few exceptions, a typical film score simply doesn't work into a good concert piece."

But, we may well ask, what precisely *is* a typical film score? William Lava, who scored numerous Westerns, remarked, "There are many beautiful themes in neglected film music, which are, when fully developed, much richer and more exciting than some concert music which has been worn thin by constant repetition." And Frank Skinner commented: "I think concert performances work out very well. A film score in its original form lacks the continuity of a concert work. However, with reconstruction on the part of the composer, a concert performance can be exciting and interesting." Skinner himself arranged a concert suite based on his score for *Tap Roots* which has been performed, with the composer conducting, by concert and university bands throughout the country; its formal structure is directly related to the plot developments of the film.

Composers of motion picture music have had to contend with considerable snobbery on the part of critics of serious music, especially those concerned with the avant-garde. Motion picture scores are often most successful when they appeal to the emotions, and this quality may not endear them to academics who like to explain works through graphs, charts, and musicological analysis. It cannot be denied that film music is primarily functional, written to serve a practical goal. So, however, were many of the great masterworks of the past, written to please patrons and to function in the church or the theater.

According to Bronislau Kaper: "There are those who even say that film music should not be good, that if the music is really good, it will work against the picture. I do not agree. This is one of those silly superstitions. Most important is the quality of the material. Decisively, I don't believe that you can have bad music, badly conceived and amateurish, which may 'fit' the picture. This is no answer to a film score." Some have gone so far as to suggest that film music be composed in a harmonic and compositional style quite different from that employed in concert music. Daniele Amfitheatrof disagrees: "I would say that the requiem I composed is germane to what I have written for the motion picture, *The Beginning or the End,* a film about the atom bomb. Both have this type of huge, religious choral feeling. I used the same approach in both compositions."

Bernard Herrmann, asked about whether motion picture music may be composed in the same harmonic style as concert music, replies: "There's no difference. It's exactly the same, it's only a question of density. In the nineteenth century, if you went to hear a musical—an operetta by Offenbach, or Lehár, or Kalman—you really heard music composed of the same materials of which concert music is made. The only difference was its weight, perhaps less inflated, perhaps more delicate. There wasn't that much difference between Lehár and 'Rosenkavalier'; it's only a question of where it arrives. The musicality is the same. Music for a film, of course, must be able to communicate instantly to someone who is listening for the first time, and with only one ear."

Adaptations of film music for the concert stage have come from the pens of many different composers. Aaron Copland arranged music from several of his film scores into a suite entitled "Music from the Movies." He also developed a concert version of his score for *Our Town*. Virgil Thomson produced suites based on several of the films he scored— *The Plough that Broke the Plains, The River,* and *Louisiana Story*. Bernard Herrmann's concert suites "Welles Raises Kane" and "The Devil and Daniel Webster," based on his early scores, were recorded only recently. Miklos Rozsa has arranged sections of his brilliant score for *El Cid* for concert performance. Prokofiev's *Lieutenant Kije* survives as a suite and *Alexander Nevsky* as a cantata. As mentioned earlier, William Walton's Shakespeare scores have been adapted into several pieces for the concert hall, and Ralph Vaughan Williams turned one of his film scores into the "Sinfonia Antarctica."

Individual sequences from a film may also be reworked for concert performance. David Raksin added to the limited literature for recorder with solos based on his music for *The Unicorn in The Garden;* his nocturne for violin and piano was adapted from *Force of Evil*. A recent concert at the Hollywood Bowl featured several composers conducting their own works: Franz Waxman, conducting the celebrated chase sequence from *A Place in the Sun;* Bernard Herrmann, his overture to *North By Northwest* and the "Memory Waltz" from *The Snows of Kilimanjaro;* Miklos Rozsa, the prelude to *Ben-Hur;* David Raksin, an unusual concert version of "Laura"; and Alex North, the processional music from *Cleopatra*. (Raksin has also sponsored entire concerts of film music, including both his own works and those of others.)

Composers naturally prefer to adapt those sections of their music that were originally developed without interruptions from dialogue or sound effects. In the words of

Jerome Moross: "In film music, every technical means is at your command. I like to make each sequence a well-formed musical piece, and I do it whenever possible. When the entire sequence can be completed as a real piece of music, it is very satisfying. Sequences that were complete pieces of music are the ones I adapted in my suite, 'Music for the Flicks.' If you're going to try to sit around and catch everything, you're going to have a problem. I catch things when they are necessary, but try to keep it at a minimum."

Ruby Raksin believes that even sequences used as linking devices should still have a sense of formal unity. "Transitions are of tremendous importance. Any symphonic composer knows that the theme is not the only element involved. It's the way in which a composer moves from one theme to another that indicates high craft on his part. This is what gives his work form, balance, and a feeling of inevitability. Music should not sound accidental. The bridges, nuances, cadences, and all the things you learn as a composer are important in the establishment of a cohesive musical composition."

According to Alex North: "The fun and the challenge of starting out as a serious composer is to write a new piece every time, an entity in itself that can be listened to in its own right. When I say that I avoid variation after variation on the same theme, I would rather write a new piece and not take the easy way out. In writing a piece of four or five minutes, I always try to write a sequence with a beginning, a middle, and an end."

A prime example of the interrelationship of film music and concert music is the career of Gail Kubik. A specialist in documentary films, Kubik extracted themes and ideas from his scores and rewrote and expanded them in entirely new ways.

Kubik, a native of Oklahoma, studied at the Eastman School of Music. At twenty-one he was one of the youngest students ever admitted to the Harvard Graduate School. By the age of twenty-three, he was teaching advanced composition at Teachers College, Columbia University. He composed music for radio programs and was appointed director of music for the Office of War Information during World War II. In subsequent years he divided his time between concert music and screen scores.

Among Kubik's documentaries were *Twenty-one Miles,* an English wartime documentary shown in the United States in 1943; *The World at War,* a United States government production feature; and *Air Pattern Pacific,* an air force short. Although excerpts from such films were never released on record commercially, Kubik decided to use themes from them in his Third Symphony, written in 1956 for Dimitri Mitropoulos and the New York Philharmonic. The slow movement of the symphony begins with a trumpet melody heard originally in *Twenty-one Miles;* an extract from *Air Pattern Pacific* (an accompaniment to a view of malaria-infested jungles in the South Pacific) is introduced as a misterioso, also in that movement; the final movement, entitled "Masquerade," incorporates several short tunes first used in an "industrial" sequence in *The World at War*.

Kubik had already enjoyed considerable success transferring film material to the concert idiom. Among his other wartime scores were the widely heralded *Memphis Belle, Earthquakers,* and *Thunderbolt.* In 1949 Kubik was assigned to compose the music for Joseph Lerner's *C-Man.* Critics spoke of his music "dominating the soundtrack even more than the dialogue." Variety praised him, declaring that "the background music has a nervous, pounding, pulse-quickening quality which, combined with the headlong action, results in a powerfully striking total effect." Kubik decided to adapt several excerpts of thematic material in a concert work he wrote in 1952, a Symphony Concertante for trumpet, viola, piano, and orchestra.

Kubik's original film score called for an orchestra consisting of one clarinet in B-flat (occasionally bass clarinet), three French horns in F, three trumpets in C, two trombones, one percussion player (timpani, snare drum), one piano, one viola, and one bass. He made skillful use of this small combination. At one point, instead of the whole group, he used a voice against a snare drum. In another notable sequence, he conveyed the impression of mechanical difficulties aboard an airplane by combining four separate soundtracks. The orchestra was divided into two uneven groups: the first consisted of clarinet, trumpet, horn, and viola; the second, of two trumpets, horns, trombones, percussion, piano, and bass. Kubik then recorded two tracks of the music written for the first group, played on a separate sound head, staggered at an interval of about 1/10 of a second. A third track consisted of a drone representing the humming of the plane's engine in flight. A fourth track, played by the second orchestral group, enabled Kubik to comment on the action taking place inside the plane itself. For a fight sequence, the composer produced a passacaglia set in 6/4, depending for its energy less upon the synchronization of music and flying fists than upon the percussive accents and biting dissonance of the orchestra.

Composers who adapt their film music for the concert stage often preserve certain sections of the original film score, restoring or lengthening portions that have been cut because of screen timings. Kubik wanted to do this, too, but he was also determined to create a work that did not depend on the film in any way for its structure. He could undoubtedly have adapted a suite based on his score for *C-Man,* but he chose not to do so. Instead of simply expanding sections of the score into movements of a suite, he used some materials from the film score, but in completely new ways.

In Kubik's Symphony Concertante, the ensemble consists of woodwinds (including piccolo, bass clarinet, and contrabassoon), two horns, one trumpet, one trombone, percussion, and a small string orchestra. In selecting thematic material, arranging, and cutting, Kubik was constantly aware of the difference between screen and concert composing. For example, he subjected the main title material to considerable alteration. It was based on two principal motifs, a six-note, angular, motto-type melody, and a short, hammered cadence of four repeated notes—elements described by Kubik as aggressive, strident sounds. In the concert work, Kubik limited this material to the chief melody, but did not include the harmony, counterpoint, or orchestration from the film score.

The airplane sequence from *C-Man* also appears in the concert work in altered form. Kubik preserved material from the four different soundtracks—the airplane motor hum, an extended trumpet melody, the same melody filtered through an echo chamber, and nervous, intense motifs from the orchestra itself. Kubik retained the overall form of the sequence, using most of the trumpet tune and having the piano play a pedal point to correspond to the airplane motor hum. He omitted the orchestral commentary on the screen action (the original fourth soundtrack).

Kubik's alterations depended primarily upon musical effects that would be appropriate in a concert hall. For example, he shortened the film toccata and introduced a new melody because a musical climax at the beginning of the third movement would have been out of place in the concert hall, as it was not in the film. Kubik composed variations on his thematic material and provided additional melodic ideas in the third movement. He decided to use the "New York Waking Up" sequence there, lifting it from the film score. In this instance, he did not need to develop his materials more fully, because they had not been truncated to allow for dialogue or sound effects. The result was a three-part, jazz-style intermezzo. The mood of the music is ideal for men and women hurrying to work in the subways.

Kubik's Symphony Concertante won a Pulitzer Prize. The work demonstrated the versatility of a fine composer, one who could not only score a motion picture, but also use the thematic materials in other ways. He comments: "A composer loves all his children, and he is not happy until they all are properly clothed and fed, sent off to college, and in short, fully prepared to make their own way in the world. If (as has happened with my scores for *Gerald McBoing Boing, The Memphis Belle,* or *The Desperate Hours*), a dramatic child of mine seems likely to enjoy a reasonable, normal span of life, having made a viable contribution to a dramatic work that in its totality adds to the country's cultural life, then that child's father is apt to be quite content with his offspring's life expectancy. But for all those dramatic children who, for whatever reason, stand in danger of an early demise, the composer-parent is always, if only unconsciously, on the watch for the opportunity to rescue them."

In 1972 David Raksin conducted what must be the most unusual performance of all film music. Appearing in Vermont as guest conductor with the Vermont Symphony Orchestra, he presented some notable sequences from motion pictures he had scored. A motion picture screen was mounted on the stage, and Raksin conducted the cues that accompanied the films. In earlier years, this procedure would have been the normal one. Today, however, theater orchestras no longer accompany motion pictures, so that this combination of symphony and cinema was a distinctive occasion.

Film scores can indeed be of high quality. Aaron Copland once dismissed some pretentious claims by a group of chamber music composers in New York with the assertion, "The boys in Hollywood do that all the time, and better than you gentlemen." Today the film score must contend with a variety of unfortunate nonmusical influences. But the possibilities on a purely artistic level are endless. Composer and critic Frank Lewin has commented: "As for what is being carried on soundtracks, that will depend on fads and fashions as it always has, I suppose. The few pieces of great craft or genius (and I would put some of Bernard Herrmann's scores in this class) will survive, and the others will be just the vast mass out of which the peaks project. That, however, has always been the case." He goes on to say: "When one considers how many operas were written and how few "Falstaffs" or "Tristans" were produced, it is clear that our situation is analogous, and that is normal, for films are today's entertainment form, which somebody in the future will enshrine as 'art.' "

Conclusion

Many of the developments in film scoring, like almost everything in motion pictures, have come about through caprice. With accident the rule, artists have learned to expect the unexpected. Even so, the present day cannot be regarded under any circumstances as a high point in the history of film music.

After achieving remarkable growth in an incredibly short time, the art of film scoring has come to be dominated by the omnipotent and ever-present influence of commercialism. Hugo Friedhofer's whimsical suggestion that "They're going to write the song first and shoot the picture around the tune" has become reality. The domination of composers by nonmusical executives has almost put an end to outstanding film music. In the earliest days of film scoring, Erich Wolfgang Korngold was allowed to perfect his art without interference from anyone. Today the composer's position is uncertain as he faces the choice of satisfying either his artistic impulses or the businessmen who employ him.

If producers, directors, and executives seem to have fared badly in the foregoing pages, it is not because of any bias against them. The evidence against them speaks for itself. Today's producers and directors are "discovering" such techniques as the repetition of a single theme, the use of compiled scores or other music unrelated to the film, and silence. All of these techniques were tested and abandoned in the early days of film scoring. And executives display an incredible lack of sensitivity about music. The story is told of a producer who heard some sounds on a scoring stage that displeased him. "What are they?" he asked the composer. "Minor chords," responded the composer. The executive promptly dictated a memo to his employees informing them that henceforth minor chords would not be permitted in the studio's film scores.

Serious composers have been inclined to laugh at the screen score, especially if it was produced by a colleague in Hollywood. Yet at a time when many composers of concert music have lost their audience en masse, interest in film music is growing daily. A new generation is discovering the achievements of the brilliantly gifted composers who provided us with our best motion picture music. They are rapidly concluding that a wealth of fine music may be awaiting discovery amidst scores of lesser consequence and, most especially, amidst the commercially prepackaged sounds masquerading as today's film music.

In an atmosphere in which genius and ignorance must function on a collaborative basis, the best composers stand above the crowd. The marvel of motion picture scoring is not that poor scores have been written, but that so much fine music has survived the circus-like milieu of the industry. At their best, film scores can be sources of delight in the theater and of fascination in music history books. At worst, they can be mundane and unnecessary. As in all musical communication, the ultimate test depends entirely upon the creator. Recognition of outstanding film music has been long overdue. Some observers predict a new cycle, a rediscovery of the musical masterworks of the screen and a newly informed public demanding that once again music play a major role in production of good motion pictures. Regardless of the future, we can only express amazement at the number of scores of high quality that have accompanied motion pictures over the last six decades. Film music began as an effort to drown out the noise of the primitive machinery used to project silent pictures. It evolved into a subtle, highly sophisticated art capable of almost limitless expression. Film scores have enjoyed a rich, brilliant past. If the most distinguished composers are given an opportunity to explore all the unique possibilities of cinema as an art form, film music may continue to develop on a high artistic plane.

Glossary

CINEMATIC TERMS

catching   Precise coordination between action and music, as in the case of a loud chord when one actor strikes another, or an orchestral sweep when a comedian slips on a banana peel.

channel   A track on which elements have been recorded.

click   A clicking sound produced when the perforation of a soundtrack is passed over the sound head of a projector.

click sheet   A written guide used by a composer to determine the precise timings and relationships between clicks and the picture, dialogue, etc.

click-track   A soundtrack containing the perforations that produce clicks.

conductor book   A bound volume of condensed versions of film music sequences. It enables the conductor to see the basic lead parts in the orchestral arrangement without reference to a full score. Conductor books also serve as legal references after recording.

cue sheet See *timing sheet*.

dissolve Visual effect in which camera shots blend from one to another.

dubbing Combination of music tracks with the sound and dialogue.

editing Cutting and splicing of tape to eliminate or combine musical sequences.

flutters Punches on film that enable a conductor to synchronize his motions with the screen action by warning him in advance of changes of action or mood.

footage counter A device that indicates how many feet of film have passed through a projector.

frame Unit of film used to measure exposure.

hurry Frantic music used in chase sequences during the silent film era, characterized by a combination of rapid, repeated chords and tremolos.

Lenatone A process for providing a quaver effect in a given sonority, named for its inventor, Harry Leonard.

lip-sync Process of synchronization in which a performer sings or speaks and then is photographed mouthing the words in coordination with the previous recording.

main title The opening sequence of a film, in which the credits appear on the screen.

"Mickey Mouse" Consistent "catching"; a composer is said to "Mickey Mouse" a sequence if his music provides an exact parallel to visual images, rising when something goes up, descending when something falls. The term comes from the

fact that the technique has been widely used (sometimes overused) in animated cartoons.

monaural   A single-channel recording.

montage   A sequence of various shots or scenes of a motion picture, each of which is presented in rapid succession to indicate passage of time.

Movieola   A special projection device through which a composer can listen to music tracks while watching the picture through a glass window.

orchestral sketch   A six- or eight-line reduction of a full orchestral score.

playback   Playing of a recorded tape or soundtrack after it has been recorded.

pre-recording   Recording music for a sequence before it is filmed.

punch   Perforation made on film.

source music   Music that is supposed to originate from a sound source on the screen, such as a band performing or a radio playing.

stereophonic   More than single-channel recording.

streamer   Line, produced by scraping on the film emulsion, used in sound synchronization.

temp-track   A music track provided for a motion picture from prerecorded sources, generally used only until the composer finishes his work.

timing sheet   Used by a composer to provide a breakdown of all dialogue and action, with precise second-by-second timings. Also known as a cue sheet.

underscoring   A dramatic background score for a motion picture.

MUSICAL TERMS

aleatory   Procedure in which musicians introduce elements of chance into a composition.

antiphonal   Alternating responses; derived from a choral technique in which one section of a choir answers another.

arioso   Lyrical, graceful style of the aria.

atonal   Without tonality. Term used to describe much contemporary music, in which materials are organized without a specific key.

augmentation   Extension of a theme or melody by lengthening the time values of the notes.

cadence   A progression of chords, usually two, giving the effect of ending a musical development.

canon   The strictest form of contrapuntal composition, in which each voice strictly imitates the other.

cantus firmus   A melody, sometimes not original, adapted by a composer as the basis for a polyphonic composition. The cantus firmus was originally a traditional church melody that served as the basis for Renaissance liturgical music.

chromatic   Proceeding by halfsteps. The chromatic scale is represented by all the black and white keys of the piano.

counterpoint   The art of adding musical lines to a single melody.

deceptive cadence Resolution of the dominant chord into another chord instead of the expected tonic.

diatonic Proceeding in order of a major or minor scale, including whole and half steps. Usually refers to a traditional key signature.

diminution Shortening a theme or melody by decreasing the time value of the notes.

double fugue Fugue on two subjects.

fugato In the style of a fugue.

fugue A composition based on a musical subject, in which voices or melodic lines enter and are developed according to specific rules. Derived from the word "fuga," the Latin term for "flight."

glissando A slurred, gliding run with a sweeping or blurring quality.

ground bass Melodic idea in a low harmonic register which is repeated over and over as the harmonic foundation for a piece of music.

leitmotif A theme or phrase associated with a specific character or idea in a music drama. Wagner is regarded as the most important figure in its historical development.

modal Describes music based upon ancient modal scales—the Dorian, Phrygian, Lydian, Mixolydian, Aeolian, and Ionian. They are based on different arrangements of half steps and whole steps than the diatonic scales.

ostinato Pattern or rhythmic figure repeated over and over.

passacaglia   Polyphonic composition based on a ground bass; a slow dance in triple rhythm.

pizzicato   Short, clipped plucking of strings; an alternative to bowing.

plagal cadence   Progression from subdominant to tonic harmony; an example of harmonic resolution.

polymodal   Combination of modes or musical ideas based on different model scales used simultaneously.

polyphonic   Many-voiced, contrapuntal in style. Refers to combination of individual melodic lines offset against each other.

polytonal   Combination of tonalities or musical ideas based on different keys used simultaneously.

scherzo   Lively, animated composition.

spartita   An Italian word meaning "partition score." Related to a complete score, in contrast to individual vocal scores written for choral compositions during the Renaissance.

spiccato   Playing strings with the middle of the bow. The performer uses a springing motion which allows the bow to bounce on the strings. The word, derived from Italian, means "separate" or "distinct."

suite   A series of musical pieces.

sul ponticello   In passages for string instruments, playing with the bow close to the bridge.

tessitura   Musical register. A high tessitura refers to extremes of the soprano register, a low tessitura to extremes of the bass register of any given instrument.

triadic   Refers to a chord with a root plus the third and fifth intervals above it.

triple fugue   Fugue based on three subjects.

twelve-tone row   A contemporary, artificial scale created by a composer who arranges twelve tones of a chromatic scale according to his preferences, and bases his compositions upon variations or transpositions of it.

vocalise   Musical passage or melody sung on vowel sounds, but containing no words. The voice is used as an instrument.

The Robe
Alfred Newman

Vertigo
Bernard Herrmann

Raintree County
Johnny Green

The Best Years of Our Lives
Hugo Friedhofer

Alexander Nevsky   *Louisiana Story*
Sergei Prokofiev   Virgil Thomson

The Rainmaker
Alex North

Spellbound   *Viva Zapata*
Miklos Rozsa   Alex North

Snow White and the Seven Dwarfs
Leigh Harline and Paul J. Smith

Gone With the Wind
Max Steiner

Index

THE AUTHOR

A young man of many interests, and the talents to pursue them successfully, Mark Evans is a composer, conductor, lyricist, author, and host of a syndicated radio talk show, "Mark My Words." Born in St. Louis, he grew up in California, graduated from the California Institute of the Arts summa cum laude, and studied for the M.A. and Ph.D. degrees at Claremont Graduate School. He also studied composition with such eminent musicians as Mario Castelnuovo-Tedesco and Roy Harris. A movie buff since childhood, he haunted studio music departments and became acquainted with many of the composers discussed in this book.

Dr. Evans also is the author of "Will the Real Young America Please Stand Up?," a study of American youth today.